THE WELCOME STR

The Welcome Stranger

Dutch, Walloon and Huguenot Incomers to Norwich, 1550–1750

Frank Meeres

Lasse
Press

First published 2018
by the Lasse Press
2 St Giles Terrace, Norwich NR2 1NS, UK
www.lassepress.com
lassepress@gmail.com

ISBN-13: 978-1-9997752-2-3

Typeset in Garamond by
Curran Publishing Services Ltd, Norwich, UK

Manufactured in the UK by
Imprint Digital, Exeter.

Contents

Maps, Figures and Tables

Maps

Figures

Tables

Abbreviations

BL   British Library
Con   Conesford Ward
Man   Mancroft Ward
NRO   Norfolk Record Office
OtW   Over the Water Ward
TNA   The National Archives
Wym   Wymer Ward

and specifically in the Norfolk Record Office:

NRO NCR   Records of the city of Norwich
NRO DN/DIS   Diocesan records, dissenters
NRO DN/INV   Diocesan records, probate inventories
NRO MC   Minor collections
NRO BOL   Bolingbroke collection
NRO ETN   Eaton collection
NRO COL   Colman collection
NRO DN/SUB   Diocesan records, subscription book
NRO FC   Free Church records
NRO PD   parish records
NRO N/LM   Lord Mayor's records
NRO NCC Wills   Norwich Consistory Court records

Acknowledgements

This book is based on records held at the Norfolk Record Office. I am grateful for permission to use images of documents held there, and to county archivist Gary Tuson and former county archivist Dr John Alban for help and support. The book could not have been written without the work of others in this field, especially Dr Christopher Joby, Dr Alastair Duke and Dr William Woods. The late Nancy Ives collected an enormous amount of material on the Strangers, now held at the Norfolk Record Office, and I am happy to acknowledge my appreciation of her work and her friendship.

Every effort has been made to acknowledge the rights-holders of material reproduced in this volume, but should any acknowledgement inadvertently have been missed, the author and publisher will be glad to rectify the omission in the next edition.

Author's royalties on this volume are being donated to the Norfolk Archives and Heritage Development Foundation, partner charity of the Norfolk Record Office.

Frank Meeres

This book is dedicated to those refugees who lost their lives trying to cross the seas to freedom, whether the North Sea in the seventeenth century or the Mediterranean in the twenty-first century.
Their names are known only to God.

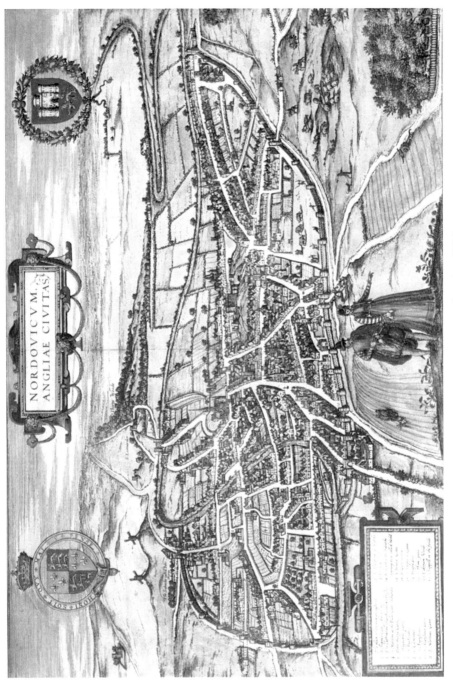

Figure 1 Norwich in the time of the Strangers: Braun and Hogenberg's map of the city, 1581

Introduction

The city of Norwich has always welcomed refugees. Several thousand came over from the Spanish Netherlands in the 1560s and 1570s, fleeing persecution by Roman Catholic authorities. Often referred to as 'Strangers', they formed two communities in the city, according to the language that they spoke – Dutch or French speakers. Several words need defining.

Stranger

The word 'Stranger' is often taken by Norwich people to mean exclusively the Dutch- and French-speaking immigrants who came over from the Low Countries in the later sixteenth century. When local people speak of having a Stranger amongst their ancestors, this is almost always what they mean. Some documents certainly do use the word in this sense, for example:

> In the time of mayor Robert Wood [1569–70] it was noted that; 'by reason of the business in Flanders the city was very much replenished with Strangers'.

A royal licence of 23 May 1570 permitted the Mayor and aldermen of Norwich to buy wool grown in the Queen's dominions and sell it to the inhabitants of Norwich 'from the relief of the city; and that its inhabitants may be instructed in the trade of making divers wares now made in Norwich by the Strangers there resident'.

However, historically the word merely means someone who was not within the legal jurisdiction of the city. The earliest time I have seen it used is in a Norwich leet court roll of 1287/8: 'Nicholas le Jay wounded a certain clerk, a stranger, and cut off two fingers': the clerk was not a 'citizen' of Norwich, but he was definitely English. Even in the sixteenth and seventeenth centuries, when the word was being commonly used for the Low Country immigrants, it was still often used in the older sense, as in these four examples from local burial registers:

> 3 July 1597: 'a begging boye a stranger' (Norwich St James Pockthorpe).
>
> 9 March 1625/6: 'a stranger from the Spittle House whose name is not known' (Norwich St Clement).
>
> 3 September 1625: 'William Galliard stranger, perished in the waves' (Norwich St Martin at Palace).
>
> 21 August 1665: 'John Allen a stranger died in the highway, supposed of plague' (Cringleford).

Human tragedies certainly, but almost certainly *not* related to the people whose story is told in this book. In some cases, when the word 'Stranger' is used in a document, for example the heading of a will or a probate inventory, it is simply not possible to be certain in what sense the word is used.

Alien

In the twenty-first century, the word alien conjures up images of creatures from other worlds. Actually, alien is the legal word for someone who is from another country. In the sixteenth and seventeenth centuries, most of the aliens in Norwich were from the Low Countries but not all: other aliens were from France and from Scotland (then a foreign country, of course) and elsewhere.

Dutch

This refers to Dutch-speaking incomers from the Spanish Netherlands. Most of those coming to Norwich arrived from the southern provinces of Flanders or Brabant, with smaller numbers from other provinces farther north, such as Zeeland or Holland.

Walloon

This refers to French-speaking incomers from the Spanish Netherlands, usually from the southern provinces, such as Picardy or Artois where French was the usual language, and from Flanders and Brabant which had large numbers of French speakers, especially towards the south. They are often referred to in documents as 'French'.

Huguenot

Protestants from France, who fled religious persecution in their home country from the 1560s and in very large numbers in the 1680s. Some authorities regard Walloons as coming within the general term 'Huguenot', others see them as a separate group. The situation is complicated because France took over parts of the Spanish Netherlands from the 1630s: a family in Picardy might be persecuted by the Spanish authorities before that date and so be defined as Walloon, but by the French authorities afterwards, and so described as Huguenot. In this book, the word 'Huguenot' refers to people from France, and those from the Spanish Netherlands are described as Walloons.

From the 1560s there was a 'French church' in Norwich. This was for the Walloon community and should really be called the French-speaking church or the Walloon church. A small number of Huguenot families did attend the church in the 1680s, but it was *not* a church founded by Huguenots, in contrast to buildings known as 'French churches' in some other communities in England.

The city of Norwich

From 1404, Norwich was a city and county in its own right. For administrative purposes the area within the medieval city walls was divided into twelve petty wards, grouped together into four Great Wards. It was run by an 'upper house', a court consisting of the mayor and aldermen, and a common council. The 24 aldermen were elected for life by the freemen of each ward (two for each ward); the common council was made up of 60 men elected annually by the freemen. The city also had jurisdiction over the surrounding suburbs or villages, which were each assigned to one of the Great

Figure 2
Chart of about 1600,
showing the route
from Brill in Flanders
to 'Easton Ness', on
to Yarmouth and
upstream to Norwich.
The inscription reads
'Between Easton Ness
and the Brill is
34 leagues or 102
miles'.
Norfolk Record Office
(NRO Y/C 37/2)

Wards. Two areas within the walls were excluded from the city's rule – the Cathedral precinct and the Castle fee.

Ecclesiastically, the city was divided into 35 parishes, each of which had its own church, with its churchwardens and overseers of the poor. The parishes beyond the walls also had their own churches and parish officials.

Chapter 1

The background

Norwich and the Netherlands

'Between Easton Ness and the Brill is 34 leagues or 102 miles': so runs the caption on a chart drawn up a few years either side of 1600. Brill is in the Low Countries; Easton Ness is by Lowestoft, the most easterly part of Britain, and only a few miles south of Yarmouth, from where the river runs up to Norwich. As this suggests, East Anglia and the Low Countries are near neighbours: indeed, Britain only finally became an island 9,000 years ago. Before then, men and animals could walk across to the Low Countries: reindeer and mammoths at first, followed later, as the climate warmed, by wild boar and cattle. The countries around the North Sea have always shared a prehistoric cultural identity: 6,000 years ago, Neolithic men mined for flint in both Norfolk and the Netherlands. Iron Age Norfolk is noted for 'Snettisham torcs' – similar treasures are found in rich, princely burials on the Continent. In Roman times Norfolk saw the import and export of goods from Rhineland and the Low Countries, including millstones, glass and pottery.[1]

It was Dr John Alban, former Norfolk county archivist, who first revealed to me a truth that is indeed self-evident: the North Sea has always been a *highway* rather than a *barrier* to movement. Anglo-Saxons, Scandinavians and Normans were able to cross and establish themselves in Norwich, and their heritage is everywhere. The Anglo-Saxons left us names ('East Anglia', 'Norwich'), as did the Scandinavians (the place-name endings '-by' and '-gate'). The Normans reclothed East Anglia in stone, moved Norwich Market from Tombland to its present site, and created the most iconic buildings in the city – the Cathedral and the Castle, built principally of stone brought across the sea from Normandy.

This heritage has been discussed in a recent book by former Norfolk county archaeologist Brian Ayers, who could be said to have achieved what King Canute could not: mastery of the North Sea.[2] In this book, the concentration is on the area known as the Spanish Netherlands in the sixteenth century, which embraced the present-day countries of the Netherlands and Belgium, and also a part of what is now North-East France. The provinces in this region include Picardy, Artois, Flanders, Brabant, Holland and Zeeland, and the archives have many records of links between Norwich and these areas from the Middle Ages onwards.

References in documents to links between Norwich and the Netherlands in the Middle Ages were drawn together by historian Helen Sutermeister. Bricks were

---

1   The chart is at the Norfolk Record Office (hereafter NRO): Y/C 37/2. It must be earlier than 1614, as it appears in Manship's list of Yarmouth records made in that year.
2   Brian Ayers, *The German Ocean: Medieval Europe and the North Sea* (2016).

imported from Flanders for work at Norwich Castle in the 1260s. Early goldsmiths in the city included Henry de Trith de Brabant (mentioned in 1296), and Edward Lamberd, probably from Flanders (mentioned in 1312/3).[3]

In 1311, a John de Frysselond owned property in Norwich. In the same year, four Norwich citizens and two from Lynn sold wool worth £1,000 in Bruges, then went to Lille fair and bought £1,500 of spices, cloth, wax and other goods for the return trip. Cloth was imported from Flanders in the early fourteenth century: in 1290 Norwich men owed £276 to Flemish cloth merchants. When Richard de Weston died in 1294 he left debts of £90 for cloth brought from three merchants of Douai, £43 to men of Ypres and £18 to vendors elsewhere in Flanders. Black salt that was brought in on Dutch ships probably originated in the Loire valley. Fine salt, either boiled down in Holland or obtained from Low Countries peat, was also imported, valued by customs at twice as much as black salt. Most was for Yarmouth, but some came upriver to Norwich.

Other imports included wax, sandals, cotton, basins, pots and pans. By the mid-fifteenth century, imports included some items of luxury furniture – cupboards and chests. Norwich merchants might well use Dutch or Hansa ships: for example, in 1447–8 they used two Yarmouth ships, 21 Dutch ships and three Hansa ships. William Heynsser, who owned the Norwich ship the *Christopher* in the reign of Richard II, was probably a Dutch immigrant.[4]

The bulk of imports were building materials – iron from Sweden, bricks like the octagonal bricks used at vaults for Norwich Guildhall and Appleyard's house (now the Bridewell museum) from Holland. Dyes were also imported to Norwich from the Low Countries. Woad was bought in via Middelburg by Dutch or Hansa merchants, such as Ellard van Fale de Hansa, who paid to take 22 pipes through Yarmouth to Norwich in 1427–8. Madder, grown on the islands of Zeeland and gathered in autumn, was important – hence the street name Maddermarket – while alum and saffron, both products of the Mediterranean, were imported to Norwich from Holland.

To see visible evidence of the link across the North Sea, you can go to Norwich Cathedral cloister. Standing in the south-west corner of the cloister, by the door leading up some steps to the new refectory, look up at the carved stone bosses. You can see the face of a 'Green Man' peeping through leaves. We know who carved this face. He was called Brice and in 1416, he was paid 4s 8d (about 23p in today's money) for his work. It took him two weeks to carve so he was not paid very much – but of course you could buy a great deal more than you can today with that sum of money.

One other thing that we know about Brice is that he was not English: he is called 'Brice the Dutchman' in the Cathedral records. Was he a refugee? The documents do not tell us, but we know that there were many incomers from the Netherlands in Norfolk and Norwich at this time, almost 600 years ago. Some were economic refugees and others fleeing from persecution. It was a time of great upheavals in their own country, some natural and some human-made. In 1420s Holland alone, there were

3   Ayers (2016), pp. 78, 97.
4   Helen Sutermeister, uncompleted thesis on the Merchant Classes of Norwich and the City Government 1350–1500 (commenced 1970) (NRO MC 146/2).

Figure 3 Green Man in Norwich Cathedral cloisters, made by Brice the Dutchman. Photo by the author.

terrible floods in 1421 and 1422, there was a civil war in 1425 and a peasants' revolt in North Holland in 1426. These disasters caused devastation to villages and towns, and many refugees made the short trip across the sea to Great Yarmouth, and from there upriver to Norwich. They included tailors, smiths, glass-makers and even an organ-maker. They also included two hat-makers, apparently bringing a new trade into Norwich. We know the names of many of these people because of the actions of the British Government – which 'registered' them by entering their names on the patent rolls – and they were also made to swear an oath of allegiance to the English Crown.[5]

The ease of travel can be shown from a typical ship travelling across the North Sea, the *Seintemarieschipp of Arnemouth*. She arrived in Yarmouth on 6 December 1388, with a cargo of alum, madder, soap, woad, cotton, canvas, flax and basins. She was soon turned around, and left on 8 December, loaded with Norwich worsted, cheese and rabbit skins. On 26 December, she was back in Yarmouth laden with a similar cargo to that she had brought just 20 days earlier.[6]

There were cultural and religious connections too. Norwich appears to have had groups of women in the fifteenth century dedicated to a communal life but without taking the vows made by nuns. These groups were similar to the beguinages in France and the Low Countries, albeit on a smaller scale. One building that they may have used is that now known as the Britons' Arms on Elm Hill. The Dutch reformist theologian Erasmus visited Walsingham Abbey in 1511, and was sceptical about the authenticity of the 'holy' relics there.

5   Nelly J. M. Kerling, 'Aliens in the county of Norfolk, 1436–1485', *Norfolk Archaeology*, vol. 33 (1965), pp. 200–15.

6   Sutermeister, using the customs accounts in the National Archives; Penny Dunn, 'Trade', in Rawcliffe and Wilson (eds), *Medieval Norwich* (2004a), pp. 224–5. Brian Ayers also uses this example.

Depositions before the mayor of Norwich in legal cases heard in the 1550s and 1560s show trade continuing between the two countries, with perhaps some hints of increasing danger as the years passed and tension in the Spanish Netherlands grew. In July 1551, the court heard a dispute about a trading contract between William Gilbert of Norwich and Hans Vossart (also called Fossart) of Antwerp. The contract was originally drawn up and signed in Antwerp in 1546, and was presumably in Dutch, as Gilbert asked Francis Wolmer of Norwich to provide a translation of it. Evidence from witnesses showed that exports included wheat, malt and beer. On one occasion, bell metal and 'certain church books' were the cargo. Imports included wine and raisins: it was the poor quality of one such cargo that gave rise to the dispute. The depositions showed that Gilbert, Vossart and Vossart's brother Cryne all regularly travelled across the North Sea.

Two years later, in August 1553, a Dutch shipman, John Gilderman, from Vandergol in Holland came to the Norwich court regarding a dispute with one John Harryson of Norwich, a basket maker. The cargo involved in the dispute was loaded at Amsterdam and Ancuse, and is listed in detail: Harryson employed Gilderman to bring in his 'hoye or boat' 54 barrels of cod, six barrels of salmon, two barrels of cods' heads, three half-barrels and a firkin of eels, and 600 staplefish.

These two cases were simply trading disputes, but five years later, in August 1558, a case came before the Mayor's Court arising from the theft of some possessions of Richard Bate, a Norwich merchant, while he was staying in 'Barough' near Antwerp (probably Bergen-op-Zoom). The case also involved William Aldriche, a Norwich merchant, who was in Amsterdam at the time, and William Becket, a merchant from Colchester, who was staying in the inn with Bate, and who was suspected of the theft. Clearly there was still regular travel between the two countries for trade. However, one detail of the evidence suggests a fear of possible danger: when Bate and Becket went into town together from the inn, Becket asked Bate if he was going to take his sword. Aldrich said that he would not as he was confident he would not get into a fight. Becket was more cautious and took his sword with him anyway!

There were always people from the Continent resident in Norwich, whether for a short time or as permanent incomers. William Duchman, from Utrecht, was a leading glass-maker in fifteenth-century Norwich. Later known as William Mounford, he worked on the windows of St Peter Mancroft church, and other churches in the county.[7]

Wealthy merchant John Asger appears to have been born in Zeeland, and to have been in Bruges in May 1426 when he was elected mayor of Norwich. His brass in St Laurence's church in Norwich describes him as 'once a merchant of Bruges'.

The parish registers of the 'market' church of St Peter Mancroft, in the heart of the city, provide several examples of incomers in the earlier part of the sixteenth century. James Lowes and Rose Harbard, 'both Strangers', married there on 5 June 1542. Four years later, the church saw an example of intermarriage: John Jowell, a Frenchman,

---

7   Ayers (2016), p. 136, citing De Biene (ed.), *Utrecht: Britain and the Continent – archaeology, art and architecture* (1996).

married Alice Dennys on 20 May 1546. The very first burial in the surviving registers for the parish is Lucy Delamote, wife of John Delamote, buried on 22 August 1554. Her nationality is not given, but she was followed six weeks later by: 'October 5: John Delamote, Frenchman'.

Several families from the Low Countries were living in Norwich even before the 1560s. Here are three examples.

The Petersons

The most important silversmith in Elizabethan Norwich was Peter Peterson, probably the grandson of 'Peter Peterson, Dutchman' who was admitted a freeman of Norwich in 1495. Peter the silversmith lived in St Andrew's parish and was one of the richest men in the city, paying tax on wealth estimated at £18 in 1576. He identified himself with the native community, specifically saying in his will, made in 1603, that he was born in St Andrew's parish in Norwich, and that he worshipped in St Andrew's parish church. He left money for repairs to that church and the poor of the parish, but revealed his roots by also leaving 40 shillings to 'the poorest sort of the Dutch nation within the city of Norwich' – and his possessions included a 'chest of Flanders make', a 'gilt bowl of Antwerp touch, to drink sack in', and a little bowl 'of Antwerp touch' from which to drink medicine.

The Isborns

Nicholas Isborn, goldsmith, came from the Netherlands to Norwich some time before 1534, in which year he paid to be admitted a freeman. He had a wife named Katherine, but it is not known whether she was an immigrant or native-born. The Isborns lived in Redwell Street and are buried in the nearby church of St Michael at Plea. They had a son, Valentine, and a daughter, Anne. Nicholas left the tools of his trade to Valentine, who became apprentice to another immigrant goldsmith, Zachary Schulte, in 1548. Quite a lot is known about Valentine as his name appears in several different documents. In 1551 Schulte's servant Katherine Grey complained that he was responsible for her being pregnant: he obviously got over this difficulty as he married Alice Albone in St Michael at Plea church in 1556. In 1562, he accused his servant Robert Cullington of stealing from him a blue sapphire worth 100 shillings. Valentine and Alice had four children but fell on hard times: Valentine's tools were distrained in 1568 and they are listed as 'pore' in the Norwich Census of the Poor of 1570, where Alice is described as 'helping others', that is, doing petty chores like taking in washing. One of their children died young, but the other three all married English spouses and had children, so that the family is a good example of how the immigrants easily merged into the native community.

The van Kurnbecks

Martin van Kurnbeck was born in Flanders, and studied medicine at Bologna in Italy. He was working in London by 1553, when he was fined by the Royal College of

Figure 4 The van Kurnbeck tomb in St Mary Coslany, erected under the will of Joan van Kurnbeck. Photo by the author.

Physicians and forbidden to practise for a time. By 1555–6, however, his degree had been incorporated at Oxford University and he had been elected to the Royal College of Physicians. He was in Norwich by 1560, and treated Bishop Parkhurst when he was recovering from fever, and for pain from a bladder stone in 1560 and 1564. In 1570 he reported another Norwich physician to the College for 'illegally licensing empirics in Norwich for pecuniary reward'.

Less is known about Martin's wife Joan or Johanna. In her will, she says that she was the daughter of Henry Leeke, a London beer-brewer. A nineteenth-century publication confirms this: her father was Henry Lake (sic), of Southwark, beer brewer, who was himself born in Germany. He died in 1559. According to this source, Martin and Joan had three children while in London – sons Simon and Henry, and daughter Genevieve. Genevieve grew up to marry a Norfolk landowner, William Dade of Witton near Blofield.[8]

Van Kurnbeck is not recorded in the 1568 census of incomers, although he was already in the city: he was presumably regarded as an English citizen, although I have found no record of any formal denization. This is confirmed by the fact that he owned property, which an alien would not have been allowed to do: he is the only 'incomer' who shows up in the 1568–70 Norwich landgable tax list. He is recorded as owning

8   Frederic Madden and others, *Collectanea Topographica et Genealogica* (1834).

two tenements by the river in St Michael Coslany, formerly owned by John Rede. His name has been crossed out in the record and replaced by another name, so van Kurnbeck had presumably sold the property by 1570.

A legal case about his house came before the Norwich magistrates in 1573: according to the evidence he gave, he was 64 at this time. He and his wife had purchased the house from Sir William Butts. Unfortunately the testimony does not give a date for this purchase. A condition of the purchase concerned one Margaret Morley, a widow who occupied a part of the house, paying 20 shillings a year. It was agreed that she should be allowed to continue to live there at the same rent for as long as she remained a widow. Van Kurnbeck later sold the house to a Richard Thurston with the same condition, and it was this that was in dispute before the court.

Martin and Joan both died in Norwich in 1579, and both left wills. Martin, who died on 9 February 1578/9, describes himself 'as Doctor in Arte and Physicke of the city of Norwich' but did not mention that he was an immigrant. Clearly a wealthy man, he left money to his two servants, John Tolye (who also received the gelding he rode on errands for his master) and Thomas Ashe. He was buried in St Mary Coslany parish church on 26 January. Joan died on 3 September 1579 (buried 4 September), leaving a will which also made no mention of any immigrant status: she asked to be buried beside her husband and requested a monument be put up in their memory. The monument was erected, and can still be seen in the church, perhaps the first in the city to members of its late-sixteenth century 'Stranger' community – if the definition of that group can be extended to include him. Perhaps he was not in sympathy with the Calvinistic religion of his recently arrived compatriots: Ketton-Cremer notes that the tomb has 'the traditional Catholic formula *quorum animabus propicietur Deus* [on whose souls may God have mercy] which the Protestant enthusiasts of East Anglia had already expunged from so many earlier brasses'.[9]

By 1579 there were several thousand Dutch incomers in the city, but these wills contained no reference to them. No money was left to the Dutch congregation or its poor; instead money was left for the poor of the parish of St Mary Coslany. Of the bequests, none was to any person with a Dutch name (and interestingly none were to any of their children, who had perhaps predeceased them). The van Kurnbecks seem an early example of a situation that became common a few decades later: incomers very quickly merging into the local population.

The Dutch Revolt

In the sixteenth century, a large part of North-West Europe was controlled by Spain under the name of the Spanish Netherlands. Broadly this comprised the areas we now call the Netherlands and Belgium, together with parts of what is now North-Eastern France. Many people living in the area would have liked to be free of their Spanish masters, and this was especially so after the Reformation spread into the country. Spain remained loyal to the Roman Catholic faith, as did many of the inhabitants of

9   R. W. Ketton-Cremer, 'The coming of the Strangers', *Norfolk Assembly* (1957), p. 128.

the Spanish Netherlands. However, a larger number embraced Protestantism based on the ideas of John Calvin, and quite a large number went further still, embracing Anabaptism, a form of faith which believed that people should be baptised as adults rather than as children.

Very few states in sixteenth-century Europe were prepared to allow their citizens to worship as they pleased: the faith chosen by the state had to be adhered to, and those brave enough to refuse to do so were liable to be imprisoned, deprived of their goods or even executed. Many would flee their country rather than suffer in this way, and thus become refugees seeking a state whose religious sympathies were the same as their own. As Spain enforced Roman Catholicism in the Spanish Netherlands, many people chose to leave. Naturally they would go to Protestant countries and many came to England, which saw itself as a champion of Protestant Europe, and to which, as we have seen, many people from the Low Countries already had close trading links. In 1560 there were already 1,000 refugees in London, and 400 in Sandwich. Others fled to Germany – there were 2,000 refugees in Emden alone by 1560.

Many chose to fight for independence. The 'Dutch Revolt' as it is now known, lasted over 40 years, and as the fortunes of war fluctuated, waves of refuges might have had to leave, or some exiles might have returned if the situation at the time looked favourable to their cause. Many books have been written about the Dutch Revolt, but in a book on refugees in Norwich only a summary can be given, noting especially events that relate to the exiled community there.

The Protestant community in the Spanish Netherlands issued the Belgic Confession, or Walloon Confession, in 1561. This repudiated Anabaptist ideas and proposed a church on Calvinistic principles. It was formally adopted at a synod at Antwerp in 1566. Even in the early years of the decade, Protestants were leaving the Low Countries to avoid persecution and were being welcomed in England as allies:

> thousands of fugitive Flemings – there were from eighteen to twenty thousand of them in London and Sandwich in 1563, and thirty thousand in 1566 – escaping from the troubled country flocked over to England to be warmly received by the queen, who gave them permission to settle, practise their trades, and worship in their own Calvinist conventicles. The immigrant foreigners were a valuable asset to the economic and industrial life of the English nation.[10]

A number found their way to Norwich. As early as 1565, a radical section of the Norwich immigrant community was apparently prepared to take up arms to support their co-religionists on the Continent. According to the historian Geoffrey Parker, 'consistories of the Dutch church in London, Norwich and Sandwich' organised and paid for Dutch soldiers to fight in Flanders: they landed on 18 September 1565. However, they were rounded up in a few days, tortured to reveal names of their backers, and then executed.[11]

---

10   J. B. Black, *The Reign of Elizabeth 1558–1603* (1959 edn), p. 121.
11   Geoffrey Parker, *The Dutch Revolt* (1979 edn), p. 110.

On 15 April 1566 some 200 Dutch nobles paraded unarmed through the streets of Brussels calling for the moderation of strict laws against Protestants and the recalling of the defunct States General. They were mockingly called 'Beggars' [Gueux], a name the supporters of Protestantism and nationalism later adopted with pride: those that operated at sea became known as the 'Sea Beggars'. On 20 September 1566, 190 members of the Reformed Community in Ypres signed an Accord there. Within 18 months, no fewer than 109 of the signatories had fled to England, including at least 17 who had arrived, with their families, in Norwich.[12]

After a Protestant prayer-meeting at Steenvoorde on 10 August, the crowd were inspired to smash religious images, seen as symbols of Roman Catholicism and therefore of Spanish rule. This iconoclasm, known as the Beeldenstorm, spread through major towns like Antwerp and Ghent. In December 1566, Protestants synods mobilised for a general insurrection. The rebels were routed outside Antwerp. Jacob Visaige, a 'Woodbeggar' captured by Spanish troops in January 1568, claimed that some of the Norwich Dutch community were responsible for uprisings in the West-erkwartier in 1567. The three consistories of the Dutch communities at Sandwich, London and Norwich had supposedly financed the activities of rebel 'Wood Beggars' there. It was in this period that many refugees fled to Norwich. For example, quite a number came from Valenciennes, where the rebels had hung on, hoping for help from French Protestants. The town fell to Spanish government forces on 23 March 1567.

Trading carried on, but under great difficulties, as a deposition before the Norwich magistrates in May 1567 illustrates. A Norwich merchant, Richard Fryer, deposed that he had gone to Nicholas Fryer, a clothier of East Harling, and probably a relative. He asked him about his foreign debts and what goods he had abroad. Nicholas replied that he owed not more than 100 marks, and that he had stock at Antwerp worth perhaps £280 to £300 – 'broadcloths, worsteds, woodnets and thommes'. Richard was surety for Nicholas, and was worried about the likely financial loss involved as a result of upheaval in the Spanish Netherlands.

Spain sent an army of 10,000 mercenaries under the Duke of Alva to restore the domination of the Catholic faith. Alva entered Brussels on 22 August 1567, aiming to establish a reign of terror. In his own words, 'everyone must be made to live in constant fear of the roof breaking over his head.' He instituted a commission (known as the Council of Troubles, or the Council of Blood) to punish those who had been involved in the rebellion. Hundreds, perhaps thousands, of people were executed, and 9,000 had their property confiscated. Towns had to pay for repairs to damaged churches, and a levy was imposed on them to pay for the occupation. Many people fled to Germany and England, where they were welcomed by governments that sympa-thised with their Protestant beliefs. Geoffrey Parker estimates that 60,000 people fled into exile during the six years of Alva's governorship. They joined with those who had left before 1567 to set up Calvinist churches in exile. In England the principal

---

12   W. J. C. Moens, *The Walloons and their Church in Norwich: Their History and Registers 1565–1832* (1887–8), pp. 217–18.

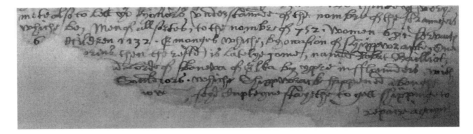

Figure 5 A 'Sea-Beggar' in Norwich (NRO NCR 17d/9). Robert Baliot's name (see below) occurs four lines up, at the end of the line.

communities were London, Sandwich – and Norwich. The year 1567 was, as far as we know, the single one in which the greatest number of refugees fled, the numbers of incomers in later years of the century fluctuating with the fortunes of the war.

The refugees remained fiercely loyal to their faith, and were allowed to set up their own churches in exile. Calvinists from the exiled groups attended an assembly of the church at Wesel in 1568, and a synod at Emden in 1571. They agreed to 53 articles which defined the discipline, theology and framework of the Dutch Reformed Church. The churches in London and Emden were recognised as the senior churches of the exiles in England and in Germany respectively.[13]

The 1568 census notes among the Dutch in Norwich the presence of one Judocus Queke, sailor, who had arrived from Flanders in 1567 with 'fifteen', presumably men: were these victims of a shipwreck or men committed to liberating their native land by force of arms?

At least one 'Sea Beggar' captain *was* in Norwich in 1569. The November head-count of Strangers records a group of 40 soldiers,

> among which by occasion of shipwreck, one more notorious than the rest is lately come, named Robert Baliot, a captain and 'lord of Skovena of Elca by Ypres in Flanders' with about 40 soldiers, which said shipwreck happened about Scarborough and now the said captain stays to get shipping to repair again to 8 other ships of his company about Emden near to the place called Flees.

Joby points out that the captain's name should be Robert de Belle, that is, Bailleul, and describes him as 'a fervent Calvinist who had served as a captain among the Water-geuzen'. The Privy Council recommended that the shipwrecked men be encouraged to leave – 'they being soldiers will not (perhaps) continue in that good quiet order that the rest of their countrymen (being artificers) do'.[14]

Both French and Dutch privateers seized Spanish ships in the Channel. By 1570

13   Parker (1979), *passim.*

14   Walter Rye, 'The Dutch refugees in Norwich', *The Norfolk Antiquarian Miscellany*, vol. 3 (1887), p. 176, quoting Lansdowne MSS vol. 7 no. 82; Christopher Joby, 'The Dutch language in early modern Norfolk: a social study', *Dutch Crossing*, vol. 38, no. 2 (July 2014), note 27.

Map 1 The Spanish Netherlands, with modern-day national boundaries
Source: notes by Nancy Ives on the Strangers in Norwich (NRO, MC 3015/3).

there were about 30 Dutch privateer ships operating out of English ports, but Queen Elizabeth bowed to pressure and expelled them on 1 March 1572. The Sea Beggars then seized the small port of Brielle and operated from there, soon gaining the support of the nearby towns of Vlissingen (which the English called Flushing), Arnemuiden and Veere. Many more towns throughout the Spanish Netherlands rebelled against Spanish rule in the summer of 1572, but the Spanish army under Alva was able to recover all its territory apart from Holland and Zeeland. They persecuted the Calvinists in each town they captured, sometimes hanging the ministers.

These events affected the Dutch community in Norwich. In 1571 Sea Beggars appeared in the city bearing letters of marque from Protestant leader William, Prince of Orange. One of the three ministers in the city, Isabrandius Balkius, opposed them, while the other two ministers, Carolus Rickwaert and Anthonius Algoet, supported them.[15]

The English authorities kept a wary eye on the refugee communities. In October 1571 the archbishop of Canterbury wrote to the Norwich authorities, telling them to make a count of the number of Strangers attending divine service in their own languages, and also the 'number of evil disposed people (under colour of religion and piety)' who might corrupt the 'natural good subjects'. The letter ordered a search for these in all the maritime counties, as they had 'lately entered at sundry ports and creeks in the realm'. On 28 October a search was made into weapons held by the immigrant community in Norwich. No armour was found, but some weapons *were* discovered – two 'calyvers', forty-five 'dags' and pistols, and numbers of halberds and bills, 'bore-spears', swords and rapiers. The officials noted that 'the quantity is not great', and did not confiscate the weapons.

As Andrew Spicer noted, the communities in exile actively supported 'rebels' in their homeland:

> The Stranger communities of Sandwich, London, and to an extent that of Norwich, played an important part in the early years of the Revolt of the Netherlands. The consistories of their communities were responsible for organising the public Reformed service held at Boeschepe in July 1562 and in 1567–8 and they co-ordinated and financed the activities of the Wood Beggars in the Westerkwartier of Flanders. Later, in 1572, the Orangist commissioner sent to Veere by the Governor of Walcheren travelled to Norwich where the Dutch community contributed 125 soldiers who were sent to Veere.[16]

The records confirm this. On 29 May 1572, Herman Modet wrote to the Dutch consistory in London saying that he had just despatched Captain Middeler and about 125 soldiers to Vlissingen in Zeeland to support the Dutch Revolt. Christopher Joby notes that 'subsequent letters from the Dutch church in Norwich also refer to the

---

15   Christine M. Vane, 'The Walloon community in Norwich: the first hundred years', *Proceedings of the Huguenot Society of London*, 24 (1984), pp. 126–7.

16   Andrew Spicer, 'Southampton, Sea Beggars and the Dutch Revolt 1567–73', in T. Hermans and R. Salverda (eds), *From Revolt to Riches: Culture and history of the Low Countries 1500–1700* (2017 edn), p. 54.

despatch of soldiers to support the revolt'. It appears that the great majority of these men were Walloons, and a much smaller number Dutch: already, some refugees were returning to their homeland. Others gave financial support: in 1573 a collection was made in Norwich, and £95 raised to be spent on training soldiers to fight on the Continent.[17]

Norfolk men still traded across the sea, at least with the northern provinces. Francis Johnson, agent for Nathaniel Bacon, wrote to Bacon from Brielle on 22 February 1574/5:

> The Prince of Orange is within Middleburg, and Arnemuiden and, so they say here, that the Prince of Orange have Dunkirk and Ostend and Nieweport and Gravelines. Much I trust in God that it will do us good with the goods that I have bought. There can come no more goods out of Flanders.[18]

A court case in Norwich demonstrates the dangers. In May 1576 John Parker, a Norwich merchant (he lived in Pockthorpe), hired a Wells boat, the *Marie Anne*, with a Wells captain, to transport nine lasts of barley and 19½ lasts of malt to Ostend. When the boat was moored up at Ostend, men from Flushing seized the cargo, claiming it as a lawful prize. The grain was sold for the use of the people of Flushing, and the *Marie Anne* and its captain returned to England empty handed.[19]

In 1573 the Spanish began to besiege Leiden, but the town held out and was finally relieved in October 1574. The States of Holland now increasingly acted as an independent country, creating a university at Leiden in 1575 (the first in the Netherlands, and one attended by a fair number of people from Norwich, both natives and members of the immigrant community), and signing an Act of Union with Zeeland in the same year. However the southern provinces, from where almost all the Norwich refugees had come, remained in Spanish hands. The war continued, with many violent episodes, such as when unpaid Spanish soldiers took Protestant-held Antwerp on 4 November 1576. Between 7,000 and 8,000 Protestants in the city were murdered and 1,000 houses destroyed.

This and similar atrocities united the people of the Spanish Netherlands. On 8 November 1576 the Protestant states signed the Pacification of Ghent, an agreement to unite to expel the occupying army. This allowed for the establishment of a Calvinistic regime for Holland and Zeeland, and a Catholic one in the other provinces. As Johnson wrote to Bacon from Flushing on 8 July 1577: 'the most of news, or men's judgement, is that it will be wars between the Prince of one part and Flanders with Brabant on the other part, viz the Papist against the Protestant.'[20]

---

17 Joby (2014), p.182, citing letters in J. H. Hessels, *Ecclesiae London–Batavae Archivum* (1887–97); Geert H. Janssen, 'Exiles and the politics of reintegration in the Dutch Revolt', *Journal of the Historical Association* (2009), p. 42.

18 A. Hassell Smith, Gillian M. Baler and R. W. Kenny (eds), *The Papers of Nathaniel Bacon of Stiffkey, vol. 1, 1576–1577*, Norfolk Record Society, vol. 46 (1978 and 1979), pp. 156–7.

19 Depositions before the mayor of Norwich in the case: NRO NCR 12a/4.

20 Hassell Smith et al. (1978–9), pp. 262–3.

One Dutch soldier from the Norwich community found himself in court in Leiden in May 1577. Gerrit Heijnricxz was involved in robbery, assault and vagrancy. He was banished for life from the Netherlands, and put on a ship taking Scottish soldiers, convicted of begging, back to Scotland.[21]

In effect, the country split in two in January 1579. By the Union of Arras, signed on 6 January 1579, the southern provinces of the Spanish Netherlands bound themselves to accept Spanish rule, while insisting that occupying troops had to go. They also laid down that Roman Catholicism was the only acceptable religion: Calvinism would not be tolerated. As this was the area from which almost all the refugees to Norwich had originated, there was no incentive to return to their homes. Meanwhile, under the Union of Utrecht of 23 January 1579, the northern provinces bound themselves to act in future as a single province. This was to be celebrated 400 years later as one of the key moments in establishing the Dutch Republic as an independent country.

From May 1585 Antwerp came under siege once more. Exiles poured in financial aid, including those in Norwich: the town records show that supporters in Norwich contributed £825, more than any other Dutch community in England apart from London. However, in August 1585 the Spanish took the city again. This time they acted with greater restraint: there was no massacre, but the Protestants in the town were ordered to leave within two years. Tens of thousands left Antwerp, and well over 100,000 people moved from the southern states still under Spanish rule to the north, where what was to become the Dutch Republic offered security to Protestants. Others may well have sought sanctuary in Norwich: people getting married in the Walloon church in the city in the 1600s include several who came from Antwerp.

The crisis of August 1585 is reflected in the Norwich archives. At the Mayor's Court on 11 August, three Dutchmen – John Fflorrett, Jacob Clynckett and George Furnell – were ordered to leave the city. However, if they decided to go abroad with 'the Dutch Captain which is here in the city to press soldiers', they were permitted to remain in the city until he went and then go with him. This may have been Captain Jacques de Hennebert, who in April 1587 wrote to the authorities concerning money he had been promised, which included £50 from the Norwich Dutch congregation and £25 from the Norwich Walloon congregation.[22]

Philip II's Spanish Armada in 1588 caused a crisis on both sides of the English Channel. On 28 June the Corporation of Norwich granted £100 to fortify Great Yarmouth, and sent 300 soldiers to defend it. After the Armada's defeat, a day of thanksgiving was held in Norwich on 26 September, with all shops closed and everyone on holiday. Although not mentioned specifically, the immigrant community would have joined in these activities – and the celebrations at the defeat of the common enemy.

In the Spanish Netherlands the tide turned in favour of the north, especially when

21   Johanna W. Tammel, *The Pilgrims and Other People from the British Isles in Leiden, 1576–1640*
      (1989), p. 115.
22   *Calendar of State Papers Foreign*, vol. 21/3/, pp. 1–14.

Philip turned his attention to war with France. The Dutch began to extend their territory southwards, although the war fluctuated and some towns were taken only to be recaptured later by the Spanish. The Dutch appointed Maurice of Nassau as their military commander in 1588. His reforms in military training and tactics over the next 20 years created Dutch forces that were not only a match for the Spanish, but also a training school for armies throughout Europe – including those later to fight for Parliament in the English Civil War. Some northern towns, such as Leiden, actively encouraged exiles in England to return. English policy towards Spain changed after 1603, as the new king, James VI, was determined to make peace with Spain.

There were English soldiers in the Low Countries from 1585, when Queen Elizabeth began an ineffectual intervention in the war. The army would have included men from Norwich. The city chamberlain's records include charges paid on 3 May 1602 for nine soldiers sent to the Low Countries, for example: according to Norwich's greatest historian, Francis Blomefield, they were part of a force of 300 men sent to Ostend. Naturally there were contacts between soldiers and local girls, sometimes leading to marriage. In 1600 Andrew Fielding, a Scottish soldier, married Lydia Jacobs from Norwich in Leiden. In 1608 Anthony Duven, a soldier from Norwich serving at Zutphen, married a Leiden girl in that town.[23]

The Truce of Antwerp of 1609 settled the independence of the northern states. The Dutch Republic was recognised by other European countries, and rapidly rose to become a great power. However the southern states, including Flanders and Brabant, from where most of Norwich's refugees had originally fled, remained under the rule of Spain. Many thousands of their Protestant inhabitants moved north to the Dutch Republic where they could worship as they wanted. Geoffrey Parker estimates that over 10,000 emigrants arrived in the town of Leiden alone. Most were coming from the southern provinces, but others returned from exile from all over Protestant Europe, including from Norwich.

---

23 Francis Blomefield, *Essay towards a Topographical History of the County of Norfolk* (1806 edn), vol. 3, p. 358; Tammel (1989), pp. 78, 88.

Chapter 2

The refugees arrive

The invitation

Medieval Norwich was heavily dependent upon one industry, weaving. By the middle of the sixteenth century the city appeared to some to be in terminal decline. It is not entirely clear to what extent Norwich as a whole was in decline before the Strangers came, but it seems that the textile industry was in a bad way. According to John Pound, the number of worsteds exported from the city via Yarmouth was between 1,000 and 3,000 a year in the period before 1535. The number fell rapidly over the next quarter-century and was a mere 38 in 1561. As early as 1536, the tax that could be claimed from worsted weavers had to be reduced. In 1549 the Common Council complained that masons, carpenters, reeders and tilers were leaving the city to find work. In the same year Norwich became the first city outside London to raise a compulsory rate for poor relief, suggesting that there were many unemployed who needed help. Joan Thirsk states, 'The decline of the worsted trade was responsible for the decay of Norwich. Plainly, a revised worsted industry would help to solve the economic malaise of Norwich and the industrial region round it.'[24]

However, other writers think that the revival had already begun. Joyce Youings says 'a revival in the making of worsted cloths was already under way', and Richard Wilson comments, 'some historians argue that the so-called 'New Draperies, itself a term never accurately defined, but essentially embracing a whole variety of light worsteds blending in mixed yarns, were already to be found amongst the city's range of cloths before the Strangers arrived.' This is the essence of the New Draperies – light mixed fabrics that took over from heavy woollen cloths. Historian Raingard Esser agrees that English weavers in Norwich were already producing ribbons and trimmings before the exiles arrived.[25]

In any case, many contemporaries *saw* the city as in decay, and some saw the skilled weavers from the Low Countries as the answer. In 1566, Norwich invited 24 Dutchmen and six Walloons over to kick-start the industry. This was done through three key documents, and the story is told in the 'Strangers' Book' or 'Book of Orders for Strangers', in the Corporation archives now at the Norfolk Record Office.[26]

---

24 John Pound, 'The social and trade structure of Norwich, 1525–1575', in Peter Clark (ed.) *The Early Modern Town* (1976), pp. 135–6; Joan Thirsk, *Economic Policy and Projects* (1988 edn), p.35.

25 Joyce Youings, *The Penguin Social History of Britain: Sixteenth-Century England* (1984), p. 243; Richard Wilson, 'The textile industry', in Rawcliffe and Wilson (eds), *Norwich since 1550* (2004b), pp. 221–2; NRO, MC 3015/18, quoting from Raingard Esser, *Niederlanische Exulanten im England* (1996). The citation is to footnote 617 in that book.

26 NRO NCR 17d; Christine M, Vane, 'The Walloon community in Norwich: the first hundred

The first part of the book records what happened when Thomas Sotherton was mayor (1565–6):

> By reason that the commodities of worsted making is greatly decayed, by the which many citizens both merchants and artisans that before that time had (of the gain thereof) their whole livings. And great number of poor of the City were set on work, by spinning, weaving, dyeing, calendaring and shearing the said cloths, which now were out of estimation and vent, that the makers and workers thereof in all the exercises aforesaid, were fain to give themselves to other exercises and trades to maintain their families which was nothing so profitable hereby people became poor, many left their houses and dwelt in the country, that the houses decayed for lack of farms and that they were let at small prices, and the city like to decay if prudent policy did not assist the same.
>
> And after many consultations and devices, what trades might be practised to redress this poor state; was given intelligence that divers strangers of the Low Countries were now come to London and Sandwich and had got licence of the Queen's Majesty to exercise the making of Flanders commodities made of wool, which strangers come over for refuge against the persecution then raised against them by the power of the Duke Alva, principal for the King of Spain.
>
> And because the poor here might be exercised in their spinning and wool work a motion was made to Thomas, then Duke of Norfolk, then lodged at his house in this City, that at his return to London he obtained of the Queen's majesty, who of her gracious goodness and merciful clemency, having compassion of the poor state of this her highness' city, did tolerate and admit to be and inhabit within this her highness' city of Norwich thirty master workmen, to have either of them ten servants, to exercise the making of these commodities, with warrant to the mayor and citizens to permit them so to do.

The Duke of Norfolk *was* able to help. Under his influence, Queen Elizabeth issued a letter on 5 November 1565 licensing the Corporation of Norwich to invite a community of 30 Strangers and their families to establish themselves in the city. The letter named only five of those invited, and did not distinguish between Walloons and Dutchmen. It specifically referred to John Powell, William Stenne, Henry Clercke, Peter van Brughen and Bartholomew Janson (also called Bartholomew Johnson in the same document), then adding 'and such others amounting to 30 Dutchmen of the Low Countries of Flanders'. Two of these five men – Clercke and Janson – were not in fact included in the 30 names of those actually invited in by the city.

The Mayor was ordered to permit the incomers to live in the city, and if any died or departed the city, he could allow others to settle in their place. The incomers were not to exceed 30 households, each of which must be made up of a maximum of ten people. They could live in the city:

> for the whole exercising of the faculties of making of bayes, arras sayes, tapesterie, mockades, stamins, kersey and such other outlandish commodities as hath not been

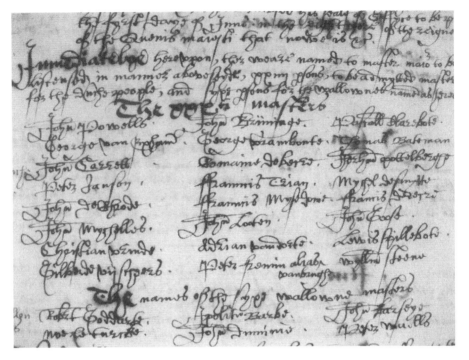

Figure 6 The invitation to 30 Dutch and Walloon 'masters' to settle in Norwich in 1566 (NRO NCR 17d/9)

used to be made within this our realm of England: may lawfully and safely inhabit within the said city of Norwich, and there exercise the said faculties above mentioned and noe other.

Almost seven months later, on 1 June 1566, the Mayor and Corporation formally invited 30 named incomers, 24 Dutch and six Walloon. As agreed, each could bring up to ten people with him. Not everybody was happy: the common council of the city refused to put its seal to the orders inviting the 30, so the mayor used his own seal of office.

The 30 needed a hall in which to display and sell their products, and the former parish church of St Mary the Less in Queen Street was set aside for this purpose. This church belonged to the Cathedral, and when it ceased to be used the city rented it from them, leasing it out for £2 6s 8d a year. The city now spent £43 on fitting it out. The city chamberlain's accounts record the profit for 'renting the onetime church of St Mary the Less for the Strangers to search and seal their bayes': they rented it from Michaelmas 1566 and the profit to the Corporation in the first year was £12 19s 10d, so the city benefitted financially from the arrangement.

Each community also needed a church in which to worship. The Dutch speakers were assigned the chancel of the former Blackfriars' monastery, the French permitted to worship in the chapel in the Bishop's palace. These arrangements are discussed further in Chapter 3.

Who were invited?

It is often stated that in 1566 the Corporation of Norwich invited 30 Strangers to come to Norwich and kick-start the declining industry in the city. Further research has produced some qualifications. Many of the 30 were already in England, coming to Norwich from Sandwich or from London, not all of them were weavers, and it does not seem that more than half of them actually took up the invitation.

Ten of the Dutchmen invited definitely came to Norwich. They included Thomas Bateman, a merchant from Flanders, who came to England in 1561 with his wife and five children. He worked as a master baizemaker in Sandwich, in which time two further children were born. He traded in cloth, for example bringing in 16 pieces of bays (as described on p. 56) worth £24 from Arnemuiden to Yarmouth in May 1566, and cloth from Ghent and Holland and 'a little chest for his own use' in the following month. Perhaps this pins down the date at which he arrived in Norwich. Bateman was one of two Strangers who had been excommunicated in Sandwich by the minister there, and who came to the bishop of Norwich asking to be restored to the church. The bishop wrote to the archbishop of Canterbury, 'they appear unto me to be very willing to be restored to the Church again and humbly to crave the benefit of absolution'.[27]

Jooris (in English, George) van Ixem, a woolcomber from Brabant, was living in London in 1561, and then in Sandwich. He came over to England with his wife and two children, and they had three more children born in this country between 1561 and 1568. He brought a maidservant with him to Norwich. He too probably came to Norwich in 1566. In that year, records show that he received a shipload of materials he needed for his business as a woolcomber, including a barrel of vinegar and a hogshead of madder.[28]

Pascal Clarebote, a woolcomber from Winnezele in Flanders, was fined for sectarian activities there in 1558 and 1566. He arrived in England in 1561 with his wife and two children. He appears on a Sandwich tax list in 1563, but seems to have returned briefly to Flanders as, according to Esser, he was again fined there for sectarian activity in 1566. William Steene [Stone] and John Powell [Paulus] were leaders of the radical party in Sandwich. They supported image-breaking there, and came to Norwich when this was rejected by the Sandwich community.

Five others came to England from Flanders between 1561 and 1564, John de Rhrode, Frauncis Tryon, Frauncis Mysedome and John Letten were wool-combers; Lewis Spillebote's occupation is not given. Another three of the 30 can probably be identified with men in the 1568 census. Ilberde Vijscheers was probably the Gisbert Visscher, tailor, who came to England from North Brabant, Peter Frenin alias van Brughe is probably Peter Firmin, and John Goose probably Johannes Goosen. Both these men were woolcombers from Flanders.

---

27 *Norfolk Antiquarian Miscellany*, vol. 3, p. 186.
28 Raingard Esser, *News across the Channel: Contact and communication between the Dutch and Walloon Strangers in Norwich and their families in Flanders 1565–1640* (1995), p. 143.

Figure 7 Blue plaque remembering the Strangers, outside Strangers' Court, Norwich. Photo by the author.

One man in the 30, Romaine Debecke, is not recorded in the 1568 census, but was definitely in Norwich by 1571: he was part of the radical group in the city. Another, John Garrett, may also have arrived later: he too is not in the 1568 census, but an incomer of this name paid tax on wealth of 20 shillings in the subsidy of 1576.

The other nine men do not appear in the 1568 census, and I have not found their names in any subsequent records of the Dutch community in Norwich. Perhaps they did not take up the invitation to move to Norwich. George Vanbroute and Frauncis Dedecre are known to have been living in Sandwich, but nothing is known of the seven other Dutch

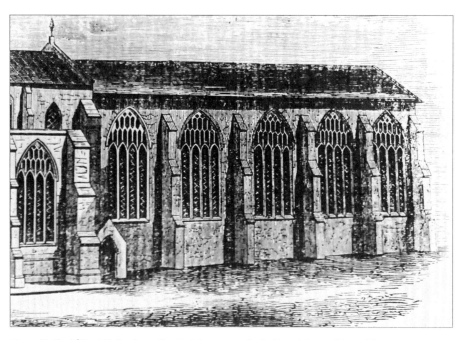

Figure 8 Blackfriars' Hall, where the Dutch community in Norwich worshipped for many years. A 19th-century engraving by G. Dorrington.

invitees: John Bruninge, Jozhm Pottilberghe, Peter Janson, John Mychelles, Christian Vrinde, Adrian van Dorte and Mychel Dosanytte.

Two of the six named Walloon masters were in Norwich by 1568: Robert Goddarte, a dealer in cloth and bays from Lille, and Noe le Turcke, a weaver from Flanders. Both had crossed the North Sea in 1564 or 1565. The other four are not listed in the 1568 census, so were presumably not then in Norwich, and perhaps never came. A lot is known about one, Peter Waolls, a farmer from Houtkerke, and a trouble-maker in Flanders – he was banished from there in 1561. He must have returned there, as he was actively involved in riots in Flanders in 1567. Nothing is known about the other three invited Walloons, Ipolite Barbe, John Dumince and John Karsye. They do not appear in any subsequent Norwich records, so might never have come to the city.

These 30 men were each allowed to bring up to ten 'family' members, which would presumably include apprentices. This would have meant a maximum of 300 people. However, fate took a hand. The crisis in the Spanish Netherlands forced many to flee, and some came to Norwich. Within two years the number of refugees in the city was not much short of 2,000.

Some Strangers had clearly arrived in Norwich before the invitation of 1 June 1566. According to a calendar produced by Dutch printer Anthony de Solemne in 1570, the Dutch church in Norwich was opened on 24 December 1565. Parker's reference to a Norwich consistory in 1565 has already been quoted. Most conclusive is the evidence found by Douglas Rickwood on bay making. In the quarter *ending* midsummer day 1566, the incomers paid tax on 162 bays. The average number of bays made in each of the next three quarters was 224, so they could hardly have made 162 bays between 1 June and 21 June! On the other hand, the fact that the first quarter on which the incomers paid duty on bays was the quarter beginning 24 March 1566 suggests that the community before that date was very small.[29]

The first rush, 1567 and early 1568

The invitation to the 30 families was made in June 1566: a year later, there were not just 300 incomers but almost 2,000. These were refugees, fleeing from the upheaval and persecution in the Spanish Netherlands described in Chapter 1. We do not know when the first invitees arrived, but by the middle of 1567 the city was probably feeling full of incomers. On 17 September the mayor (Thomas Walle, who we are told 'had no liking of the Strangers') ordered the leaders of the new community to bring him a list of the 300 people to be licensed and named to live in the city. They promised to do so, but there is no record of such a list.

As the refugees arrived tensions rose, with several disputes reaching the Mayor's Court in the spring of 1568. In February the city's glovers and white tawers (leather-workers) complained they could not get sheepskins from the city butchers because the Strangers were buying them up. The Court ordered Strangers not to buy any sheep

---

29   Douglas Rickwood, *The Norwich Stranger Settlement* (1989), vol. 1. I have confirmed his figures
     in the original record: NRO NCR 17d/10.

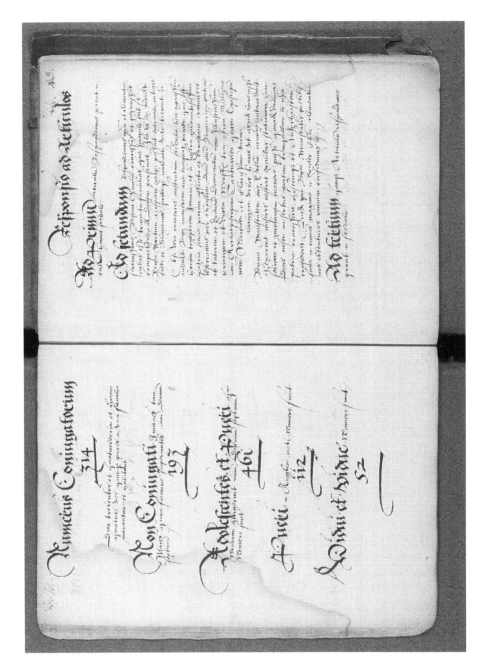

Figure 9 1568 census, numbers of Dutch – the total is wrong as it ignores wives! (NRO DN/DIS 10)

skins, lamb skins or calf skins from any butcher. A dispute between three English tawers and incomer Peter Byllett in the following month led to Byllett's imprisonment. Vincent Tesmond, Simon Sallett and Thomas Tesmond complained about Byllett, who lived in St Michael Coslany: they had gone to his house 'to understand the manner of pulling the sheepskins'. Byllett called the Tesmonds 'knaves', and said he would not teach anyone his skills unless they would be his apprentices for four or five years. As a result, the mayor ordered that neither Byllett nor any other Stranger could buy woolskins in the Market – and sent Byllett to prison. This was followed four days later by an accusation against five immigrants who had set up as joiners: Raynold Louys, Robert Gosens, John Foos, Nicholas Varbraband and Andrew Funnevex. They were told to shut their shops and work with Englishmen – or else to leave the city.

As these incidents show, refugees were moving into Norwich and, in a small number of cases, coming into conflict with the locals. In fact, many hundreds of incomers had arrived in Norwich by the summer of 1568. We know a great deal about these incomers because a detailed census was made, giving names, family size, occupation and place of origin.

The process leading to the census is known. Under orders from the Queen, the archbishop of Canterbury wrote to the bishop of Norwich on 16 May 1568 asking for the count. The results were sent back by the bishop on 4 August 1568. There is no way of telling when, within these dates, the census was actually taken. I suspect it was early in this period: only three Dutch families are recorded as arriving in 1568, so either the rush of incomers was over or the census was taken before the year's rush had arrived. (It must be remembered that the year began on 25 March, so any arrivals in January to 24 March 1568, as we now style it, would be counted as arriving in 1567.) There is a copy of the census in the Norfolk Record Office, and I have analysed this to find out exactly who the incomers were.

Numbers

The census gives the names of individual heads of households, says whether they brought their wives with them, and gives the number of children, distinguishing between those born abroad and those born in England. Each group counts the number of incomers: the Dutch give their total as 1,132, the Walloons as 339. However, the Dutch figures do not tally with the actual numbers of incomers as given in the census. I think the explanation of the discrepancies in the figures lies in the way that married couples were counted. It seems that the original figures included married couples as *couples* rather than as individuals. The Walloon census-taker rightly doubled the figure of married couples to get the correct total of *individuals*, but the Dutch census-taker did not do this, so his 'total' is more than 300 short of the real total of individuals.

I have been through each family in the census and counted 1,480 Dutch incomers and 339 Walloon incomers. It is not possible to be absolutely accurate, as half a dozen families are recorded as having 'children' without specifying the actual number. There are also the 16 'men' mentioned in the previous chapter, perhaps ship-wrecked soldiers and not permanent residents, and who might not be included in the

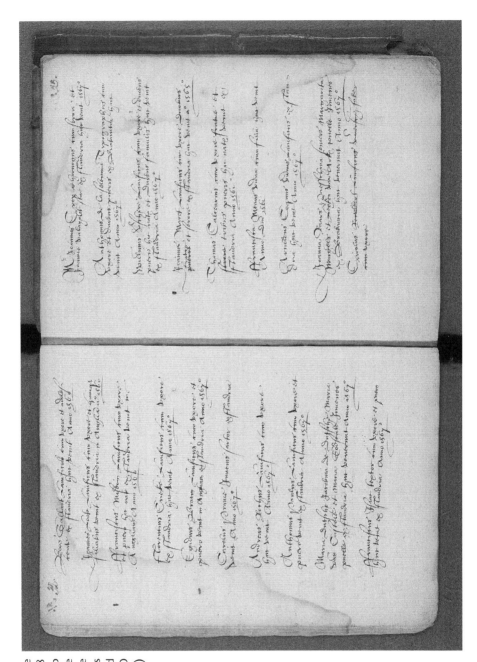

Figure 10 The census of 1568 – John Crop and Anthony de Solemne are the two first entries on the right-hand page (NRO DN/DIS 10)

totals. However, the picture is clear, remarkably precise in fact for sixteenth-century statistics: by May 1568, there were about 1,800 incomers from the Low Countries in Norwich – and this in a city whose 'native' population was probably 13,000 at the most (this calculation is explained in more detail later).

The figures were drawn up by the church authorities of the two groups of incomers, and they employed different methods in some calculations. For example, Dutch servants are not listed separately, so are presumably are included in the single men and women. A search through the individual entries shows up 27 maidservants, three manservants and eight just called servants. Related entries include 'four young people', 'two young people', 'three youths', 'two workmen', so that working apprentices and household servants are not always clearly distinguished.

One purpose of the census was to sort out dangerous elements coming in with the honest refugees, just as ISIS supporters are suspected of coming in with genuine refugees in the twenty-first century. The authorities asked whether the incomers included any 'with dangerous opinions contrary to the faith of Christ's church as Anabaptists and other sectaries, and such also as be doubted of to be guilty of some horrible crime of rebellion, murder, robberies or such like committed by them in the parts from whence they came'. The ministers did not identify any murderers or rebels, but did divide the incomers by the strength of their faith. This does not show up in the version of the census printed by W. J. C. Moens, which just lists the whole lot in alphabetical order.

The Dutch authorities listed the names in three categories: sworn deacons and other brothers (318 names, with their families about 1,170 individuals); those who were not formally members of the church but attended it diligently (70 names, about 255 family members) and finally those who were considered 'unsatisfactory': just eight names, all male, and no indication whether any had family. These were the ones of whom the ministers were critical: four were drunkards, and two were apparently followers of Luther rather than Calvin. The Walloons made similar distinctions: 76 people (totalling 281 if their families are included) were faithful in the church, nine including their ministers (44 counting all family members) were 'faithful', and just six were not in communion with the church (one had a wife, five children and a maidservant, making 13 individuals).

One enquiry was whether they went to parish churches. The Walloons replied that they did not go to parish churches as they did not understand the strange language, but all diligently frequented their own church. In the case of the Dutch, some were reported as being 'not of the flock', as we have seen, but the ministers were optimistic: 'these not to be despaired of'.

Where they came from

The authorities in most cases recorded the place in the Low Countries from which each incomer originated. The Dutch always recorded the province of origin, the Walloons sometimes the province and sometimes the town of origin. Out of 392 Dutch heads of households who give their province of origin, no fewer than 309

Map 2 1568 census, where the immigrants came from. Underlined figures represent Dutch families, those in circles Walloon families. Base map from Frank Meeres, *Strangers* (2012), figures added.

came from Flanders, with 39 from Brabant, 26 from Zeeland, and very small numbers from other provinces. Out of 90 Walloon households, 29 gave their place of origin as Flanders, followed by nine from Artois and five from Hainault; just two came from Brabant. Others gave their town of origin: 28 from Lille, four from Valenciennes and smaller numbers from other towns. One man came from France. These are presumably the places in which they last lived, not necessarily places of birth. One entry suggests further travel: Anna Gomerspach is said to have come to England from Flanders in 1567, but is described as 'of Cologne' in Germany, so had moved at least twice. We will probably never know the full story of the travels of this enterprising spinster.

What they did

The great majority of the incomers were connected with the weaving industry, with wool-comber as the most common single occupation. The others had an enormous variety of trades. No fewer than 204 of the Dutch heads of households were wool-combers or weavers. The next largest groups were merchants (23), tailors (18), smiths (13) and carpenters (11). Those with more unusual occupations included four booksellers, two printers and two gardeners. The Walloons were also mainly in the textile trades, 41 describing themselves as woolcombers, weavers, fringemakers (no Dutchman described himself as a fringemaker) or drapers. Nine called themselves merchants. There were no booksellers, printers or gardeners among the Walloon refugees. The occupations of the incomers are discussed in more detail in Chapter 3.

One group of refugees who arrived in Norwich together must have been in a desperate plight. They came from North Flanders, but arrived in Norwich in a boat from Dieppe in France, so the boat trip was the last leg in a lengthy flight – and they made the journey in winter! The group consisted of five women, 12 children and just one man: Maria, widow of John Faber with seven children; the wife of Peter de Paisetts with three children; Jacob de Poultier with his wife and two daughters; Joanna Clapettia, and Joanna la Dente, widow. Such a group would be in immediate need of support from the community. At least they made it. Although there are no records, common sense says that there must have been some who, like refugees crossing the Mediterranean in the twenty-first century, died on the way.

The great majority of incomers were married couples, with or without children. There were also a number of men travelling without women; a few were widowers with children. Those arriving on their own could have been bachelors (this was explicitly stated in a few cases) or widowers (this was never said). A few had other forms of description – one was called a student, one 'noble', one an old man. The Dutch ministers were not above passing the occasional moral judgment, such as their comment on a carpenter named Jasper Aert – 'so deeply addicted to drunkenness that he seems to have been born for potations rather than piety'.[30]

Just over 70 women arrived on their own. This at least means their names are given in the census: the married women were always just described as 'wife of xx'. The

---

30   R. W. Ketton-Cremer, 'The coming of the Strangers', *Norfolk Assembly* (1957), p. 119.

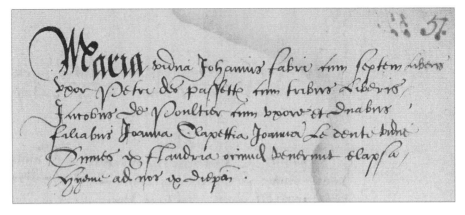

Figure 11 The census of 1568 – Maria Faber and her companions (NRO DN/DIS 10)

women were almost always described as spinsters (26 cases) or widows (31 cases); the latter sometimes brought children with them. In a small number of instances (four Dutch women, two Walloon women), no status was given, but this was probably just poor recording by the census taker.

Ten women among the Walloons were described as wives, but their husbands were not with them. Only two were given their first names, Clara Baileu and Philipotta Halle, the others being described simply as 'the wife of …'. Four were said to be from Lille, and one each from East Flanders, Hainault and Artois (in three cases places of origin were not given). Presumably the husbands remained in the Spanish Netherlands, while their families escaped to a place of greater safety. Eight of the wives were said to have children with them, the number varying between one and four, and in two cases specifically said to be infants. The woman bringing four children was the previously mentioned Philipotta; her husband, Hieronymous Halle, was recorded as a surgeon. I have seen no record of him, or any of the other nine husbands, ever coming to Norwich. No unaccompanied woman in the Dutch census was described as 'wife'.

Some 11 Dutch women (six widows and five spinsters) were recorded as having an occupation: ten of these were wool-combers. The only other occupation was that of midwife. None of the unattached Walloon women was assigned an occupation.

A few of the Dutch women were not assigned any status, such as Clara Dathen, and Elizabeth Sanders with her three sisters, 'girls over 16 years of age'. All came from Flanders in 1567, and all five were almost certainly spinsters. Just one Walloon woman was not given a status: Barbara 'of Harmani Moded'. She was in fact the daughter of Herman Modet, a well-known preacher in the Low Countries, who himself was in Norwich in 1578, but had returned to Utrecht by 1586.

The Dutch census records that 112 children of the incomers had been born in England. As the great majority of the incomers had only been in England about a year, very few had more than one child born in England, just nine families having between two and four English-born children. These were clearly families who had

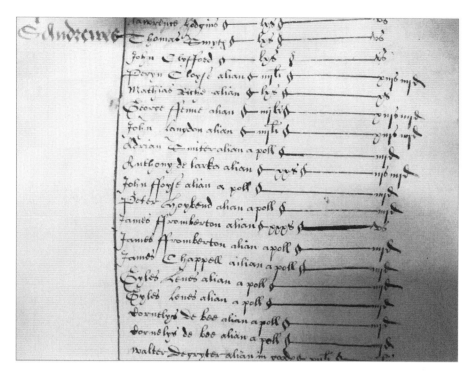

Figure 12 George Fenne and Walter Gruter in the 1576 subsidy (NRO NCR 7i box 3)

arrived in the country several years earlier. The largest families were the Hornes and the Maeschers, each with four children born in England. The families had arrived in England in 1561 and 1562 respectively. Just two families that arrived in 1567 had two children rather than one, having either given birth to two in very quick succession, or had twins.

By far the greatest number of Walloon refugees in the 1568 census, about 70 families, had come over in the spring or summer of 1567, almost all even before the Duke of Alva had entered Brussels. One group from Namur, the Morimontes, make a sharp contrast with the desperate families of East Flanders. Gaspar de Morimonte came with his wife, two children and a maidservant, while Pierre de Morimonte brought his wife, five children and a maidservant. The men, very likely brothers, were wealthy merchants, dealing in corn. They came over in June or July 1567, and by 1568 Pierre was established as one of the elders in the Walloon church in Norwich.

Smaller numbers of Walloons had arrived in England in earlier years, about a dozen families in 1565 and half a dozen in 1566. A few had arrived in the previous decade, the earliest in the census by far being Nicolas Carron, a wool-comber from Lille, who had arrived 19 years earlier, which would be in about 1548 (unless there has been a scribal error, and 19 *months* was really meant).

First impressions: writing home

We are incredibly lucky that the text has survived of over 60 letters written by the incomers on their arrival to Norwich. They were written by them to relatives and friends in Ypres, and survived because they were seized from houses in Ypres as incriminating evidence. They were stored with the archives in Ypres Town Hall, and when that building was destroyed in the First World War the letters went too. Fortunately, their importance had already been recognised by historians. The letters were published by H. Q. Janssen in 1859 and 1861, after that by Pieter de Smedt had been published by I. L. A. Diegerick, the Ypres archivist, in 1852. They are in Dutch, of course; the most recent and best translation is by Alistair Duke. Like all archives they need to be set in their context. The writers are trying to persuade relatives and friends to come over to Norwich: 'That a country that is poor, rainy and cold, and populated with hostile and unfriendly Englishmen and women cannot look too attractive for a prospective migrant is obvious.'[31]

The two earliest letters from Norwich were both written to Oliver Keeuwere in Ypres in July 1567: recognising the dangers, he tore them up, so they presumably existed in this torn form until their eventual destruction in the First World War. They were written by the minister, Karel Rijckwaert, and by Thomas Willemot, a wool-comber. Two letters were written in the last days of August, one in September and ten in the first four days of October. Just one writer wrote twice in this short period, Clais van Wervekin writing to his wife on 21 August and to Jooris Tooris on 4 October. Later letters included ones from Adrian Wallewn, 7 January 1568, and Gilles Navegeer, 13 September 1569.

The letters include one from Pieter de Wulf to his nephew Victor Fruutier in Ypres, written on 8 July 1568. Wulf was the only person in the 1568 to be described as 'nobilis': according to Duke, he was one of the richest Calvinists in Ypres, from where he was formally banished. In the letter he comments that he does not think he has done anything wrong, as he did not go to Reformed services until they were allowed under an agreement drawn up in September 1566. On a practical note, he asks Fruutier to look after his possessions left behind in Ypres – and to send him money.

Some letters describe the journey from the Spanish Netherlands to Norwich. Pauwels de Coenes urges his wife and children, who are still in Ypres, to sell everything she does not need and come over. He sends her a barrel of herring to sell to provide ready cash so that she can come over quickly, 'for the journey, as we understand, is every day becoming more dangerous'. She presumably soon came over with the children, as the 1568 census lists Coenes, a smith from Flanders, as being with his wife and five children.

Clais van Wervekin has heard that the recipient of his letter is thinking of going to Friesland, but he recommends Norwich instead as the cost of living is cheap and the people are very friendly. Tanneken van der Haghe gave practical advice to incomers: they should go to Nieuwpoort and take a ship to Yarmouth and then come on to

---

31   Esser (1995), p. 142.

Norwich. To go via Sandwich would cost them twice as much. Clement Buen recommended an inn in the town, the *Halve Maan*. However, Jan Philipeel had problems in Nieuwpoort: the people there treated him and his wife and six children meanly, forcing them to spend the night without a bed.[32]

Leonard Teerlinck was a wool-comber from Flanders, with a wife and five children. He had had a letter from his brother-in-law in Ypres asking if Leonard thought he could make a living in Norwich. He replied that he was sure a living could be made 'for you buy more here for a stuiver than, so I hear, in Ieper [Ypres] for three'. He also had practical advice: come before the winter, and only bring what is really needed, 'for the freight is expensive'. In contrast, Clement Buen advised his wife to 'bring also with you all your clothes and your daughter's clothes, for people go about decently dressed'.

Pieter de Smedt wrote to his son Salomon Faber in Ypres describing the journey made by family members. Salomon's little brother Jacobellus had been sent ahead by their mother, duly arriving on 29 September [1567]; the lady herself had suffered from seasickness but had soon regained her strength. He urged Salomon to join them: it was only a day's journey from Leuven to Antwerp, and 'the journey from here [Norwich] to Antwerp is not at all difficult'. However, the journey could be dangerous. Maerritgen Vrancken wrote to her son to say that if was unable to make a living, he could come to her with his wife and family: he must, however, lie low 'for they're keeping a strict watch to arrest people'. Olliver Cuvelier had come to Norwich with his children, leaving his wife Paescincken in Ypres. There were rumours in Norwich that she had died there, so he wrote anxiously to her for news.

Those still in Ypres would naturally be worried about employment prospects in a new city, and several letters addressed this. Clement Buen told his sister-in-law that her husband Lein could not practise his craft in Norwich, 'for they only make bays'. Hans Losynghier wrote back to Ypres that now he was in Norwich, he found that his old craft was not practised there, and he was now learning to comb. The census says that he came with his wife but no children, and does indeed describe him as a wool-comber.

Nicodemus Navegeer, wool-comber, arrived in Norwich 1567 with his wife and four children. His son Gilles wrote to his grandmother back in Ypres that he and his family 'are living in great quietness and peace'. The family had been able to find employment of various kinds – his brother was learning the trade of a cutler, one sister worked in a brewery, another younger one spun thread, while a third sister Synken, presumably just an infant, 'played all day'. Gilles himself also had to learn new skills when the family came to Norwich: he had spent 18 months there learning bookbinding, but finding it did not pay he had turned to a new (unspecified) craft. His father wound reels for spinning yarn, while his mother did the same (unspecified) work as she had done in Ypres.

Some letters give other first impressions – how some things differed in Norwich,

---

32 Janssen had difficulty reading the original, suggesting the name Baet as a possibility. Duke suggests Buen, who was indicted by the Council of Troubles and who is in the 1568 census, and I follow him here.

and also how supportive the Norwich people were to the incomers. Clais van Wervekin wrote: 'when you come, bring with you, if possible, a dough trough for you don't find any here; they knead everything in earthenware which is most disgusting …. Will you also buy two small wooden dishes for making half a pound of butter. The Netherlanders or Flemings make all their own butter, for here they only use lard.' He also commented, 'You'd never believe how friendly the people together are, and also how well-disposed the English are to our nation.' Wervekin had been a hat-maker in Ypres. A keen reformer, he had had one of his children publicly baptised by the Reformist preacher Robert Flaminius.[33]

Other letters stressed that the incomers were a community in the city: many immigrants already knew each other from home. When Clement Buen arrived in Norwich on 3 September, he was, he wrote, joyfully received by 'Clement van Tanne's aunt and her husband, Jan Langedul, Thomas Vilgemo, meester Pieter de Smet, Franchoys Tybaut, Thomas Bateman, Jan Bateman, Claies Victor and others'.

Pieter de Smedt asked his son to send over the chair on which her mother sat at outdoor services, and her two best rings, if these items could be recovered from the Ypres bailiff. If they did arrive, they would probably have come via Wulfaert Boetman who ran a ferry service between Nieupoort in Flanders and Great Yarmouth. A regular carrier, he is mentioned in several of the letters.

Most of the letters are from men, but there are a number from women, providing an authentic female voice from almost five centuries ago. Mayken de Wert and her cousin urged their parents to come to Norwich: the two girls were both learning to spin bays. The unnamed wife of Jaques Rollier wrote to her son that she had arrived in Norwich on 29 September [1567], after a good journey, and her health was good. She asked that her things be given into the care of the wife of Adrian Wallwyn or given to Wulfaert Boetman, who would presumably bring them over to her. In another letter, to a friend, she said that she was living in a good 'passage' where many people walked by and which was close to the market and the church. Tijnken Peer, who according to Alistair Duke's notes was lodging with Thomas Bateman, wrote back to her father that 'so many people have come across that it's incredible'.

Perhaps surprisingly, a significant number of these letter writers do not appear in the 1568 census, including Pieter de Smedt and Olliver Cuvelier: either they had already moved away, or the census is not as complete as it is generally assumed to be. The name De Smedt does not occur in this form, in the Latin form, Faber, or the English form, Smith. A man of this name, a common one of course, does occur in the London Dutch Church register of 1561, and the next list of names of incomers in Norwich, the 1576 subsidy, *does* include a Peter Smet, but it is impossible to say whether these refer to the same individual.

Some of the other letter writers probably did only stay a short time in Norwich, such as William Bricxes who wrote from Norwich to his wife in Ypres on 1 October 1567. It is known that he *left* Ypres at Whitsun 1569, so he must have gone back there from Norwich fairly soon, to leave the town again! We know of his movements

---

33   Esser (1995), p. 139.

because he was arrested as a supposed rebel in July 1570. Another letter-writer, Joos Dateen, was also a known 'trouble maker', taking part in image breaking in Ypres in 1566, and may have moved on fairly quickly.

These letters are a unique record of the feelings of the immigrants, and any historian must be grateful to Janssen for his original transcription of them, and to Alistair Duke for making them available in English.

Another collection of letters was confiscated when Henry Fleel, alias Floeau, and his ten-year-old companion were captured near Calais by Spanish troops on 26 February 1570. He had 79 letters on him destined for various places in England, including five intended for Norwich: they were written between November 1569 and February 1570. They included one to Jan Kacaut, who is listed in the 1568 return as a carpenter.

There is one other letter that describes the life of the refugees, though it was written some years later. Walter Gruter, his wife Catherine and their four children, from Brabant, arrived in Norwich in 1567. A quarter of a century afterwards Catherine, then living in Danzig, wrote a letter describing the flight. This is now in Heidelberg University. It records that the family, probably like many others, first arrived in London. Gruter's story gives a personal example of a tendency noted by Joyce Youings, the dispersal of Strangers from the capital, where there were thought to be too many immigrants, to the provinces.[34]

They decided to leave London, 'then we journeyed 90 miles with four children for two months by land on a wagon, and came to a town called Norwich where there were about 1,200 Flemings and among them all not one person that I had ever seen before'. Finding work also proved difficult:

> we did not know what to do to earn our living there. The trade was the spinning of wool and preparing of bays, in which we had no skill, so we had to join together with other people and bought wool and supplied the poor people with wool and took bays in exchange and sent them to London to sell them there. There we chanced upon a merchant, who, when the time came for payment and we thought to have our money was bankrupt, and £450 Flemish was lost: that was our first welcome. The second was that the same man who was in partnership with us left England secretly to cross to Flushing with £300 sterling and on arrival at Flushing he jumped into the water for fear of the Spaniards who came alongside, and sank with all the money and never came up again. And so we lost that too.

Despite these difficulties, the family eventually did flourish in their new homeland. One of the children was Janus Gruter, born at Antwerp in 1560. He went on to Cambridge University, and later became one the greatest literary figures in the Europe of his day.

---

34   Youings (1984), pp. 242, 348.

Later incomers, 1568 onwards

There is no later equivalent to the 1568 census with its list of names of households, occupations, and details of where the incomers came from and how long they had been in England. However, the city authorities kept a wary eye on numbers, and head-counts were made in 1569 and 1571. There was a further headcount in 1583. Other lists give names of householders or taxpayers only: taxation records, muster lists, and the 'Return of Strangers' of 1622: the number of dependants can only be guessed. The numbers were certainly in decline by the early years of the seventeenth century and the actual highest number on record is that of the 1583 headcount: however, there are good reasons for thinking the highest number in the city was in the early months of 1579, as we shall see.

The headcount of 1569

On 16 November 1569 Thomas Walle, the mayor, wrote to the Privy Council with a count of the number of Strangers now in Norwich. There were 752 men, 681 women, 262 servants and 1,132 children, making a total of 2,827. No distinction is made in this return between children born abroad and those born in England. [35]

The last figure of the number of servants has been lost in the entry in the Norwich Strangers' Book, although it was still legible when a transcript of it was made in 1913. However, it must be 262 to match the final total. As there were only about 40 servants recorded in the 1568 census, the word is probably being used here to include young workers as well as household servants.

The Dutch said that because of the persecution in the Low Countries:

> many poor Christians which (rather than they would forsake Christ and his Gospel) left their houses, lands and friends, and took refuge in this your Majesty's realm. And many of them came to Norwich aforesaid, using all means to get their living in the sweat of their brows in the said sciences, rather than that should be chargeable to any man.

Perhaps surprisingly, Walle agreed: 'All which company of strangers, we are to confess, do live in good quiet and order, and that they travail diligently to earn their livings.' The Privy Council recommended that the incomers (apart from the shipwrecked men mentioned earlier) be allowed to stay provided they behaved themselves 'quietly and in good order'. However, no others should be permitted to settle in Norwich from Sandwich or elsewhere in England.

In the 18 months since the census of May 1568, the number of immigrants in Norwich had almost doubled, going from 1,480 to 2,827.

The headcount of 1571

In October 1571, it was the central authorities that took the initiative. The archbishop of Canterbury wrote to the mayor and Corporation telling them to make a count of

---

35 NRO NCR 17d/9.

the number of Strangers attending divine service in their own languages, and also the 'number of evil disposed people (under colour of religion and piety)' who might corrupt the 'natural good subjects'. The headcount was conducted in Norwich on 16 November 1571, exactly two years after the previous count.

The total number of Strangers was 3,993 (1,056 men, 1,095 women and 1,862 children). After taking the count, the authorities made a list of 48 'disordered persons' (all men) who were to leave the city. They included William Steene, one of the original 30 invited to the city. They then gave the Privy Council the information that the number of Strangers in the city was 3,925 (868 men of the Dutch nation, 203 men of the Walloon nation, 1,173 women of both nations, and 1,681 children under the age of 14, of whom 666 were born in England). The smaller figure is presumably because the 48 (perhaps with their families, nothing is said of them) had been driven out, and so are no longer included in the count.

Not counting those banished, the immigrant population had risen by just over a thousand in a year. The city itself calculated that 355 people had arrived in the six months since 25 March 1571, made up of 85 Dutchmen, 25 Walloon men, 85 women and an unspecified number of children – and also one Frenchman from Dieppe. So, every month in the summer of 1571 saw about 50 incomers arriving in the city. The figure probably dropped during the winter months, but the authorities must have dreaded what might happen the next summer. However, no more headcounts were conducted until 1583.

The 1571 headcount is the only one that counts the number of Strangers in each ward, so that we can see where they tended to settle, and also make some comparisons with the English population. Fell uses the figures for the English population given in John Pound's edition of the *1570 Census of the Poor* for the Norfolk Record Society (themselves based on the names of the poor, those paying poor rate and an estimated 40 per cent of others). She gives these figures:

Colegate, and Middle Wymer: Strangers make up 59% of the total population
West Wymer: Strangers make up 58% of the total population
North Conesford: Strangers make up 46% of the total population
Coslany: Strangers make up 39% of the total population
Fyebridge, and St Giles: Strangers make up 37% of the total population
South Conesford: Strangers make up 32% of the total population
East Wymer: Strangers make up 26% of the total population
Ber Street: Strangers make up 20% of the total population
St Stephen: Strangers make up 14% of the total population
St Peter Mancroft: Strangers make up 13% of the total population.[36]

It is no surprise that the number of incomers was noticed by other visitors to the city. On 21 April 1575, Thomas Kendall wrote from Norwich 'the city is filled with strangers'. By the 1570s, the Norwich community was the largest in England with

36   John Pound, *The Norwich Census of the Poor,* Norfolk Record Society vol. 40 (1971), p. 107.

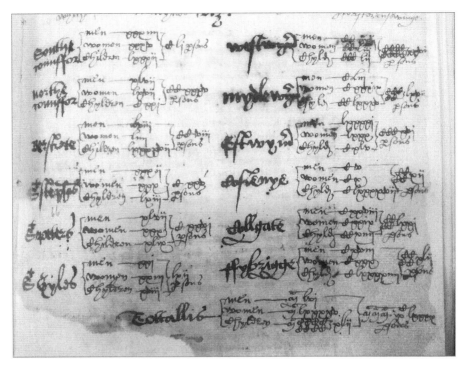

Figure 13 The headcount of 1571, showing number of Strangers in each ward, from the Norwich Strangers' Book (NRO NCR 17d/9)

4,000 or more refugees in the city. This compares with 3,500 in London, 1,200 in Sandwich, 800 in Canterbury, 200 in Colchester – but with over 5,000 in the German town of Emden.[37]

At least one in four, and possibly considerably more, of the inhabitants of Norwich in 1575 were immigrant refugees who had arrived in the previous ten years, who spoke different languages in the streets (in the main, Dutch; a sizeable minority, French), and whose first loyalty was to their own incomer community rather than to the parishes or wards in the city in which they lived. Of course, there were *some* tensions. It is amazing that there were so few: the overwhelming spirit in the city was one of welcome to the stranger.

The 1576 subsidy

The next 'count' of incomers was not for the city but for the government, the subsidy of 1576. Subsidies are national taxes on land and possessions, and are very important for the study of incomers for two reasons. In the first place, they list all the incomers wealthy enough to pay the tax, along with those English rich enough to do so. In fact, the aliens stand out as they had to pay double! In practice, they are also distinguished

---

37   Figures as given in Geoffrey Parker, *The Dutch Revolt* (1979 edn), p. 119.

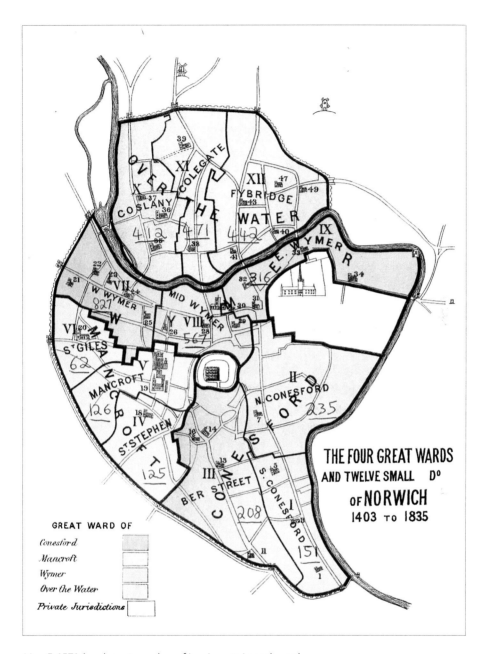

Map 3 1571 headcount, number of immigrants in each ward
Source: Base map from W. Hudson and J. C. Tingey, *The Records of the City of Norwich* (1906).

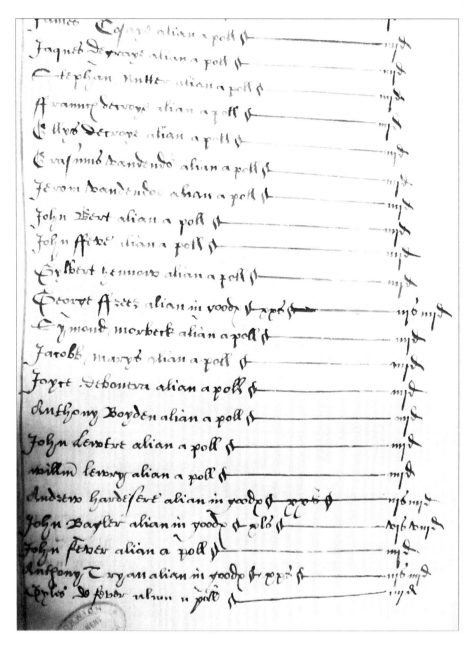

Figure 14 The subsidy of 1576, a unique listing of the Strangers in the years before the great plague (NRO NCR 7i box 3)

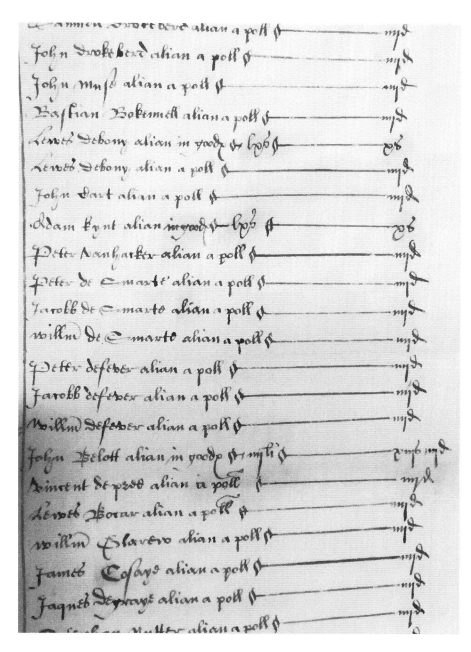

Figure 15 Strangers in St Martin at Palace parish, from the 1576 subsidy. They include the merchant Adam Kyndt (NRO NCR 7i box 3)

by the word 'alien' being added to their names. The second reason is that each time there was a subsidy, all incomer households had to pay a tax of 4d, which natives did not have to pay. So, a subsidy list consists of the names of both English and immigrants rich enough to pay, followed in each parish by the names of the immigrant households too poor to pay any tax on their possessions, but compelled to pay their 4d. It is a great source for the names of immigrants, their wealth and for identifying where they lived.

The important of subsidies as a source has long been recognised: several are printed in Moens, for example. Like everyone else, I have made use of these. However, I am breaking new ground by concentrating on the 1576 subsidy, which has not been used before. This has the advantage that it gives the number of immigrants exactly ten years after the original invitation – and, above all, before the disastrous events of 1579 cut into the incomer population.

In this subsidy, 210 'aliens' had enough property to pay tax on it, and a further 1,321 paid their 4 pence, making a total of 1,531 named people. This invites the question of how many non-taxpayers – wives and children – need to be added to obtain the actual number of individual immigrants. Multiplying the taxpayers by three would produce a figure of 4,593 people, and multiplying by four would produce a total of 6,124: the real number of incomers in 1576 probably lies somewhere between these figures.

Almost half the aliens, 711, lived in Over the Water (OtW) ward, and 505 in Wymer ward. There were 201 in Conesford ward, and just 114 in Mancroft ward. In terms of parishes, four parishes had over 100 aliens in the subsidy: St Michael Coslany, St Peter Parmentergate, St Augustine and St Gregory. In contrast, in a few parishes the number of aliens did not reach double figures; St Peter Southgate and St Etheldreda combined had only three, as did St George Tombland. St John Sepulchre had only seven.

The subsidy as a whole raised just about £500, the wealth divided in this way between the four wards: Wymer 44 per cent, Mancroft 24 per cent, OtW 22 per cent, Conesford 10 per cent. The 'wealth' of the aliens was very similar, being divided like this: Wymer 48 per cent, Mancroft 32 per cent, OtW 32 per cent, Conesford 6 per cent. The parishes with the highest amount of wealth among the alien community were St Michael Coslany, followed by St Laurence and St Michael at Plea. Some of the parishes that contained most immigrants had very little wealth: only four of the 103 aliens in St Augustine paid tax on their possessions, and only eight of the 101 in St Gregory.

The subsidy lists mainly adult males, but the names of several women do occur, mainly widows as we might expect. There are a few other females, such as these on the list of those living in St Peter Mancroft: Barbara (no surname), servant to Matthew Farhagan; Mary Malard, daughter of William Malard; Frauncis Kynne, Katherine Kynne, Dorathe Kynne, Jone Kynne – an ambiguous list. I take the last three names to be female, but none to be a wife (no married women are named in the subsidy), so perhaps the women are sisters, or grown-up daughters.

The year 1576 may represent the highest point for the number of immigrants within Norwich. In that year, William Tipper secured a royal patent for the 'hosting' of merchant strangers throughout England, that is, placing Strangers with English hosts. He enforced his rights in Norwich through his deputy William Rookewoode, and their control was so draconian that, according to Dr John Pound, 'many newcomers left the city and others prepared to follow suit'.[38]

The city could not allow this to continue: after negotiation, the city authorities paid Tipper 100 marks (£70 13s 4d) to take over the role of deputy themselves as it affected Norwich. Norwich authorities told the immigrant communities in the city that they had done this to protect them from further molestation. The city 'borrowed' the money from the city's corn stock, returning it to that account in 1579.

The visit of Queen Elizabeth

In 1578 Queen Elizabeth came to Norwich. This was a great event, the first royal visit since King Henry VII almost a century earlier: many citizens of Norwich never got to see a monarch. It was also an important occasion for the incomers. Their pageant represented no less than seven looms showing off their techniques – worsted, russel, dornix, mockado, lace, caffa, fringe. Hermanus Modet, the Dutch preacher, made a long speech in Latin (translated here):

> The very calamity of godly men, and tears of the afflicted, the tears I say of faithful *Christians*, have thoroughly moved thee to defend and protect the miserable and dispersed members of *Christ* exposed to every kind of injury, frightened by a thousand deaths, with the safety and preservation as well of mind as body. For these thy singular benefits of godliness towards us, and that we live under so good a tutor, as the magistrate in this thy city of *Norwich*, which thy Majesty hath of clemency granted unto us for a mansion place, which were banished for *Christ's* religion: and moreover for that we find the minds of the people favourable towards us, first we give immortal thanks, not such as we ought, but such as we are able unto *God* the father, and the *Lord* our only *Saviour Jesus Christ*: and then unto thee most merciful Queen.

Modet gave the Queen a silver gilt cup worth £50 on behalf of the two foreign congregations. In return, as the Mayor's Court Book for 30 August 1578 records, Queen Elizabeth gave £30 to the relief of the poor among the immigrant communities in Norwich. On this day, the money was handed to Thomas Layer as mayor, and immediately handed over to the deacons, Anthony de Solemne and Zegor Wittewrongle for the Dutch, and Jan Debraban and Thomas de la Tombe for the Walloons. The Dutch were given £19, the Walloons £11, presumably in proportion to their numbers. This was done in the presence of Modet as minister of the Dutch congregation, and Leodowycus Maupin, minister of the Walloon congregation.

This was perhaps the high point of immigration in Norwich. In the following year, there was a crisis. An outbreak of plague killed many thousands of people in Norwich, including at least 2,500 incomers. This is discussed more fully in Chapter 5.

---

38   Pound, in Rawcliffe and Wilson (2004b), p. 43.

Figure 16 Queen Elizabeth's visit to Norwich in 1578 as portrayed in the programme to a pageant by Nugent Monck, 1926 (NRO MC 26/211)

The city was becoming more wary of refugees. At the Mayor's Court of 16 March 1580, eight 'stranger' newcomers were commanded to leave the city, saving one young maid and two children of 10 or 12 years old who were allowed to remain. The water bailiff and four Elders of the Congregation were told to convey the newcomers to Yarmouth 'with all speed'. A fortnight later, the court had to deal with a further 11 strangers who had turned up in the city. Again, the court looked at the individual circumstances of the incomers: all were told to leave the city and go overseas except for one man, named Maund. He had come from Sandwich with his wife and three children, and a testimonial letter from the mayor of Sandwich; the family were allowed to stay. These are the only two entries of this kind in the mayor's court books, and may reflect the fact that it was a time of plague, when incomers were naturally received with great suspicion. On 29 October 1580 each alderman was ordered to search [out] and certify the strangers in his ward, but this does not appear to have been carried out.

The subsidy of 1581

The subsidy of 1581, which is printed in Moens, shows a sharp fall in the number of alien taxpayers compared with that of 1577: 166 paid tax on property, and 850 paid the 4d, making a total of 1,026 people. Using the same multipliers, this would represent between 3,048 and 4,064 individuals. The parishes where the most wealth was concentrated were St Mary Coslany (£30), St Michael Coslany (£29) and St Andrew and St John Maddermarket (£26 each). The poorest areas were St Swithin and St James Pockthorpe, where 52 incomers paid the poll tax but none of them had any taxable wealth.

There had been a great decline in both alien population and alien 'wealth' in the five years between 1576 and 1581. In Conesford Ward, the number paying tax fell by 79, and wealth fell by £16; in Mancroft Ward, the number paying tax fell by 51, wealth by £34.10s; in Wymer Ward, the number paying tax fell by 76, wealth by £82; in OtW Ward, the number paying tax fell by 301, wealth by £29.

Of the 27 aliens who paid tax on wealth of £5 or more in the 1576 subsidy, just five appeared in the same parish in 1581, and two others had moved to different parishes. No fewer than 20 of these wealthy aliens have disappeared in the intervening five years. Two are known to have moved away (Thomas Bateman and Walter Gruter) but the fate of the other 18 is not known, many no doubt being victims of the 1579 plague. The fall of 505 aliens in five years reflects deaths by plague, returns to Europe and moves elsewhere, balanced by an unknown number of new incomers.

The headcount of 1583

The next head count was taken in 1583, and we have more details of how it was done. On Saturday 26 October, the Mayor's Court ordered the aldermen in each ward to find out how many Strangers, men, women and children, were in their ward on the following Tuesday. Three of the aldermen reported their results on Wednesday 30 October:

> Thomas Layer, alderman of Colegate ward brought in the certificate of the Strangers: men 139, women 170, children born abroad 115, children born England 229. Total 424.

> Nicholas Sotherton of St Giles ward: men 24, women 20, children born abroad 9, children born in England 20. Total 53.

> Mr Yarrington of Ber Street ward: men 20, women 24, children born abroad 11, children born in England 18. Total 55.

Mathematically minded readers will at once notice that the totals are all 'incorrect', and will soon see why: the aldermen have *not included the children born in England* in their totals. Layer, Sotherton and Yarrington are known as supporters of the Strangers, so they produced the lowest figures. The city's official statistics give a much higher number. This playing about with the statistics of numbers of immigrants was an issue in the sixteenth century, just as it is in the twenty-first century debates on the same subject.

The other nine wards must also have bought in their certificates. The actual figures for these were not recorded in the court book, but at the court on 10 November the totals were announced: 1,128 men, women 1,358 women, 815 children born abroad, 1,378 children born in England: total 4,679. The city's official count *has* included the children born in England, and this is the figure recorded in the State Papers, 'being Dutch refugees and others'.[39]

The total of 4,679 represents an increase of 754 since the previous headcount 12 years earlier, but this hides the fact that in between, over 2,000 of the refugees had died of plague. The figures for the three wards that record the numbers in 1583 suggest a change in the pattern of where the immigrants lived, either through plague deaths or because of physical movements of people over the years. Between 1571 and 1583 the immigrant population of Ber Street ward fell by 134, and the small population of St Giles by 11, whereas that of Colegate ward rose by 182. This confirms the general impression of later documents that Colegate and West Wymer were the areas where the incomers increasingly tended to congregate.

A few years later the city authorities, like many governments since, attempted to control immigration by punishing those who actually transported the newcomers. At the Mayor's Court of 27 March 1585, the Norwich authorities threatened to punish Henry Ford and Thomas Weems, the two city carriers: they were told not to bring any 'aliens or strangers' into the city apart from those already living there, on pain of imprisonment.

The evidence of muster rolls

All able-bodied adult males had the duty of appearing at the musters every year with such arms and armour as they could produce. The only likely enemy was Roman Catholic Spain, which both the native English and the incomers would have seen as a deadly foe.

Although as we have seen there were large numbers of incomers in the city by the early 1570s, they did not appear in muster lists for a generation. The 1574 muster of all able-bodied men of the four great wards has no mention of aliens. The 1578 city muster list also has no separate list of incomers. Anthony de Solemne and George Fenne both appear, without comment, among the list of *Englishmen* bearing arms, no doubt a responsibility that came with taking up the freedom (see Chapter 3).[40]

I have found entries in the muster accounts that show immigrants making a contribution to the organisation in the 1580s:

1587: To two 'Strangers fluters' on Musters Day 3 shillings

1587: To Jacques the claspmaker four shillings for 3 pounds [weight] of brass plates to make new spoons for the guns.

1589: Receipts of money from 'dyverse citizens and alians' for gunpowder at the feat;

---

39 *Calendar of State Papers Domestic, Queen Elizabeth 1581–90*, vol. 163; November 1583.
40 NRO NCR 13a/7.

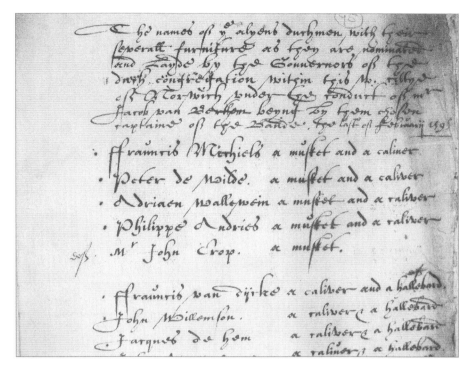

Figure 17 The start of the Dutch musters list, 1595 (NRO NCR 13a/7)'

from Thomas Bonnell and Jacques Wallwyn for 30 pounds of gunpowder spent at the feast. Also, paid to Jacques Wallwyn, alien, 8 shillings for a dozen flash strings for muskets; to Thomas Bonnell, alien, three shillings for a staff with a head [for a banner][41]

In 1595, separate lists were made of the Dutch and Walloon men bearing arms. A series of confusing and overlapping lists suggests that this was being done for the first time. The lists show that the incomers did not serve with the English companies, but formed their own – one for the Dutch and one for the Walloons. The lists should contain the names of all males aged between 16 and 60 capable of bearing arms.

The view was held on 10 August 1595. The English men were arranged in their wards, with a total of 1,908 men (422 from Conesford, 414 from Mancroft, 468 from Wymer and 604 from OtW). There are various versions of the lists, with differing numbers of names: a transcription by Thomas Tallack of one version gives a higher number of 2,276 English names.[42]

The Dutchman numbered 401, and the Walloons (the list is headed 'Walloons or

---

41 NRO NCR 13a/9.

42 NRO NCR 13a/7 for the original lists, NCR COL 8/16 for Tallack's transcription, which is of the English names only. There is another, undated, list of Walloons in NCR 13a/3, to which a later hand has added in pencil '1574', but this is clearly wrong: it is another version of the 1595 list.

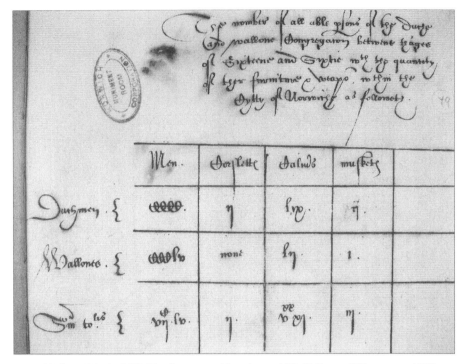

Figure 18 The militia in 1595. The figures read Dutchman 400, Walloons 355, sum total 755 (NRO NCR 13a/7).

Frenchmen') 359. By any calculation, despite losses by plague and people returning 'home', between 25 and 30 per cent of the adult males in Norwich in 1595 were immigrants. In terms of equipment however, the incomers were very much less well equipped than the native residents. They did have their share of calivers – the English had 316, the incomers 119. However, when it came to muskets, the English had 88, the incomers just six. It was even worse when corseletts were counted: the English had 154, the incomers none at all. The Walloon list is subdivided: 65 who had arms, and 294 who had no arms at all to offer. (The Dutch list is not divided in this way.)

Sixteen years later, in 1611, there were about 3,000 names altogether in the muster lists for the city. This included 325 Dutchmen and 282 Walloons, now making a total of 607, or about 20 per cent of the adult males. The numbers declined quite rapidly as the years went on: in 1619 there were just 106 Dutchmen and about 90 Walloons bearing arms.

The last surviving lists are for 1627–8, at which time about 45 Walloons are named. The final Dutch muster lists are far more complex and not as neatly written as the earlier documents: names were quite often paired, and the person present was often not the person supplying the arms involved. In 1627 for example, when Tobias de Hem was named as lieutenant, 33 corselets and 34 muskets were available for inspection, but the number of individuals presenting them was well over a hundred. There was also mention of poor attendance and shoddy equipment: in 1628, Matthew Boyes 'should have shewed', but 'makes default'; he was a wealthy merchant and draper, who was withdrawing from the Dutch community, like several others, as we shall see. John Letten showed a corselet 'not allowable' and there were unspecified 'other small faults'.[43]

In 1631, the Lord Lieutenant of Norfolk suggested that the Dutch and Walloon companies be merged into the English companies of each ward, a sign that they were no longer regarded as separate communities within the city. However, we know from the French Consistory Act Book that the Walloons vigorously opposed this. The reaction of the Dutch is not known as their Act Book does not survive.

Later 'headcounts'

The very fact that the city made no headcounts of incomers after 1583 suggests that the crisis was thought to be over, and all sources confirm the evidence of the muster lists: the number of members of the Dutch and Walloon congregations was in decline. They also suggest that the proportion of Walloons within the immigrant community was rising. This was natural: from 1608, the Dutch speakers could go to the newly independent – and Protestant – country of the Dutch Republic. Walloons could go there too, of course, and undoubtedly many did, but *their* homelands were still under the control of Roman Catholic Spain.

Another subsidy was ordered in 1597, and assessed in 1598. This time, the poll tax on individuals was doubled to 8d. Not only that, but in Mancroft Great Ward – and in that ward alone – married couples were counted as two people and had to pay 16d. A total of 743 people were listed in the subsidy. If the wives of Mancroft are excluded to harmonise with the figures given in earlier subsidies, the total comes to 721. Applying a multiplier of three would mean 2,163 incomers, and a multiplier of four would produce 2,885. The number of 'aliens' in the city had fallen to about half of the figures of 20 years before.

The parishes with the largest number of alien taxpayers in 1598 were St Mary Coslany with 55, St Margaret (52), St Augustine (52) and St Paul (44). The wealthiest of the aliens was Jaques de Hem in St Michael at Plea, with wealth of £8, followed by Abraham van Ixem in St Gregory (£6), and Adrian Wallwyn in St Peter Mancroft and Bastian van Burren in St Andrew (each with wealth of £5).

A note in the city archives summarises the position in the first third of the seventeenth century:

> The number of persons in the Dutch congregation in Norwich, men, women and children in the year 1612 [altered to 1613] was 1200.
> In the year 1624 the total number was but 999.
> In the year 1634 the whole number of souls was but 678, whereof aliens 103, native born 575.
> Of these were communicants, male and female 396, whereof aliens 103, native born 293.

---

43   NRO NCR 13a/31–33.

Figure 19 Cottages beside St Swithin's churchyard, an area where many immigrants lived. The large windows on two of the attics may be to let in light for a loom. The painting is probably by Leonard Bolingbroke, the man who 'saved' Strangers' Hall (NRO BOL 4/34).

Of the persons able to do service, being from the age of 16 years to 60, the whole number is but 103 besides the officers. Whereof there be trained 66 and untrained 37.

Of the French (or Walloon) companies, the trained are about 32, and the untrained (as the list was lately in) 120.[44]

The government ordered a Return of Strangers in 1622. This lists 331 aliens in Norwich, 168 born in England of parent strangers, 163 born beyond the seas: these are householders not individuals, so a multiplier is needed to get the actual total. There is nothing to say how long those born overseas had lived in Norwich. A few may even be those who were listed as children in the first census of all, 54 years earlier. I would guess that very few were recent incomers: any who found conditions in the Spanish Netherlands intolerable could much more easily move to the prospering Dutch Republic.

The communities were very small by the 1630s. I have taken samples of the records of baptisms in the first six months of 1631, 1633 and 1635. A total of 1,011 were recorded in these 18 months: 940 were baptised in the English churches, 42 in the Walloon church, and 29 in the Dutch church.

Burials show the same pattern. There were 125 burials in the city in the first four

44   NRO NCR 10h/11.

months of 1633: just ten of those buried were 'Strangers' (no distinction being made in these cases of death between French and Dutch). In the 1570s, incomers made up over 30 per cent of the city's population: 80 years later their descendants using their churches made up no more than 6 to 8 per cent of the total. On this basis also, the Walloons were now more numerous than the Dutch. Many of the incomers, or their descendants, had returned to Europe, and many more had merged into the English parish communities in the city. The apparent fall was also partly because of a rapid increase in the population of the city, presumably this time through incomers from the countryside rather than from abroad. Campbell estimates the population of Norwich to have been 20,000 by the 1620s.[45]

A 1635 list of the members of foreign churches in England says the Dutch church in Norwich had 363 (another version says 393) members, and that there were 396 Walloons (still a large community: by this time the church at Yarmouth had just 28 members).[46]

When the Dutch artist Willem Schellinks came to Norwich in 1662, he estimated that there were 100 communicants at the Dutch church. A 1677 document lists about 77 members contributing to the support of the Dutch church, with 21 other 'poor members', and another 13 who had just joined after a 'Confession of Faith' or recruiting drive.[47]

---

45   James Campbell, *Historic Towns: Norwich* (1975), p. 18.
46   Joby (2014), p.158, citing a document in Hessels, III, ii, 1678.
47   *The East Anglian* new series vol. 1 (1885–6), pp. 58–60.

Chapter 3

Work and discipline

The making of livings

The normal arrangements in a city like Norwich were that only registered freemen could carry on a trade. The usual way to become a freeman was to serve as an apprentice to an existing freeman for seven years. These arrangements could be circumvented in several ways: the city could grant the freedom if it wanted, or an incomer with capital could purchase the freedom. Alternatively, the city could classify the incomers as a special case, and allow them to trade without going through the usual formalities.

The richest incomers purchased their freedom, such as George Fenne, who paid £2 in April 1567, Anthony de Solemne, who paid the same sum in 1570, and a generation later Jaques de Hem, who paid the enormous sum of £50 in 1601. As freemen, they could not only trade in the city but also buy property, as de Solemne and de Hem both did; Fenne does not appear to have entered the land market. Fenne and de Hem both also took out letters of denization, but de Solemne did not: it appears that it was the freedom of the city that allowed these men to own property.

In 1598, members of the Stranger community born in England were admitted to the freedom for the first time, and once freemen, could buy and sell as readily as an English freeman. In 1612, by order of the Privy Council, it was decided that Walloons need not serve apprenticeships: this was in response to the fact that 'certain busy promoters' had been complaining that Walloons in the city had not been obeying the laws governing apprentices.[48]

Weavers and wool-combers

When the Strangers were first invited to Norwich, it was with the intention of reviving the weaving trades in the city. The great rush of refugees brought in men with an enormous range of skills, but the overwhelming majority were weavers, wool-combers or merchants dealing at least in part with woven products.

The weaving process is very well summed up in a letter by Martin Man to Sir Nathaniel Bacon explaining how the Strangers in Norwich worked (I have modernised the spelling):

There are employed this year [1608] by the Walloons and Dutch in this city of fleece wool and skin wool [wool from dead sheep] about 8,100 tods [a measurement of weight, usually equalling 28 lbs]. And of this there is bought of the fellmongers in Barmesey

---

48   NRO 16c/5 fo.266; NRO FC 29/7.

Street in London by the Walloons (being wool of the shires near adjoining) about 5,700 tods which is combed by the Walloons in Norwich and put out to spinning by the poorer sort both in the city and in Norfolk. And the yarn here employed about the making of the new draperies, and there is bought also by the Dutchmen of this city of the clothiers in Essex of combed wool unscoured (being fleece wool of Northampton-shire and Buckinghamshire) about 2,400 tods, and of the Dutch combers within this city being skin wool (and about 180 tods).

We do learn that the nyles, or coarser part of all the said wool, arising to about 1,300 todde, is sold to freemen of this city, and by them put out in part into Essex for bayes and says making, and in part into the West Country for kerseys. We do likewise find that of the aforesaid wools, combed, about 400 todde of the finer sort is sent to Yarmouth and is there employed in fine stockings only. And lastly we cannot by any means discover, by examination or otherwise, that any of this wool is sold beyond the seas.[49]

Thomas Deloney, silk weaver and poet who lived in Norwich, described a 'Norwich cloathier' or cloth merchant. In one room, men worked on looms, each with a boy beside him making quills. In another room:

An hundred women merrily
Were carding with joyful cheere
Who singing sat with voices cleere.

In another room 'maidens' and children sat picking wool. The girls:

In petticoats of stammel red
And milk-white kerchiefs on their head.
Their smock sleeves like to winter snow
That on the western mountains flow.

Children were also expected to work:

And these their labour to requite
Had everyone a penny at night,
Beside their meat and drink all day
Which was to them a wondrous stay.

Elsewhere were shearmen, helped by 'rowers', a dye-house and a fulling mill.

The large-scale operations imagined by Deloney do not square with the usual view of Norwich weaving, which is assumed to have been conducted mainly by weavers working in the attics of their own houses. Daniel Defoe, writing in 1722, noted how empty the city streets were, 'the inhabitants being all busy at their manufactures,

---

49 NRO MC 1872/31. Transcribed (in its original spelling, which I have modernised) in G. Alan Metters, Victor Morgan, Elizabeth Rutledge and Barry Taylor (eds), *The Papers of Nathaniel Bacon of Stiffkey*, vol. 6, Norfolk Record Society, vol. 81 (2017), p. 79.

dwell in their garrets at their looms, and in their combing shops, twisting-mills, and other workhouses, almost all the works they are employed in being done within doors'.

The whole process was covered by very strict rules. Indeed, it was the strictness of the regulations that guaranteed the high standards of Norwich stuffs, and led to their international success. John Strype, talking about the merchants of London, wrote of stuffs from the immigrant communities in Norwich and Colchester: 'they were made so well, and so strictly examined every Piece, that they carried a Reputation throughout the world'. He was so impressed that he spent two pages describing all the stages of inspection, from the wools themselves and the bay weavers' houses through scouring and fulling, onto the final inspection at the Sale Hall.[50]

The Dutch and Walloons used different methods and produced different products. The Dutch specialised in wet and greasy drapery, known as the *baytrie*. The *warps* (of worsted) were specially supplied by the worsted weavers and the *weft* was of good carded cloth. After being woven, the cloth was scoured (to remove the grease that had been added to the wool when it was combed), after which it was *fulled*, that is, laid out in water and trampled on: this why the incomers lived near to the river. After fulling, the *nap* of the cloth was raised by using king teasels, after which it was sheared, leaving a soft downy face to the cloth.

Dutch 'Orders' (rules) for making bays were first drawn up in 1570, not without difficulty. Four 'masters' – Anthony Pascheson, Anthony Paulus, Jacob de Vos and John Gherarde – resisted the mayor, the aldermen and their own countrymen and withheld the book. They were sent to prison, retracted after seven days and handed the book over, upon which they were released. This Book of Orders has been lost. The version that now exists was ratified by the incomer community on 13 August 1581. It is attested by the clerk, P. Langhelets, and the four governors, Christian Verking, Francois Tryon, Jan de Turk and Adriaen Cabilliau. As an illustration of the dramatic changes that can occur in the lives of any family, almost exactly 15 years earlier the last two of these men had set their names to a very different public document, in different circumstances and in a different country: an accord signed in Ypres by supporters of the Reformed Religion in 1566.

The orders appear to be exact copies of those in a book in English entitled 'Orders concerning Wooll' which is dated 1577 (and which includes some other sets of orders not included in the Dutch book). However, the 'Dutch' version is in fact in a curious version of that language: *perhaps* it was actually written by an Englishman not as good at the language as he thought! It would nicely match Norwich's reputation as a trilingual city if there was also a version of the Orders in French for the Walloon community, but if one did ever exist, it has not survived.

Many of the incomers were specifically combers of wool. Wool was combed to make the fibres lie straight and parallel. Combs came in pairs and might be imported: a Dutch baker paid duty on 30 pairs of wool combs in 1584.

One set of churchwardens' accounts throws further light on another process in

---

50   Stow's *Survey of London,* pp. 299–300.

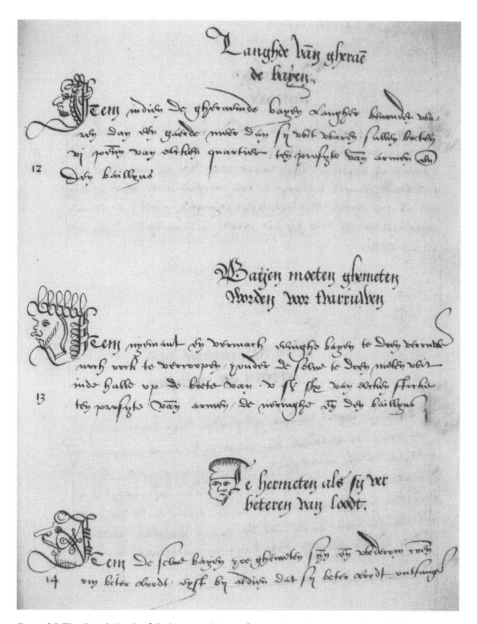

Figure 20 The Dutch Book of Orders, regulations for immigrant weavers written in their own language (NRO NCR 17d/12)

which the immigrants were involved. As early as 1569, an unnamed Dutchwoman paid a penny for bleaching in the churchyard at St Margaret's, and the same or another Dutchwoman gave 3d for doing the same. In 1581, the account records 'received of the Dutchman for bleeching in the churchyard 5s. 8d'. In 1582, Francis Tryon paid 5s for hire of the churchyard, no doubt also for use as a bleaching ground. I assume this

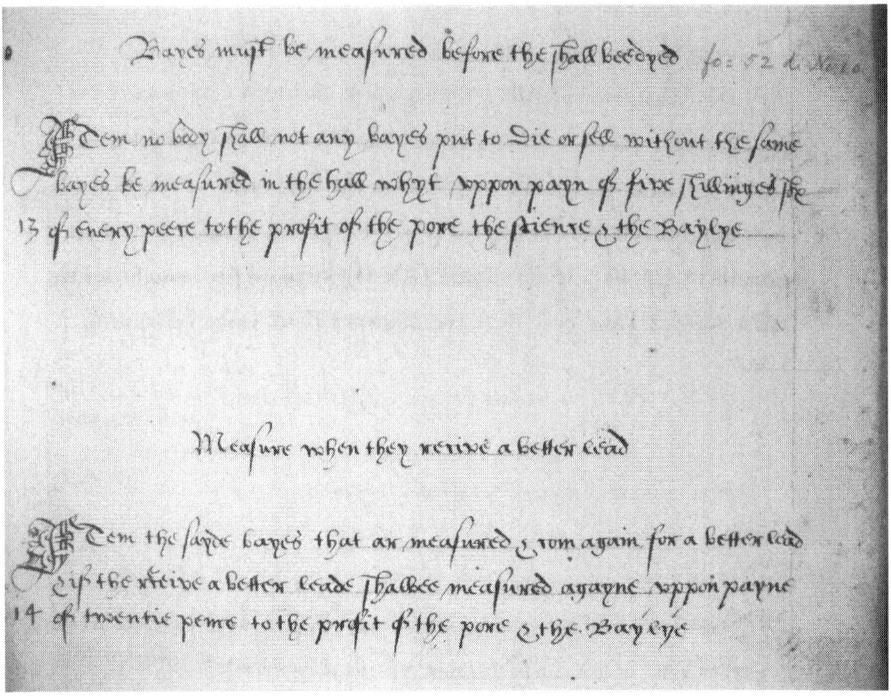

Bayes must be measured before they shall be dyed fo: 52 l. Nota

Item no body shall not any bayes put to Die or sell without the same bayes be measured in the hall whyt uppon payn of five shillinges the
13 of every peere to the profit of the pore the seienre & the Baylye

Measure when they retive a better lead

Item the sayde bayes that ar measured & com again for a better lead yif the retive a better leade shalbee measured agayne uppon payne
14 of twentie pence to the profit of the pore & the Baylye

Figure 21 (above) Two of the same clauses in English (NRO NCR 17d/11)
Figure 22 (below) The Dutch Book of Orders, detail (NRO NCR 17d/12)

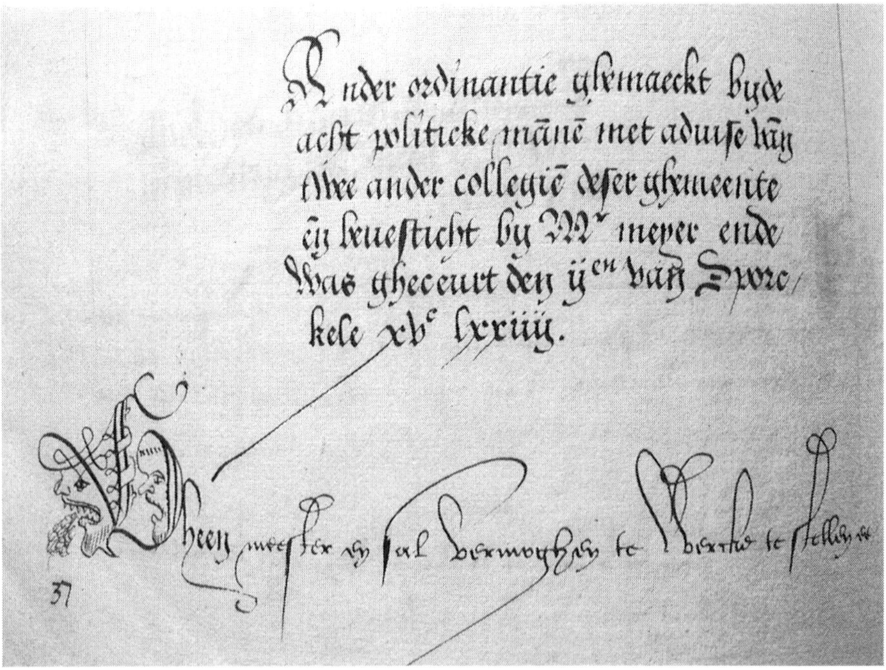

Ander ordinantie ghemaeckt byde acht politicke mānē met aduise van tHee ander collegiē deser ghemeente ēn bevestight by Mr meyer ende Was gheceurt den ijen van Sporkele xvc lxxiiij.

Gheen meester en sal vermoghen te verwen te stellen
37

was the part north of the church, still a very large space today although part has been lost for road widening.[51]

The Walloons specialised in dry and coloured stuffs known as the *cangeantrie*. As Richard Wilson puts it, they 'used scoured, dyed yarns and introduced silk thread to produce much lighter cloths which when finished achieved a lustrous effect.' E. T. Blakely agreed: 'the Walloons introduced the manufactures of woollen, linen- and silk-weaving, dyeing, cloth-dressing, silk-throwing etc, and instructed the English in the art of making bayes, sayes, camblets and other light stuffs, and the striping and flowering of stuffs and damasks.'[52]

There were occasional disputes between the two communities, which were brought to the Mayor's Court. In 1575, the leaders of the Dutch community came to the court with a new product, 'bombazine'. They wanted to be given a monopoly of its produc- tion, but the leaders of the Walloon community objected. The Dutch won their case. Two years later it was the Walloons who came to the court, asking for protection for a product of their own – 'mockadoes', a woollen fabric in imitation ('mock') of velvet.

The incomers were naturally protective of their skills. In September 1581, the mayor and Corporation asked the Dutch to take on four Englishmen and train them in the art of the Dutch 'bayetree', but the Dutch replied that there was no reason to do this as they had so many of their own to set on the work.

In fact, infringements of the regulations were a source of income to the city. In October 1571 Adrian Buffytt, Dutchman, tailor, was fined 20 shillings for making of English work contrary to the order of the book. In June 1576, 'Adrian Wallwyn, Stranger' was charged with selling wool that had not been sealed: he admitted his guilt. Another new rule was laid down by the Mayor's Court in September 1601: wool-combers of the Dutch and French congregations could now sell their flock and nyles anywhere in the city, as long as they only sold to freemen, and weighed and paid duty on their products in the usual place.

From their arrival in 1566, both nations had used St Mary the Less as their trading hall. In 1571, each nation was given their own hall. The baytrie (Dutch) continued to use St Mary; the cangeantrie (Walloons) began to use a building on the north side of the former cloister at St Andrew's Hall, which soon became known as the Walloon Hall.

The amount received by the city from the Bay Hall and the Camiant Hall (the cangeantrie) was roughly the same in the 1570s, but the Walloons flourished over the next decade while there was a decline in the production of bays. In the third quarter of 1576, for example, 2,623 bays were produced, which at 2d a piece brought in £21 17s 2d. The Walloons produced 4,689 tuft mockadoes, grograynes and carrels in the same quarter, which paid 1d a piece, bringing in £19 10s 9d. However, in the quarter ending Lady Day 1589, the Dutch produced only 875 bays bringing in £7 5s 10d, while the Walloons produced 6,890 pieces, bringing in £28 14s 2d. Indeed, as John

---

51   NRO PD 153/42.
52   Richard Wilson, 'The textile industry', in Rawcliffe and Richard Wilson (2004b), p. 222; E. T. Blakely, *History of the Manufactures of Norwich* (undated, c.1870).

Pound noticed, it was the Walloons rather than the Dutch who benefited Norwich in the long run: 'The English, although never mastering the art of bay making which declined with the Dutch congregation, took more easily to the Walloon grograynes, mockadoes, vellums, buffins and other caungeantry, and by the last year of Elizabeth's reign the manufacture of traditional worsteds was all but extinct.'[53]

One of the fascinations of archive research is that even the most apparently dull document has human stories to tell. The city accountant very occasionally noted cases of hard times among the immigrants. In the third quarter of 1577, for example, he made allowance for 'a poor man in prison', and another man 'that is sick and not able to pay to the accountant'. In the first quarter of 1579, he allowed for four incomers who had become bankrupt, including one woman, 'widdow Gemdrell'. Their stories are only known through the recording methods of a city official four centuries ago.

The incomers were continually inventing new products. When the city accountant began to note income from the Strangers' products in 1566, he made provision for Flemish cloth, bays, says and stammels. Within a few years, half a dozen new products had been added, including mockadoes and vellure. By 1607, some Dutch weavers were making 'cloths of new devise, being dry and coloured stuffs'. The Corporation ordered that all dry cloth, whether made by Dutch or Walloons, should go to the Walloon Hall, and all greasy cloth, whether made by Dutch or Walloons, should go to St Mary the Less, which was known as the Dutch Hall, or as Strangers' Hall.

A letter of 1601 listed a bewildering variety of fabrics being manufactured in the city: 'arras, bays, bewpers, boulters, boratoes, buffins, bustyns, bombacyes, blankets, callimancoes, carrells, chambletts, cruell, dornicks, duraunce, damask, frisadoes, fringe, fustyans, felts, flanells, grograines, garterings, girdlings, linsey woolseyes, mockadoes, minikins, mountaines, makerells, oliotts, pomettes, plumettes, perpetuanas, perpicuanas, rashes, rugges, russells, sattins, serges, syettes, sayes, stamells, stamines, scallops, tukes, tamettes, tobines, and valures'.[54] Some of these new names may have been marketing ploys rather than new products: as Fuller wrote in the 1650s describing Norwich stuffs: 'a pretty, pleasing name, complying with the buyer's fancy, much befriendeth a stuff in the sale thereof.'

In any case, it was the new draperies as a whole that changed Norwich, not any individual product, as Joan Thirsk saw:

> The New Draperies represented innumerable different kinds of cloths whose number was constantly being enlarged: their spectacular success as a group has totally smothered curiosity in the history of each individual type of cloth, as well as obscuring the fortunes of associated handicraft industries which developed alongside the New Draperies and were also large, but separate, employers of labour. In Norwich, one of the first centres in which the New Draperies started, lace making, ribbon making and stocking knitting

---

53   John Pound, *Tudor and Stuart Norwich* (1988), p. 60.
54   Quoted in L. F. Salzman, *English Industries of the Middle Ages* (1970 edn), pp. 243–4.

Figure 23 A Norwich weaver's probate inventory, in the garret a loom – and a bird cage
(NRO DN/INV 82a/138)

all became thriving, expanding occupations, simultaneously stimulated, if not started,
by foreign craftsmen'.[55]

Even if all the official documents regulating weaving had been lost, the importance of
the business in the lives of the immigrants would be obvious from the many references
in wills and probate inventories. Matthew Ployart's probate inventory, for example,
lists the tools of his trade. They included 14 looms with the harness and stays belonging
to them, two presses, coloured yarn and silk – 541 bobbins with silk on them were
valued at £81. Lowysken van Rokeghem bequeathed to her brother her 'shuttle to
weave says with', and a candlestick for the loom; Hubrecht Wiltens bequeathed 'all
my mocado looms and my shirts'. William Moens' inventory mentions 'one say loom
with all the things ready for work withal': 30 shirts and smocks together for men,
women and children, about 100 kerchiefs or handkerchiefs. Vincentiana Heijtes died
in possession of 'certain instruments to dress flax', bags of linen cloth, and three dozen
lamb skins. The contents of Martin Balden's [work]shop included tub vessels, shears,
small amounts of cloth, crepes, yarn, frees, damask and silk. The inventory of Jane
Jakemine Begots included 14 parcels of wool, while that of William Powells included
£28 worth of raw silk and small amounts of white and orange-and-green silk.

The probate inventories of two wool-combers, Giles Tettart and Jacob le Poultre,
reveal much about their way of living. Tettart, of St Augustine's, died in 1588. He was
owed £26 8s, some of it for wool and yarn, but his actual possessions were valued at
£56 14s 10d. No less than £50 of this was 'fleece woaded'. Nancy Ives says that this
was fleece already dyed blue, so that the yarn would be coloured – 'one of the features
of the Walloons was that they wove in colour on the loom, so that they were able to
create designs'. Jacob le Poultre, of St George Colegate, died in 1589. His inventory
shows the tools of the trade of the woolcomber:

2 pairs of wool combs
20 pounds of whey butter [for greasing the wool before combing]
3 bushels of charcoal [for heating pots in which combs were dipped]
2 small wheels [used for spinning Jersey yarn, or yarn for Says]
4 pounds of combed wool

55   Frank Meeres, *Strangers* (2012), p. 44; Thirsk (1988), p. 44.

Figure 24 Norwich Guildhall, the seat of the city's governance. Source: Norwich HEART, previously published in Frank Meeres, *Strangers* (2012).

Figure 25 Flemish weavers' tapestry, church of St Peter Mancroft, Norwich. The figures at the centre represent Mary Magdalen mistaking the risen Jesus for a gardener: did Dutch gardeners in the 16th century dress like this?
Source: Norwich HEART, previously published in Frank Meeres, *Strangers* (2012).

32 pounds of bay yarn
4 great bay wheels [used to spin weft yarn for bays]
1 say loom [for Jersey yarn]
1 yard of say cloth
6 pounds of fine noils [combings: fine noils were carded, and may have been used for blankets and kersey cloth or Dornix]
2 pounds of coarse noils [coarse noils were used for making garters, swathe bands, reins]
Weights, beams and scales.

Weaving continued to be the main business of the incomers throughout their time as a distinctive element in the city. The 1622 Return of Strangers includes 111 weavers and 82 combers: in fact, as Fell points out, almost two-thirds (63 per cent) of the Strangers in the return were involved in the textile trades.[56]

This was the basis of Norwich's fame. When Schellinks visited in 1662, he noted that 'a large number of Dutch craftsmen live at Norwich, who have taught the English the weaving of all kinds of cloth, and Norwich is famous for the quantity and quality of the cloth which is produced there'. Almost a century later, the Marchioness Grey came to the city:

> I was disappointed in not being able to see any of their Manufactures at Norwich. I expected to have seen some kind of Public buildings for carrying them on, or large work-rooms belonging to the several weavers, but there is no such thing, and the workmen I was told have all their separate looms in their own houses; and mounting up into a Garret to see a single loom was not worthwhile.[57]

A characteristic Norwich probate inventory is that of Anthony Tills, weaver, who died in 1753. In his garret he had his loom 'with the appurtances belonging to it' – and a bird-cage. A weaver working alone in a garret, perhaps with a canary for company: on this, the wealth of Norwich was built for the next 250 years.

Hosiers

No hosiers (makers of knitted stockings) are recorded in the 1568 census of Strangers, but over the years many of the immigrants took up this trade, several becoming very wealthy in it. It was something in which children could play a part: at the City Assembly on 25 January 1577, the employment of unapprenticed children to work on hose was made a punishable offence.

Things changed in April 1614. The Mayor's Court decreed that only freemen and denizens could work freely as hosiers. Anyone else could buy a permit to work

---

56 Glynis Fell, 'The spatial impact of the immigration of the Strangers', Cambridge University BA dissertation, unpublished (1975), p. 12.

57 Quoted in Wilson, in Wilson and Rawcliffe (2004b), pp. 219–20. The original journal is in the Bedfordshire Record Office.

without having gone through an apprenticeship. It was agreed that the Dutch could manufacture hose without being freemen: they were to pay a 'foreign fine' for this privilege. Those who were already denizens were to be 'to all purposes as those that are English born'. The elders and politic men who were present are said to have 'thankfully accepted' this.

About two dozen incomers did so in the next two years, some after haggling about the price. On 27 April, Peter Wallwyn was offered the concession for a price of £20 – he suggested that he pay £5. George Fox offered to pay 30 shillings, which the city rejected. Nicholas Priem offered to pay 50 shillings: this was also rejected. On 3 May, Priem appeared again and in view of his 'weak and poor state' was offered toleration for £10. Richard Culen was offered toleration for £15. On the following day Gilles Sondeville and his wife paid £20, and Peter Wallwyn now agreed to pay £20.

On 7 May, William Vertegans alias Rottengoose, Gilles Sondeville, Oliver Dacket, George Fox, Peter Wallwyn and Nicholas Priem all turned up and paid, some of them second instalments. Four days later George Holwicke, Andrew Allyard and John Wittewrongle refused to pay. Allyard said he was about to leave the city. Wittewrongle refused to pay more than 20s, saying he was about to depart beyond the seas to live – he asked that his wife and servant be allowed to continue trading for eight weeks, but the city allowed them just three days. However, he then agreed to pay and turned up with four bills each worth £3 6s 8d, which he presented to the court.

Other immigrants paying to be allowed to work as hosiers included Peter Verbeck, John Letten and Jan Cruso. It was very much a business for incomers – 17 out of 29 registered hosiers were of Dutch or Walloon descent. On 16 July 1615 toleration was offered to Malliart Browne and his wife to deal in fringe, lace and stockings: they paid £12. At the same court, John and Ellen Cueleman paid £5 to be allowed to deal in the buying of bone laces and other small wares.

One surviving document gives an authentic picture of how the hosiery business worked. Peter and Susan Backowe, of St Gregory's, hosiers, died within a year of each other in 1597–8. Their executor appears to have carried on the business. He took from the house a 'debt book' that contained details of what yarn had been put forth to knit, and accounted also for 'certain hose which he received weekly coming by the knitters out of the country'. These details, preserved by chance, give an insight into how a family like the Backowes worked, parcelling out yarn for knitters to work on in their own homes outside the city, receiving back the finished hose. William Vandercamme's shop contained 414 pairs of knit hose, yarn, and 100 pairs of leg boards (used to shape stockings) at the time of his death.

Both incomers and natives made stockings, which became a Norwich staple. Joan Thirsk describes how the business developed:

The new vogue appears to have developed because of an improvement in knitting techniques, partly connected with the use of finer wools, but also perhaps with the better shaping of stockings over the ankle and foot. Jersey wool, one type of fine wool increasingly used after the 1560's, was spun on a Jersey or Guernsey wheel. The technique was evidently derived from the Channel Islands and passed from there to Norwich, soon making Norwich the foremost centre for knitted jersey stockings.[58]

In the 1620s half of the richest members of the incomer community described themselves as 'hosiers'. They were almost all Dutch: only one Walloon, Elias Des Bonny, is described as a hosier. The 1622 Return of Strangers lists 31 hosiers (some combining it with other occupations), of whom 14 were born in England and 17 born over the seas. They included three widows, probably taking up the trades of their late husbands; one, 'widow Wollewyn', was probably the former wife of the Peter Wallwyn mentioned above.

Merchants

Merchants among the incomer community had to tread a fine line to remain within the law. Adam Kyndt (see below) and James Wallwyn, with other aliens, came before the Mayor's Court in May 1583, charged with buying up corn and sending it overseas, leading to scarcity and high prices on Norwich Market. The court ordered that henceforth no alien could buy corn except for the needs of their own households. In March 1584 seven alien merchants were charged with buying up commodities in Norwich and selling them at a higher price in London. The men were Jacob Buskyn, Segar Wittewrongle, George de Roe, John Bagler, John Billet, Lewes Quinten and Malliard Rickwaert. They promised not to use factorship to the harm of those English people who were trading between the two cities.

In 1578 two royal officials, Sir George Delves and Sir William Fitzwilliam, were appointed aulnagers to collect the special customs duties levied on the transport of the New Draperies for seven years. In 1579 they demanded £70 from the Dutch and £8 from the Walloons. Norwich Corporation bought out the last five years of the contract, farming the aulnage directly from the Crown between 1580 and 1585: they made a profit of £616 from this. The Corporation offered 400 marks (£266 13s 4d) and an annual payment of £5 for a further 12-year contract, but were outbid.[59]

Aulnage accounts survive for the years 1582 to 1610 and have been transcribed by Douglas Rickwood. The first year, 1582–3, names some 20 men importing goods into the city, and also about a dozen people who are not named, a typical entry of this sort reading 'A Dutch widow for two sacks of hops'. Many of the names are those known from other sources to be leading merchants. For example, the 1594–5 list contains nine entries for imports by Jaques de Hem (all relating to wool or cloth), and four entries for cargoes of Malliard Rickwaert (including wine, raisins and figs).

By the 1590s Jaques de Hem was very much the dominant trader. In 1592–3 he traded in yarn, cloth, flax, fustian, raisins, hops, brushes, pots and warming pans. In 1599–1600 he almost monopolised the accounts, paying tax on his imports which included trusses of cloth, yarn, coverlets and linen yarn, sacks of wool, and he also

58 Thirsk (1988), p. 45.
59 Pound, in Wilson and Rawcliffe (2004b), pp. 43–4.

imported one tun of wine. There is only one other entry for the whole year – Oliver Dackett paid duty on bundles of grey paper.

The natural route for merchandise was through Great Yarmouth, but alien merchants might use other Norfolk ports. John Williamson, a Norwich clothier, and an alien despite his anglicised name, had interests at Cley. In 1604 he complained to the Norfolk justices of the peace that his house and property (corn) there and at Glandford, and a parcel of jersey stockings sent beyond the seas, had been seized by a man named Thomas Chambers. The result of the case is not known, but it shows the range of interests an alien in Norwich might have. Another Dutch merchant, Adam Kyndt, traded between Blakeney and Rotterdam in the 1580s. He imported hops, stone, bricks, Spanish salt and onions, and exported wheat, barley and malt. He also traded through Norwich, where he lived at one time: he paid tax on wealth of £5 in St Martin at Palace parish in 1581. By the time of his will in 1597 he was living in Cley, where he owned substantial property, including a brewhouse.[60]

The 1622 Return of Strangers lists nine alien merchants in Norwich, two born beyond the seas (Jaques de Hem and Peter Beck or Verbeck), and seven born in England (Daniel Bunnell, Joel Desormeaux, John Rockingham (the English version of Rokeghem), Jan Cruso (a hosier as well), Philip Andries (a draper as well), Tobias de Hem and Francis Dackett).

Gardeners and farmers

The census of May 1568 included two of the earliest of many gardeners within the Dutch community. Odard van der Somevelt, gardener, came from Flanders in 1567 with his wife, who was possibly pregnant: the census records that they had one son, born in England. He was followed by Joos van Brake, gardener and seller of herbs, who came from Zeeland with his wife and son in 1568.

In 1575 a Dutchman, perhaps one of these two men, was paid 3s 4d for travelling from Norwich to Hengrave Hall in Suffolk to view the orchards, gardens and walks there. He was paid a further 40s for 'clipping the knotts, altering the alleys, setting the grounds, finding herbs and bordering the same'.[61]

Two minor criminal cases before the Mayor's Court reveal the Dutch love of gardening. In 1582 three English men, perhaps boys as one was described as an apprentice, were whipped for breaking into the orchard owned by Giles Vanderbrook, alien, and stealing apples and pears. Eight years later five Norwich men were charged with breaking into a close outside St Stephen's Gates and stealing roots, the property of a 'Mr Vertngoose'. There is a Flemish-style tapestry in St Peter Mancroft church which shows the scene where Mary Magdalen mistook the risen Jesus for a gardener: with his hat and spade, he probably represents just what the Dutch gardeners in late sixteenth-century Norwich wore.

60   Victor Morgan, Elizabeth Rutledge and Barry Taylor (eds), *The Papers of Nathaniel Bacon of Stiffkey*, vol. 5, Norfolk Record Society, vol. 74, pp. 148–9; *Maritime Trade of Blakeney, Norfolk 1587–90,* Norfolk Record Society, vol. 8 (1936), *passim.*

61   Frederick A. Norwood, *The Reformation Refugees as an Economic Force* (Chicago, 1942).

Two probate inventories show that some incomers had quite sizeable plots of land. Adrian Coesse died in December 1595. His inventory mentions a plot of ground set with turnips and roots, beds set with herbs, and seed of root vegetables. Francis van Dyke died in May 1597, leaving crops growing in 8 acres of land: 2 acres were of roots, which at £10 were the most highly valued, worth more than his crops of barley, wheat and rye. The immigrants may even have exported these crops back 'home': the city chamberlain's accounts in the first half of the 1590s record payments from 'certain strangers for loding Rootes at the Blackfriars Bridge'.

The Vertegens or Verdegans family were known in English documents as Rotten-goose, the literal translation of the name, or, as above, a combination of the Dutch and English elements. Pieter and Jakemyn Vertegens were living in St Laurence in 1612. They had three children baptised in the Dutch church: Debora in 1606, Abraham in 1607 and David in 1612. By the 1620s Peter Vertegens was living in St Benedict's.

A related characteristic of the new Dutch residents of Norwich was their love of flowers: they introduced the tulip (originally from Turkey) into England. According to Thomas Fuller, they 'brought hither with them, not only their profitable crafts, but pleasurable curiosities'. He praised their cultivation of tulips 'feathered and variegated, with stripes of divers colours', and said that they also brought a particular variety of rose (Rosa Mundi) to the city.[62]

Norwood says that new flowers not previously known in England like 'carnations, Provence roses and gilly flowers' appeared in Norwich. Some had flowers in their own homes, such as Jane Begots, whose probate inventory included two flowerpots. William Powells' probate inventory included 'one picture of a flower pot': this might not have been one of the masterpieces of Dutch art familiar to us from art galleries, being valued at a mere shilling. By the early seventeenth century 'Florists' Feasts' were being held in St Andrew's Hall, with displays of flowers and entertainments, poetry being read and plays performed. They were no doubt attended by both Dutch and English, acting as the Chelsea Flower Shows of their day.[63]

Gardening continued to be a popular occupation. The 1622 return lists six immigrant gardeners: Mallyard Wyboot, Bowgin Porter, David Dewalue, Christian Vervinke and William and Peter Rottengoose (the last being both gardener and hosier). Three second-generation immigrants, born in England, are also listed as gardeners: Tobias Barton, David Dam and Jacob Boy. These men were all Dutch: no gardeners are recorded among the Walloon community.

Wyboot paid tax of £7 in 1625, more than any other immigrant, and Peter Rotten-goose was also among the ten wealthiest aliens, paying £4. Wyboot was the only wealthy immigrant residing beyond the city walls, living in Trowse or Carrow: his wife was named Joan and their daughter Debora married wealthy English hosier Richard Puckle, probably a relation of Samuel Puckle, mayor in 1656. On his death, Wyboot

62   R. W. Ketton-Cremer, *Norfolk Assembly* (1957), p. 124.
63   Ketton-Cremer (1957), p. 132; Amy M. Charles, *The shorter poems of Ralph Knevet* (1966), pp. 24–5; J. S. Burn, *The History of the French, Walloon, Dutch and Other Protestant Refugees Settled in England* (1846) has the phrase about gillyflowers, p.196.

left £100 to Debora and a mere £3 to his youngest daughter Jeane. His bequest of 20s to the poor of the Dutch congregation was not over-generous for such a wealthy man. Perhaps he saw himself as being as much English as Dutch.

Medical men

Medical men from overseas were a recognised part of Norwich life. We have seen that Martin van Kurnbeck had arrived in Norwich by 1560. Jon de Marbier, a French surgeon in Norwich, became naturalised in 1541.

The longest serving immigrant medical family was the Cropp family, described in Chapter 6. In the early 1570s the City employed 'a Dutch man' to cure the swelled knee of a poor patient and 'a Dutch surgeon' to cut two poor children. Medical men recorded in the city at Bishop Redman's visitation in 1597 included the two Cropps and Petre de No, a Frenchman practising surgery: he may have been the unnamed Walloon surgeon banished from the city in 1599.[64]

Matthias de Rijcke was another medical incomer. Born about 1530, he and his wife Barbel Clouckaerts were condemned at Messines in 1567, and came to Norwich with their two children, one of whom was named William. Matthias lived in St Mary Coslany in 1576 and was a wealthy man, paying tax on wealth assessed at £5. He acted as executor to the will of Joos de Ram 1577, and paid tax, and poll tax for his son William and a servant, in 1580. A member of the Consistory of the Dutch church in 1571 and 1584, he was buried in St George Tombland church on 7 July 1593.[65]

Another is known only from an entry in the Mayor's Court Book for 18 February 1608:

> Peter Astoe, the Dutch surgeon. Upon complaint of neighbours of the ill rule and misbehaviour of poor Peter otherwise called Peter Astoe surgeon towards his wife and for beating her in most extreme manner, it is ordered that if he shall hereafter beat his wife or be drunken, then to be banished from the city or whipped at the post in Mr May's his discretion.

Mr May was the ward constable.

Another surgeon from Norwich, Abraham Langebillinck, shows up in the Leiden betrothal registers twice in less than three years. He married Fijtgen Gedeons in August 1614, and after her death married Lijsbeth Adrians in January 1617. Both women came from Leiden, so Langebillinck had probably moved there.

One possible midwife occurs in the 1568 census – the unnamed widow of Henry Brabant, 'obstetrix'. If she pursued this occupation in her new environment,

---

64   Margaret Pelling and Charles Webster, 'Medical practitioners', in C. Webster (ed.), *Health, Medicine and Mortality in the Sixteenth Century* (date), p. 224. See also p. 223 for Marbier, p. 225 for de Noe.

65   Leonard Forster, *Janus Gruter's English Years* (1967), pp. 41–2. Forster thinks the parish register entry is a record of the death rather than a burial entry. It is true the actual word 'buried' does not appear, but it seems most unlikely that he would have been buried anywhere else.

she would have been the only midwife we know of in sixteenth-century Norwich.

The 1622 Return of Strangers lists three medical men in the city: surgeon John Cropp, physician Abraham Hacker and barber-surgeon Peter Hiborne.

Preachers and schoolmasters

The 1568 census lists four Dutch and two Walloon schoolmasters. The Dutch were Johannes Ruytinck, Egidius Honnenagel, Jodosorus van Slaet and Richardus van der Varent. The Walloons were Pierre du Rieu from Lille and Adrian Claess from Antwerp.

Johannes Ruytinck, a leading Calvinist in Ghent, left Flanders in 1567 and was in Norwich by 1571, working also as a notary. In 1577 the Dutch consistory asked him to train as a minister. He declined, saying that he taught French to Flemish and English children and that there was no one else in Norwich who could do this;

> furthermore, recently some boys were sent to me from Flanders, whom I received [and provided with] board and lodgings along with a good numbers of others who also live with me; all of these and many others who attend my school would be without a means of learning French here, since I am the only one who instructs the Flemish and English children in the French tongue.[66]

Another schoolmaster is recorded in the Mayor's Court Book for 5 September 1590. Furmyn Vanwater was charged with keeping a school during a time of plague. He refused to come before the court and was ordered to be put in the stocks. He was told to appear before the court the following week with the minister of the Dutch congregation, but there is no record that he did so. Other educated men, ministers and doctors for example, might well have taught children privately. According to Christopher Joby, Matthias de Rijke is recorded in the registers of Gonville and Caius College as the teacher of Jan Gruter when the latter was in Norwich.

As always in education, the wealthy could afford to pay for the best, and several incomer families were able to send their children to Norwich Grammar School. Seventeen of these boys went on to Gonville and Caius College, Cambridge University, between 1592 and 1663. They included Gruter, who afterwards moved to Leiden and later to Heidelberg, and Aquila Cruso, who settled in Norwich after obtaining his degree. His son Francis Cruso followed him to Norwich Grammar School and on to Gonville and Caius.

The 1622 Return of Strangers records two schoolmasters: John Cokele and Francis Boy. Both were born beyond the seas.

Printers and bookmen

The Dutch immigrants introduced the craft of printing to Norwich. Anthony de Solemne arrived from Brabant in 1567. He combined printing with the selling of

---

66   Joby (2014), p. 169.

wine from the Rhineland. He purchased the freedom of the city, as the City Assembly book records:

> Anthonius de Solen, printer, non-apprentice, is admitted citizen under condition that he shall not occupy any trade of merchandise either from the parts beyond the seas or from London but only his art of printing and selling of renysh wine, and this he hath agreed: to pay 40 shillings.

De Solemne presumably brought his printing press with him. His press operated in Norwich between 1568 and 1572. The first books published in 1568, within a year of his arrival in the city, were religious: a book of psalms – a Dutch translation of John Calvin's French Genevan Psalter – and the Confession of the articles of the Christian religion (the catechism). In 1569 he was commissioned by a preacher in London, Antonio del Corro, to publish a 'Tableau' of the works of God: this was written in French. Corro used de Solemne because he was prepared to print 100 copies of the work. London publishers would only do a minimum of 1,500 copies. De Solemne showed it to the minister of the Walloon church in Norwich who thought it was heretical, but de Solemne went ahead anyway.

His next work was in English, verses written by Thomas Brooke while in Norwich Castle awaiting his execution (see Chapter 7). This was followed by a 16-page calendar or almanac. De Solemne was also used by St Andrew's church to print proclamations, and by the Corporation of Norwich to print handbills: in 1570, he was paid 15s for printing bye-laws relating to passage boats, reed-roofed houses and scavengers.[67]

The press closed down after just four years, but other books were published later that falsely claimed to have been printed in Norwich. De Solemne remained in Norwich and sold wine in the city. We know that he did practise this trade – the Yarmouth customs accounts show that in 1579–80, for example, he paid cranage on two tons of imported wine. He presumably prospered as he was one of the richest alien taxpayers in the 1581 subsidy, paying tax on wealth assessed at £8.[68]

De Solemne exhibited a bill of complaint against John Henonde before the Mayor's Court on 4 May 1580, and was before the court again two years later regarding a financial dispute. He is described as 'vintner' so it was presumably connected with this business rather than his publishing concerns. The case was first raised in the summer 1582 and finally heard in May of the following year. On 15 May he brought before the court his 'book of reckoning', from which an entry, obviously crucial to the case, was copied into the Mayor's Court Book and certified. The entry reads: 'Received the last day of September 1573 of Mr Anthony de Solemne the sum of £49 11s 8d, which is in full payment of one obligation due to Roger Barnye the 29th day of the month'. We do not know the details of the case, or why it was being raised nine years later, but it gives us a unique insight into business life and record-keeping in the Dutch and English communities in the city. There is no record of De Solemne in the city after

---

67   NRO NCR 15/2 (Norwich Clavors' book, 21 May 1570).
68   NRO Y/C4/273.

this case, and he had already sold his house in 1581: perhaps he returned to the Low Countries.

There was a second printer in the 1568 census, Albert Christian from Holland. No books printed by him in Norwich are known: perhaps he worked under de Solemne.

Four booksellers, all Dutch, are recorded in the 1568 census. Joannes Paetz is recorded as arriving from Holland with his wife and two boys in 1567. He was in fact a printer from Leiden; by 1572 he had returned there. The other three were Cornelis van Hille, Pieter Jass and Anthony Rabat. There was at least one bookbinder in the community in the 1570s: Joos de Ram, who died in 1577 and left a bequest of books in Latin and in Dutch.

No printers are listed in the 1622 Return of Strangers. In fact after de Solemne had stopped, no more printing was done in Norwich for another 140 years.

Goldsmiths and clockmakers

These skills were particularly associated with men from the Low Countries: the careers of two such families, the Isborns and the Petersons were described in Chapter 2. There were many others. Jaques van Barton was probably the son of Jacob Bertin who came over from Brabant in 1567 with his wife and five children. Jaques was living in St Michael at Plea in 1599, his name appearing in the lay subsidy roll. He took up the freedom of the city as a merchant in 1605. He was captain of the Dutch militia in 1621. His son James took up his freedom as a clock-maker in 1629, and two other apprentices, David van Barton and Samuel Barton, were probably also relatives judging from their names. The last took up his freedom as a clock-maker in 1628. Peter de Keyser, an alien living in Norwich, was fined in 1593 by the Company of London Goldsmiths' searchers for having substandard articles of silver. Other alien goldsmiths in the city included John Vanderpone of St Gregory's, described as a goldsmith in the 1576 subsidy (in which occupations are not usually given).

The origins of goldsmith George Fenne are something of a puzzle. He was sometimes as known as 'Dutch George'. (He seems to have attracted nicknames: Joos de Ram called him 'Honest George Fenne' in his will.) He owned property in Utrecht, where his father and wife were both apparently born, and his will was actually written in Dutch, but his letters patent of denization describe him as a subject of the duke of Holstein, who controlled the northern part of what is now Germany. In his will he stated that he was born in 'Eastland'. Fenne took on two apprentices, James Grundy and Matthew Cobbold, in 1583. Grundy was certainly English, being the son of Roger Grundy of Bolton, Lancashire. He became a freeman himself, as did three of his sons and two other men who served as apprentices to him. One of these men employed at least one apprentice who became a freeman himself. In this way, the skills brought to Norwich by Fenne benefitted several generations of the English community.[69]

Ahasuerus Fromanteel was baptised in the Dutch Church in Norwich on 8 March

---

69   He was called by the nickname 'Dutch George' when fined at Stourbridge Fair for 'mis-working' in 1568.

Figure 26 The New Hall, on Thomas Kirkpatrick's prospect of 1724: the part in which the Dutch worshipped is marked '6' (just over half-way down, about a quarter of the way across).

1606/7, the son of Murdoch and Leah Fromanteel. Murdoch was a turner and chair maker. Ahasuerus was a clock-maker, moving from Norwich to London in 1629. According to Christopher Hanson-Smith, 'he is reputed to have introduced the pendulum to England'.[70]

Andreas Priem, the son of Andries and Susanne, was born on 11 April 1619 in St Andrew's parish, and baptised in the Norwich Dutch Church. He grew up to become a clock-maker, but lived most of his life in London. In 1646, he married Elizabeth, the sister of Ahasuerus Fromanteel: the marriage took place in the London Dutch church at Austin friars. In 1668, the Mayor's Court asked the Dutch community to provide a new clock to be set up on the newly repaired steeple at the New Hall. Presumably nothing was done, as in 1675 the Court resolved to ask Mr Prime and his son 'of London now being in Norwich' to repair the clock at a cost of not more than £15, to be split three ways between the City, the Dutch congregation and the Russell Company. Priem was living permanently in Norwich by 1684. He died in 1710. The clock was presumably on the tower when it fell in 1713.

---

70   Christopher Hanson-Smith, *The Flemish Bond: East Anglian and the Netherlands: Close and Ancient Neighbours* (2004), p. 106.

Potters

Jasper Andries and Jacob Janson, potters, came to Norwich from Antwerp in 1567. They are believed to have produced the first tin-glazed earthenware in England, making tiles, and also pots for apothecaries. The evidence in support of this is in Strype's edition of *Stow's Survey* and in a letter in the British Library. Strype wrote: 'Jasper Andries and Jacob Jansen, potters, came from Antwerp and settled in Norwich, where they followed their trade, making galley paving tiles and vessels for apothecaries. They moved to London in 1570.'

The letter is a petition from Pastor Balkius and 20 members of the Norwich Dutch congregation in favour of the pair, and recites their history:

> In most humble ways shown your orators Jasper Andries and … anss both of Antwerp: That whereas to avoid persecution and for their conscience sake they came into this your Majesty's realm and continued … almost three years, exercising the making of galley paving tiles and vessels for potycaries and others very artificially, even as it may appear by the chest with their handiwork by them to your Majesty presented, and forasmuch as they are the first which brought and did exercise the said science into your Majesty's realm, and have been at very great charges before they could find the materials in this realm, and that the same science was so acceptable unto King Henry VIII of most famous memory your highness' father, that his Majesty offered to the said Jasper's father good wages and houseroom to exercise the same in this realm, which then came to none effect. But now your orators do only beseech in recompense of the cost and charges that it may please your Majesty to grant them houseroom within or without the liberty of London by the waterside, an privilege for the time of twenty years and that none but they, their wives, children and assigns may exercise the said science in this your Majesty's realm of England, and to sell and transport the same as well outward as inward unto all men free from all custom. And they shall pray to the living Lord for your Majesty's godly and prosperous success.[71]

However, it is difficult to find any evidence of their time in Norwich. There is a Jacob Jansen in the 1568 census, but he was a minister; there is a Jasper Andries in the census, but he was described as a merchant (and condemned as a drunkard!). The only potter in the census is Georgius Andree, who came with his wife and son from Brabant in 1567. Antwerp is in Brabant, so there must surely be a connection: is there an error in the forename, or was Jasper Andries perhaps the son?

There are no potters listed in the 1622 Return of Strangers.

Sellers of aquavitae

The sale of aquavitae – a strong spirit – was not the sole prerogative of the immigrant community. John Pound refers to its sale by the Norwich poor in his work on the 1570 census of the poor. However, it appears to have been particularly associated with the incomers. A mayor's order of 6 November 1574 (when Christopher Soame

---

71   BL, Lansdowne MS vol. xIi 58 and 59.

was mayor) said that no Stranger was 'to sell in any street or house any aquavite or aquacomposita (made by them or by other people) to any other Stranger; nor to drink in any Inn or tippling house on Sundays or other days, except in their own houses'. Fine: two shillings for each offence. When Soame became mayor for a second time, he said that the offences had of late grown again, leading to complaints, and reissued the order on 15 March 1580.

The will survives of John Decock, aqua-vitae seller, made in 1603 (curiously, he describes himself in it as 'son of George with the beard'). He bequeathed to his cousin Anna Moniers of Lynn three 'akavita kettles, with four serpents and all things belonging thereto'. Zacharias Piters, shoemaker, was to have a beer firkin of aquae vita, and all the aqua vitae that was in the house of the testator's cousin in Lynn.

The Return of Strangers of 1622 included three aqua vitae distillers, all born overseas: Jacob Tevell, Peter Hosbert and Joan Dorpin, widow.

Bakers

No bakers are listed in the 1568 census, but there were soon several bakers among the immigrant community. Disputes arose about the kinds of bread they made, and whether they could sell bread to the English or just to other immigrants. In September 1570 the wardens of the [English] Bakers' Company complained about Strangers making and selling bread to other Strangers. Six men in the immigrant community were appointed bakers to the Strangers – Jan Aernondes, Gabriel Aernondes, Jan Vander Helst, Adrian Mys, Mallyarde de Swicheter and Geeraerd de Lere. In October 1571, the 'Strangers Bakers' were ordered not to buy any wheat or bread corn on the Common Market before 1 o'clock on any market day. It was also complained that the Dutch bakers used to 'colour' their bread with eggs, 'whereby great numbers of eggs were wastefully spent'. They were ordered to stop. In 1573 they were told they could come to the Market and sell their bread without any interruption.

No Stranger was allowed to bake any kind of white bread, only 'bread of meal as it doth come from the mill'. Any Stranger who wanted to buy white bread could get it from English bakers. The Strangers were also forbidden to make or sell cakes, or other spiced or white bread called sweet cakes.

The rule that only six incomers could work as bakers was being flouted by the end of the century: in 1598 the Mayor's Court even sent six Dutch bakers to prison for baking bread! One incomer, John de Wylde, took his case all the way to the Privy Council, which ordered that he should be allowed to bake bread and sweet ginger-bread. On 10 November he triumphantly produced letters in the Mayor's Court from the Privy Council permitting him to continue his trade of making and selling gingerbread. The Council decided to write back saying that much corn was wasted in making this kind of bread, but bowed to the inevitable and allowed him to continue. This is the only occasion I have seen when a decision of the Mayor's Court in Norwich was overruled by the government.

Eight bakers were recorded in the 1622 Return of Strangers. Five were born in

England of parent strangers, including 'Elia Flepoe' (Elias Philippo) and two with the appropriate name of Whitebread. The other three were born abroad.

Dyers

Five dyers were recorded in the 1568 census, four Dutch and one Walloon. They very soon came into conflict with English dyers. In July 1569, English dyers complained to the Mayor's Court that certain strangers were 'wood setting' – they were called into the court and told that no one should do this hereafter.

Details of a new skill are revealed in Mayor's Court entries in 1590. Giles Cambye, a Dutch immigrant dyer living in Norwich, told the court that he was trading with Arthur Rotye, another Dutch immigrant, who lived in London. Rotye was an expert in the use of green dyes, and Cambye wanted him to come to Norwich. Rotye did come, and he taught his skills to an English dyer in the city and his apprentices.

The colours were mostly derived from plants, such as woad for blue and weld for yellow. A case involving a new dye, cochineal, derived from South American insects, is described in Chapter 7.

One dye, madder, is especially interesting to Norwich people because it has left a place name, the Maddermarket, although there is no indication that madder was sold there at the time of the Strangers. Madder was imported from the Low Countries in the Middle Ages. The immigrants of the sixteenth century did the same. A Dutchman named only as Adrian (perhaps Adrian Wallwyn) paid duty on madder valued at £30 in 1588–9, and Mallyard Rickward paid for a bale in 1594. The main importer was Jaques de Hem, who paid duty on madder on six occasions between 1591 and 1599, importing between one and three bales on each ship. The value of each bale varied between £10 and £13. In December 1600 he was before the Mayor's Court, for selling four bales of madder to Cambye: the sale was *not* in the Maddermarket but in St Peter Mancroft parish, which is where the Market Place is. However, the offence was not in where it was sold but because buyer and seller were both foreign.

Nine dyers were listed in the 1622 Return of Strangers, six born in Norwich (including Samuel Cambye, probably a son of Giles), and two born beyond the seas.

Drainage engineers

No immigrant in the 1568 census was described as a drainage engineer, but the Dutch have shared with the people of Norfolk the need to struggle against the sea and to improve the drainage of their low-lying farmland. A 1525 inscription in Dutch in Haddiscoe church commemorates Peter Peterson, a dyke-reeve. The Dutch type of mill called the smock mill was used for drainage in the Fens and the Broads. In about 1640 a Dutch mill was actually brought to Lynn and erected there.

Sir Cornelius Vermuyden, born in the Netherlands in about 1590, worked on fen drainage between 1634 and 1655, the greatest land drainage scheme in England and bigger than all the land reclaimed in the Netherlands between 1540 and 1690. His daughter Deborah married Sir Francis Bickley of Attleborough in Norfolk: there is a memorial to her in Attleborough church. In 1568 a Dutchman, Joas Johnson, was called in to supervise the new harbour works at Great Yarmouth. It was he who stabilised the harbour mouth in its present position. The way the river turns sharply to the east at Brush Quay is a lasting reminder of the contribution of the Dutch to the landscape of Norfolk.

Governance

The incomers can be classed overwhelmingly as refugees fleeing persecution, although as Douglas Rickwood suggested, some may have been economic migrants also: 'it is equally open to argument that the Netherlanders who had fled to England were as much driven by the need to seek a safer location in which to earn their daily bread as they were by the desire to worship God according to their own beliefs.'[72]

The refugees were united in their Calvinistic faith, and their churches were the centre of their lives. The ministers and elders were responsible for the social organisation of the Strangers. The 'Book of Discipline for the French church' of 1589 survives and gives a clear idea of how the Walloon incomers were organised. No similar record survives for the Dutch community, but the organisation would have been very similar.

The **pastors** and **ministers** were to be of pure doctrine, learned, irreproachable and of good fame. Chosen by the elders and deacons after examining the candidates in life and doctrine and hearing them preach. The office was for life.

The **doctors** were to maintain sound doctrine, search the scriptures and prepare students for the ministry. The order included schoolmasters, who were required to teach true preaching and the catechism.

The **elders** ('anciens') needed not be learned but did have to be sound in the faith. They could summon a delinquent to the Consistory and punish them by a mild admonition, or by suspension from communion. All ways were to be tried to bring a brother back, but if recalcitrant he could be cut off from communion. Persons of scandalous life had to be expelled, and other churches informed. There was no set number of elders and the office was temporary, usually for three years.

The **deacons** were to watch and help the poor. This was done through weekly meetings, but an individual deacon could give away up to a shilling on his own authority. Deacons were to make collections at the church, and hand the money to the deacon in charge of the purse. They were expected to visit each poor and afflicted person every three months. The office was temporary, usually for three months. They also gave hand-outs to *passants*, short-term residents. At the 1595 colloquy of the French church, the deputies from Norwich and Canterbury complained that this was being abused.[73]

These 'Orders' together made up the Consistory. The Dutch Consistory met in one of the rooms in the St Andrew's Hall complex. They probably met at first in the rooms

---

72   Douglas Rickwood, 'The Norwich Strangers 1565–1643: a problem of control', *Proceedings of the Huguenot Society of London*, 24 (1984), p. 121.

73   Vane (1984), p. 137.

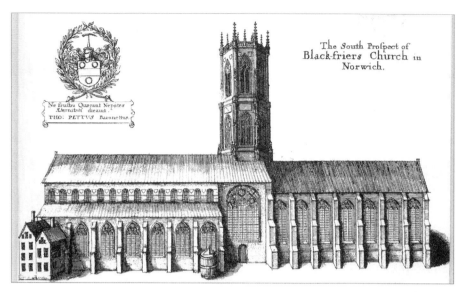

Figure 27 St Andrew's Hall, showing the rooms over the porch. Print produced for Dugdale's *Monasticon Anglicanum* (late 17th century).

over the south doorway to the Hall: Giles Langhelett is recorded as paying 55 shillings a year rent for this building in the early 1580s. From 1596–7 the Dutch congregation paid 20s a year rent of their 'Consistory Chamber' in the New Hall. The Consistory heard cases of blasphemy, false doctrinal opinions and improper behaviour.[74]

Personal expressions of faith can be found in almost all the wills left by the incomers. A typical religious preamble is that of Gerarde Vervincke, who died in 1613: 'I commit my soul into the hands of God my Creator, with an assured hope that he has forgiven me all my sins for the merit of Christ his son my only Saviour and Redeemer.' The longest expression of faith came from Hugh Herbert:

> I do bequeathe my soul from henceforth and ever here after in the hands of God my creator and merciful father through Jesus Christ his son, our only saviour, mediator and intercessor, by whose death passion and resurrection I do firmly believe and embrace my salvation. And concerning my body (God having withdrawn the soul to himself as it hath pleased him to bestow the same) I do ordain the said body to be buried after the Christian simplicity of our reformed church, waiting and looking for together with all the faithful for the resurrection of the said body on the last day, when or in which day I do assure myself to see my redeemer and to enjoy the everlasting and blessed life. And this faith and hope of my salvation grounded upon the word of promises of God in Christ I do assure myself not to perish by any means.

Services were simple ones with Bible readings and a sermon. In 1570, the elders who read on Sundays before the sermon were told to read out the Ten Commandments and

---

74   NRO NCR 18a/10; Vane (1984), pp. 134–5.

the 'beleve' [the creed] after the Bible reading. The Dutch church in Norwich began using the Dutch psalter of Petrus Dathenus, before it was adopted by the London Dutch church in 1571. Joby suggests that they probably used the edition printed in Norwich by de Solemne.[75]

There is one hint of something more dramatic. In 1574, according to Bishop Parkhurst, a young Dutch girl, a servant of the preacher of the Dutch church, was 'most miserably troubled by Satan' for a whole year. She remained strong in faith, and eventually the demon left her, entering instead into the body of a son of a Norwich alderman, aged 13 or 14. However, after some weeks, the Lord took pity on the boy and 'overthrew the enemy'.

The Dutch church

Two letters went to the Archbishop of Canterbury on 28 December 1565, asking that the Dutch be given a church for their own use in Norwich. The duke of Norfolk wrote that since he had returned to Norwich, the Strangers had come to him asking to be allowed to have a church; he pointed out that 'here be churches I know that be void'. The postscript to his letter added that 'the like had been granted here in King Edward's days'. This is the only known reference to a Dutch church in the city in earlier times (Edward VI was king between January 1547 and July 1553). However, Helen Sutermeister found a reference to money spent on wine (for communion) and wax (for candles) used by Strangers in an account for the year 1545, so there may have been a Dutch presence here even before the time of King Edward.[76]

The bishop of Norwich supported the request, saying that the incomers wanted a church where they could hear the word of God 'according to their former manner in the town of Sandwich'. He had spoken to the mayor but found him 'somewhat strange therein' so he was writing directly to the archbishop. The archbishop agreed that the Strangers should be granted a vacant church in the city, and proposed that the bishop should have authority over their religious practices. He was wary of their Calvinistic ideas, 'wishing that they might be persuaded to recede as little as might be from the common order of prayers, and administration of the sacraments as is used by authority in the realm'.[77]

The Dutch were given permission to use part of the former friary building now called St Andrew's and Blackfriars' Halls. The first service appears to have been held as early as 24 December 1565. It is not clear if these first services were held in Blackfriars' or St Andrew's Hall, but they were eventually established in the former. This was on an informal basis at first – members of the congregation brought their own chairs with them for the services – and with no charge. The lack of chairs may have been standard practice; in 1567 Pieter de Smedt asked a relative in Ypres if the chair

---

75 Christopher Joby, 'The Dutch language in early modern Norfolk: a social history', *Dutch Crossing*, 38(2) (July 2014), pp. 154–88.

76 Helen Sutermeister, *The Norwich Blackfriars* (1977), p. 12.

77 Moens (1887–8), p. 253; Rye, 'The Dutch refugees in Norwich', *The Norfolk Antiquarian Miscellany*, vol. 3 (1887), p. 197.

on which his mother used to attend 'preachings' could be brought over, while, in 1586 James Dehorn paid duty on a dozen sermon chairs.

John Kirkpatrick thought that the Dutch worshipped in St Andrew's Hall until at least 1619, and an entry in the Mayor's Court book for that year may support this. In November 1619 the city authorities were planning to fit out the chapel for use by the Walloons (see below). They noted that 'the Dutch have long used the New Hall without recompense to the city for the same'. However, Moens was sure that it was the 'choir' of the old friary, that is, Blackfriars' Hall, which was used from the beginning.[78]

The situation was regularised in 1625. From then on the Dutch had a secure lease on the Hall, for which they paid 6s 8d a year. They began to add permanent fixtures to the Hall, and hired an adjacent room for their administrative business. In 1651 the city decided to use the building as a preaching place instead of the Cathedral. It was suggested that the Dutch use the church of St Peter Hungate instead, and they moved there, ceasing to pay rent on the chapel in the year 1651–2. When Schellinks visited the city in October 1662, the Dutch were still at St Peter Hungate, but they were soon back at Blackfriars' Hall: they resumed paying rent for the chapel from Lady Day 1663.

In 1687 the Roman Catholics in the city petitioned the city authorities for the use of the chapel, but, after the Dutch sent in a rival petition, it was eventually decided that the Dutch could remain. In 1713 they were granted a formal lease for 200 years, at the same rate of 6s 8d a year and on making a one-off payment of £30 to the city. An annual service in Dutch continued to be held in Norwich well into the twentieth century.

The Dutch church naturally had its own pastors. The first was Hendrick van Schoonberg, apparently in 1565, followed by Pieter Hasaert and Carolus (alias Theophilus) Ryckwaert, who had been banished from Ypres (where, Christopher Joby notes, he had preached *in French*) in 1567.[79]

The most well-known ministers were the Elisons, father and son. John Elison, born abroad in 1581, and educated at Leiden University, became the pastor of the Dutch church in 1603, and served for 36 years until his death in 1639. In 1634 John Elison and his wife Marie had their portraits painted by Rembrandt when they were on a visit to Amsterdam, the only people from Britain to have been accorded this honour. The paintings are now in the Boston Museum and Art Gallery in the United States.

Elison died in 1639, having made his will five years earlier. He left 40s for the Dutch poor and 20s to the English poor of the ward in which he lived. His eldest son John was to have the silver wine cup which had been bequeathed to him by his grandmother, Anne Bonkenell.

Elison bequeathed all his books and papers in his study chamber to his son

---

78 Moens (1887–8), p. 23; John Kirkpatrick, *History of the Religious Orders and Communities and of the Hospitals and Castle of Norwich* (written about 1725, published 1845), pp. 61–4. He quotes an entry in the Mayor's Court Book for 1619 that says that the Dutch had 'long used the new hall'. He thought the term meant St Andrew's Hall, but perhaps it could also cover Blackfriars' Hall, in which case there would be no conflict in the sources.

79 Joby (2014), p. 168.

Figure 28 (above and right)
Twentieth-century 'Strangers' (American servicemen) at play in front of the memorial to John Elison in Blackfriars' Hall, Norwich; and outside the building. MC 371/77/333 (interior), MC 376/350/4 (exterior) 1942–5, photographers unknown. From the 2nd Air Division Memorial Archive at the Norfolk Record Office.

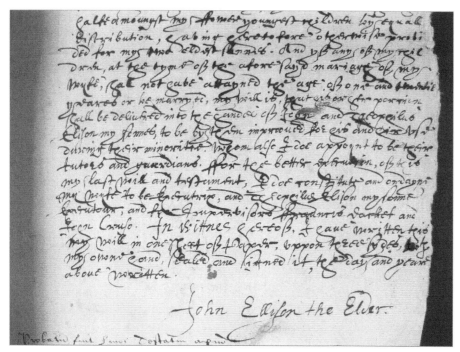

Figure 29 Original will of John Elison, pastor of the Dutch community in Norwich, with his signature (NRO NCC WILLS)

Theophilus, described in the will as 'the scholar', except for four folio volumes. These were reserved to three friends: two to fellow minister Charles Liebaert, one to Francis Dackett, merchant, and one to Jan Cruso, 'captain of the Dutch company'. They were to make their own choice of books from his library.

Elison's younger sons Jacob and Francis and his daughters Ann and Joane were each to have £10 on reaching the age of 21 or on marriage, this having been bequeathed to them by their grandmother Ann, the late wife of John Bonkenell. All other goods were left to his wife Mary if she remained a widow. If she did remarry, they would then be divided, half to Mary, half to be split among his four youngest children. Elison requested that his body be buried in the Dutch church, and there is a monument to him in Blackfriars' Hall. The text is in three languages (Dutch, English and Latin).

Theophilus was a 'native': he had been born in Norwich in 1609. He also went to Leiden University, and in 1640 he followed his father as pastor of the Norwich church. He also served for 36 years, dying in Norwich on 1 June 1676. A wealthy man, he bought a property in St Andrew and St Michael at Plea, presumably on the border between the two parishes and very near to the Dutch church, in 1664. There is a smaller monument to him in Blackfriars' Hall.

A list of communicants at the Dutch church in 1679 had about 105 names, many of them designating families rather than individuals, whereas an early nineteenth-century list of members of the church had just 38 names. Eventually the weekly services in Dutch at the Hall dwindled to just a few services a year. Only a very few families were still enrolling themselves into the Dutch church in the late nineteenth and early twentieth centuries. Some have the names of incomers, such as the Boltz family, but others have completely English-sounding names. The last two admissions in the church register are of Sarah White in 1911 and Stephen White in 1912, the son and daughter of Stephen and Mary Ann White (and adults themselves: Stephen was 34, his sister 17 years old). Stephen senior had himself been admitted in 1869, and his father Henry had been a member before him, so the impression is of a very small number of families perpetuating the tradition of membership of the Church over several generations.

The French church

The Walloons were allowed to use the Bishop's Chapel in the Cathedral Close as their place of worship. Bishop Parkhurst had himself been a religious exile when he fled the persecutions of Queen Mary: his time in Zurich may have made him especially sympathetic to the problems of refugees.

The church flourished. There were almost a hundred baptisms in one year alone, 1600. The first minister was Jan Helmich, who came over from Utrecht in 1567: however he died in 1568. Jean Marie and Nicholas Basnage, the next two pastors, were from France and are discussed in Chapter 9. Then two ministers, Aaron Capel and Jaques Polyander, came from the Low Countries, but Pierre de Laune was also a Huguenot. The next minister was the first to be native-born: Philip Delme born in Norwich in 1588, and studied at Leiden, becoming assistant minister at Norwich in 1615 and minister in 1616. He went on to the French Church at Canterbury in 1620.

As the years passed, the bishops became less tolerant of the use of their chapel. In 1603, the Mayor's Court ordered the city chamberlain to confer with the minister and elders of the Walloon congregation, suggesting that they take over the New Hall chapel. Nothing came of the proposal. In 1619 the bishop asked the Walloons to leave his chapel, and suggested they could worship in the Hall with the Dutch speakers. The city authorities were prepared to allow them the use of the chapel there 'if they shall desire the same', and, as the city would have to bear the cost of fitting it out, hoped they and the Dutch could share the building and contribute to the costs of maintenance. However, the Walloons said it was too small for both sets of worshippers, and that as they held their services at the same time of day, 'the voice of the one congregation, in singing psalms and the like, will hinder and disturb the other'. They continued to worship in the Bishop's Chapel.

On 26 December 1634 Bishop Richard Corbett wrote to the Walloons: 'You promised me from time to time to restore my stolen bell and to glaze my lattice windows. After three years I see nothing mended.' A petition of 1638 says that when they first used the Bishop's Chapel, in about 1565, they 'found it was more like a dove house than a church, full of mud and ordure, the roof decayed and the windows broken'. They paid no rent for it but spent a lot of money on it, so that they had in fact repaired the chapel – after which, they claimed, the Bishop had started using it again! Now, in 1638, they claimed it was 'well glazed and supported': thanks to them the roof beam was sound.

Figure 30
The Walloon church
in Norwich, formerly
the parish church
of St Mary the Less
and then a cloth hall.
Photo by the author.

Corbett told them to leave by Whitsun: 'Your discipline, I know, cares not for a consecrated place, and any room in Norwich that hath but breadth and length may serve your turn as well as a chapel. I say: Depart and hire some other place for your irregular meetings.' However, Corbett died in July 1635 with the Walloons still in possession. He was succeeded by Bishop Wren who again gave them notice, and urged them to follow the example of the French community at Axholme who, he said, used the English liturgy (translated into French).

It was time to move on. The Walloons obtained a lease for 40 years from the city for the former church of St Mary the Less, which as we saw had earlier been used as a Sale Hall. They promised to repair and make it fit, and also to repair the yard on the north side; the work cost them £160, as they complained, a large sum 'to repair a poor little forlorn church granted them by the city's favour'. They promised to maintain the church and steeple and also the yard adjoining it to the north, paying 20s a year rent for the yard and no rent for the church itself. Perhaps they entered the church through the yard rather than the 'main' entrance on Queen Street: the wooden carving over the

Figure 31
North door of St Mary the Less: 1637 in the oval commemorates the date when the Walloon community began to worship there. Photo by the author.

north door bears the date 1637.

The original lease was for 40 years, but in fact the building was used by the Walloon or French-speaking church for almost 200 years, from 1637 to 1832. They were already a small community, describing themselves in 1638 as 'a poor decayed congregation'. They first paid rent on Lady Day in 1640, but this was for three whole years so they must have moved in about Lady Day 1637. They then paid 10s rent every year for the courtyard (they must have obtained a reduction from the city), including the Commonwealth period: unlike the Dutch, they were not disturbed even in that turbulent time.[80]

As the Dutch and French churches declined in numbers, they sometimes shared a pastor. Pierre des Reaux, appointed minister of the Dutch church some time between 1690 and 1692, was appointed pastor of the French church as well in 1712, holding down both jobs until 1736. John Bruckner, born on the island of Cadsand, in what is now Belgium, in 1726 and educated in Leiden, was elected minister of the French church in Norwich in 1751, and to the Dutch church in 1766. He could preach in four languages (French, Dutch, English and Latin), but it appears that the few worshippers at the Dutch church were by now French speakers rather than Dutch speakers! He remained in both posts until he was just a few years short of 80, but on 12 May 1804 he was found hanged in his house in St Benedict's.

A reminiscence by Amelia Opie gives an impression of how cold and damp these churches might have been by the late eighteenth century, by which time they were little used. One day she visited the Dutch church in Norwich. It was so cold inside

---

80   NRO FC 29/13; John Browne, *History of Congregationalism* (1878), pp. 83–4.

that she broke into a little dance – only to look down and see to her horror that she was literally dancing on the grave to her one-time dancing master, Mr Christian. As a story it is somewhat negated by the fact that no memorial of this man ever existed in the Dutch church. Rye wondered if she was thinking of the French church, dancing masters being more characteristic of that nation, as the Noverre family demonstrates, but nothing is known of such a memorial there either.

In fact neither church is rich in memorials. Moens has a list of those in the French church in 1838, many of which have since disappeared; none were earlier than 1726. The only two prominent ones today are those to the Martineau and Colombine families. The church is privately owned and only occasionally open to the public. Blackfriars' Hall is usually open, and the monuments to the two Elisons can be seen on the wall. Other memorials in the Hall included those to members of the de Cleve and Athow and families, and also to the family of John Smith (died 1779). These are not now visible as they are hidden beneath the present wooden floor.

Religious disputes

The incomers, the Dutch especially, were split by issues of religion on several occasions: 'The Dutch seem always to have been much more unruly and turbulent than the Walloons.'[81]

On 7 May 1570 agreement was reached by members of the Dutch church to keep the company in good order: no ordinances were to be made except those which 'accord with the word of God or at least to the quietness of the church'! Twelve elders were to be elected each year to still all contentions, and also to ensure that drunkards were expelled out of tippler houses. The elders were to patrol the streets on Sundays and Holy Days and make people come to hear the sermon. They were to punish fighters, drunkards, street walkers by night, and contentious and rebellious persons. Four brethren were to be chosen to care for 'the widows and fatherless'. All 'impenitent and obstinate rebels' who would not repent were to be excommunicated.

Most incomers took their religion very seriously, and the community was occasionally divided by theological controversy. The Dutch congregation was split by a dispute in 1571, Minister Balkius leading one party and Ministers Ryckewaert and Algoet jointly leading the other. The bishop of Norwich favoured Ryckewaert's party but the mayor and Corporation favoured Balkius and put Ryckewaert and Algoet in prison, eventually expelling them and their supporters from the city. On 16 September 1571 it was decided that all three ministers should be displaced from the ministry, and that John Paules [Powell] of Sandwich should forthwith depart Norwich. Ryckewaert became minister of the Dutch church in Thetford, where his son was born, but soon returned to the Low Countries. He was at Leiden by 1577 and back in Ypres in the following year. Balkius, who had come to England from Friesland, also left Norwich in 1571. He was Minister of the Dutch church in Stamford in 1572, and at Sandwich

81   Vane (1984), p. 126.

between 1572 and 1578. He then returned to Friesland. Algoet remained in England, being recorded at Colchester in 1583.[82]

Bishop Parkhurst wrote to Protestant reformer Heinrich Bullinger that silence had been imposed on 'three quarrelsome preachers' in the Dutch church in Norwich, and two others appointed. Without the troublemakers, 'the greatest quiet and concord prevails in the Dutch church'.

However there was more trouble in 1575. The Dutch and Walloon Strangers' Book includes a letter from the 'Commissioners' to the mayor of Norwich dated 7 June 1575, which notes that 'sundry strangers born in the Low Countries … had been found to maintain the horrible and damnable error of the Anabaptists'. All Strangers in Norwich had to give their assent to a series of articles which included rules that infants could be baptised, that Christians could take oaths, that it was lawful for a Christian to go to war, that Christians should hold their possessions as individuals and not in common – and also that it was lawful for a magistrate to execute obstinate heretics! The whole company in Norwich set their hands to these articles on 27 June 1575. The Mayor's Court became involved on 2 July 1575. Aldermen of each ward, together with the ministers of the Dutch and Walloon nations, were told to call before them those Dutch and Walloons 'as well men as women' remaining in the city who were not of the congregation nor of the church, to examine them and try to bring them to reformation and to be of the church. If any of them refused to conform, the aldermen were to inform the court so that they could be banished without delay.

In fact it was not always easy to keep recalcitrants out. The Mayor's Court Book for 21 October 1579 records that:

> Leonard Foxe, alien, lately sent to prison because he would not leave the city when he was commanded to, is to be taken by the gaoler and placed in a boat and so conveyed to a place beyond the seas. If he is found again in the city, he is to be tied behind a cart and whipped about the Market Place and then sent to prison again.

He did return, and on 5 March 1580 the Court ordered the punishment to be carried out.

The authorities in the immigrant community attempted to limit the job opportunities of those of whom they disapproved. One rule in the Book of Orders ratified by the Dutch community in 1581 ordered that 'no person of our nation that live disorderly and are not of the congregation of God and do take the bread-winning of the brethren of the church' could work in the drapery trade. The only people who could come into the trade were those who were part of the congregation of the church, or who had a certificate of approval from the minister of the church.

In 1585 there was more trouble. On 6 March the politic men of the Walloon congregation asked for three of their number to be banished for their 'ungodliness' – John Kentyng, John Porryn and Mary Valdyr were 'lewd persons'. The Mayor's Court

---

82   Forster (1967), p. 43.

ordered them to 'return to the places from whence they came'. If they dared return they would be publicly whipped around the Market Place, tied to a cart.

This was followed by the politic men of the Dutch congregation, who on 10 May came to the Mayor's Court with a list of names of 'wicked and ungodly' people they wanted banished. As we have seen, there had been a similar banishment in 1571. The mayor and aldermen tried to contact them, but those they could find were contemptuous of their authority. The Court supported the politic men and issued a letter to be read out in the Dutch church. The names were to be read out and they were to be told to leave the city within __ days [the figure is left blank in the record]. The names are recorded in the court records: Pieter de Smedt and 43 others were ordered to leave the city. If they did not, they would be whipped out of town. The offenders were mostly male, but did include several women, such as Catherine Hackett, Lowystken the wife of Adrian de Sorge, and Mary Doneck, widow.

A group of people, both Dutch and Walloon, were presented to the Mayor's Court on 4 August 1585 by elders of both congregations as persons of lewd behaviour, drunkards, and of no church. Twelve people were ordered to leave the city, taking their wives and families, and never return. To make sure they left, they were to be whipped every Market Day that they remained. The list included a few new names, such as John and Philip Ras, but most were people who been banished earlier in the year, but who presumably had ignored the previous order. These repeat offenders included the one woman on the list, Mary Doneck.

Discipline and control

The incomers were controlled by their own leaders, and also subject to regulations laid down by city authorities. The latter drew up a set of 'Orders' to take effect from St Andrew's Day 1570:

1 Mayor and aldermen to determine all disputes between the city and the Strangers. Those between Dutch and Walloons on religious matters to be referred to the bishop of Norwich.
2 Every Stranger to come before mayor and aldermen, bringing a list of the names of their family members, and a certificate of their 'good conversation'.
3 If any Stranger come to the city, mayor and aldermen to be informed within two nights, on penalty of a fine of 5s for each additional night.
4 Aliens to pay rates to the local parish church, and to pay 'watch rate' to the parish constable. No Stranger to be found on the streets more than half an hour after the St Peter Mancroft curfew bell has been rung 'without urgent and reasonable cause'.
5 Strangers to choose officers to view and search commodities every year, and give list of names to the mayor.
6 Strangers to elect arbitrators – eight for the Dutch community, four for the Walloon community.
7 Strangers to render account every quarter for duties due on their products.
8 The officials of the Hall to have half the money, the remainder to go to the city chamberlains.

New laws would be introduced at different times, such as the Order issued by Mayor Pecke on 11 June 1573: no Stranger on any Sunday or Holy Day was to walk about the streets or out of the city gates, to play, or to sit to talk in the time of sermons or prayers. Neither during that time or any at other time were they to drink or eat in any 'inn, tavern or tippling house'. Fine: 5s for the first offence, 10s for any subsequent transgression.

The Dutch and Walloon authorities could admonish, excommunicate or even fine offenders, but they had no prison. They had to turn to the city authorities for the imposition of physical punishments – whipping or imprisonment – on offenders in their communities. There are several examples in the records of the Mayor's Court, although remarkably few for a community making up one-third of the city's population. Sentences such as the public whippings given to aliens George Haessacke alias Vandebuske, for 'evil rule' [drunkenness] in 1570, Jane Eade, for stealing money from a shop in St Augustine's in 1582, or to Allen Floren and Mary de Post for fornication in the following year, may seem harsh today, but were just the same as those given to members of the English community for similar offences. Proof of this is in the record of the Mayor's Court of 7 July 1576. Arnold Polertys, a Dutchman, and Jacoby Gooderskall, a Dutch woman, were punished for 'evil rule'. They had to ride about the Market in a cart with a paper on their heads proclaiming their crime, and were then set in the stocks, still wearing the paper. Exactly the same punishment was imposed on five English women by the Court on the same day.

As we have seen, the authorities had an extra weapon in their armoury when dealing with incomers: they could be banished. John Muryes was told he would be banished if he did not improve his behaviour when before the court for drunkenness in 1582. In 1585, three Dutchmen were presented to the Mayor's Court: they were told to leave the city within six days and take their families with them. Eight years later, the Walloon authorities complained that Frances Demmer and Jacob Grenegote were common drunkards. The two men were put in prison until they could find sureties, and their families ordered to leave the city.

The politic men

Under mayor Thomas Parker (1568–9), an order was made that the incomers elect their own governors – eight for the Dutch, four for the Walloons. They were to be elected every year, and the mayor was to approve the names. These were the 'politic men' – *politijcke mannen* or *hommes politiques*. They were to act as arbitrators of petty causes between community members. No English official was to interfere in the Strangers' affairs apart from the mayor himself. An Order of 1573 gave the politic men the additional duty of examining all newcomers and their guarantors, before they were presented to the mayor for approval.

In 1569 the elders of the Norwich Dutch Congregation presented to the mayor 24 articles designed to maintain their church 'in Christian peace and tranquillity'. These gave more details of how the eight Dutch politic men were elected and what they were to do. Every year, shortly after the election of the mayor in the third week of June,

24 men were to be put forward from which the eight were to be chosen: eight carried over from the previous year and 16 others put forward by the preachers, elders and deacons. The congregation was to choose the eight politic men for the ensuing year from these 24. Naturally there was a great deal of continuity, with the same names occurring every year – Bonnell, Desbonnet, Wallwyn. The same people often served as deacons or elders before or after their service as politic men. No doubt the Walloon politic men were chosen in much the same way.

These men were to punish 'any fighters, drunkards, whoremongers, street walkers by night, contentious or rebellious persons, and made provision to care for orphans within the community'. They also dealt with testamentary affairs, and disputes between masters and apprentices. In the sixteenth century, decisions about orphans were made by two or three politic men; in the seventeenth century all 12 had to be present. They were fined for non-attendance – and for falling asleep at meetings![83]

Norwich appears to have had the first immigrant community to appoint politic men. In 1582 Canterbury did the same, deliberately following the example of Norwich, but as Esser says, 'in the London Dutch and French churches, it was the consistories that dealt with the cases that were referred to the politic men in Norwich'.[84]

Two volumes recording the work of the politic men have survived. We have already mentioned the so-called Strangers' Book at the Norfolk Record Office. It was mainly concerned with appointing guardians for orphans. The Book of the Norwich Dutch Church at the British Library is the minute book of the Dutch politic men covering 1605–15. It too has a good deal about the guardianship of orphans but also covers other matters: the settlement of disputes between masters and apprentices, the punishment of those breaking trade regulations, and matters of probate. The politic men punished people for scandalous talk, violence, drunkenness, gaming and dancing. To take two examples, in 1608, two Dutchmen were fined 6s each after being found drinking in a pub called the Bull during the time of the sermon. In 1613 five people (three women and two men) were each fined 6s 8d for aggressive behaviour.

The politic men often translated wills from French or Dutch for the English probate courts, and made or testified to probate inventories. One inventory, that of Jacob Somerman, 1585, is actually entered into the Strangers' Book, in Dutch of course. However, it is not for probate purposes, and presumably relates to some form of dispute.

The Dutch and Walloon Strangers' Book, also called the Book of Orders for Strangers

The Assembly Books show that the Corporation decided in 1570 to create a separate volume to record matters relating to the Stranger communities, and the process of its creation can be traced in detail. The Assembly of 24 February 1570 ordered eight of its members (whose names are given) to make and establish a book for the order of the

---

83   Raingard Esser, *Social Concern and Calvinistic Duty: The Norwich Strangers' Community* (1992), p. 178.
84   Esser (1992), p. 182.

Dutch Strangers and to take such orders to them as they shall deem good. This was to be done by the next meeting. However, when the Assembly met on 10 March it had clearly not been done, and they were told it was to be ready by the next meeting. In fact it was not until the 16 June Assembly that the book was produced, and it was agreed that it should be established as 'law'. However, this took more time. At the Assembly of 16 November, the 'Book for the Order of the Strangers and the Strangers' Hall' (or the 'Strangers' Book' as it is called more simply in the margin of the entry) was finally presented. The Assembly, having perused it, agreed that it 'shall stand and remain in strength and effect' from the feast of St Andrew coming, that is, from 30 November 1570, nine months after the idea was first mooted. This is the volume now generally known as the Strangers' Book. It is possible that the present book is a copy of the first one. Douglas Rickwood thought that it was actually written in the late 1570s. Entries before that date are retrospective, and therefore perhaps copied from the other book, those after that date being added as they occurred.[85] (The Strangers' Hall referred to above is not the building in Norwich now called by that name, but the former church of St Mary the Less, later the French church, which was then used as a sealing hall for the wool produced by the Dutch and Walloon communities.)

The book records the articles made by the eight men who had been appointed by the Assembly, with a further series relating to the regulation of business at the Strangers' Hall. Another set of orders was drawn up by the eight 'persons for the city', this time with the co-operation of four representatives of the 'alyans' – Johannes Ruytinck, Peter Obrii, Francis Tryon and Mahui Priem. These are followed by a series of orders, dated 1570 and 1571, and similar to those in the 'Dutch Book of Orders' (see below).

Entries continue into the seventeenth century, but become less frequent, finishing with a complaint about the quality of 'a piece of tufted buffyns' in 1617. The book then concludes with a series of 'Articles to be inquired of by the bailiffs for the year 1642 before William Gostlyn Esq, Mayor of Norwich for the French and Dutch congregations to be inquired of and to present all offenders in these articles comprised made and sett downe'. The 29 articles are repeated for the following year and the next mayor. The articles appear restrictive. Incomers had to enter into a bond with their politic men that they would not become chargeable upon 'the common purse'; any women who remained in the city after their husbands had left had to 'repair to their husbands' or pay a fine of £5 a month. The age when the incomers were welcomed for the benefits they brought to the city appears to have passed.

Decline

By the early seventeenth century, the churches were trying to hang on to members who wanted to leave the community church and worship in their local Anglican parish church. One issue was money, since the Stranger churches wanted members to contribute to supporting their poor. Members of the Dutch and Walloon congre-

---

85   Rickwood, (1989), vol. 1, p. 169.

gations had to pay rates to both the Anglican parish in which they lived and their own church. For example, in 1602–5 the English parishioners in St Laurence parish contributed £17 12s 1d to the rates of the parish church. The Dutch living in the parish contributed £8 17s 7d in the same period. Not only did they receive almost nothing for this, as they worshipped in and maintained their own church and received no handouts from the parish overseer when in need, they had to contribute to their own church funds as well. It is little wonder that many of them felt aggrieved.[86]

There was a whole succession of such cases among the Walloons. In 1601 the Walloon church took action against Peter Truye and Nicholas Corte for failing to contribute money to support the Walloon community. In 1608 the Walloons appealed to the bishop to mediate and try to bring 'these two strayed sheep into their own sheepfold', and not to allow others to leave the community.[87]

The muster roll of the Walloon Company for 1618 shows up another man trying to leave the community: there is a note beside the name Peter Desbonnet recording that he 'refused to come saying he was of the English Company'.[88]

In 1621 Dennis Lermytt refused to pay Walloon dues or attend the Walloon church. He said that he was attending his local parish church and paying church rates. He was joined by Joel Desormeaux and Samuel Cambye, who were already in dispute with the pastor of the Walloon church. These two were second-generation immigrants as they were born in England, but according to the 1622 Return of Strangers, Lermytt had been born overseas.

Samuel Cambye made a statement before the Mayor's Court in 1621:

> I am born here in this city of Norwich, and the King his majesty's subject by birth, am fully and firmly resolved to frequent as a parishioner my parish church and continue during my life in the performance of all the duties belonging to a parishioner as by the laws of this realm of England I am bound. And I will have nothing to do with the Walloon church at all.

Desormeaux also refused to be part of the Walloon congregation, and to pay dues to the minister. He told the court that he was a freeman and English born, though of Walloon parents. He admitted that he had been baptised in the Walloon church, and even held office there, but resolved to count himself as English and not go back to the Walloon church. The case went up to the Privy Council, which ordered that all such 'Strangers' should continue pay dues to the Walloon church as well as to their local parish church, as had been the case since 1565. Desormeaux was ordered to pay the arrears due to the minister and poor of the Norwich Walloon congregation, which had by this time built up to £24 16s, and told that he must henceforward pay his dues to the congregation.[89]

---

86 Figures from NRO PD 58/38.
87 Vane (1984), p. 140, citing Lansdowne MS vol. 841 no. 31, fo 53.
88 NRO NCR 13a/15/20a.
89 NRO Rye 33, vol. 7, p. 111.

In 1630, the Mayor's Court wrote to the Privy Council in London on the behalf of the Strangers. They were afraid that many people would plead poverty in view of 'the scarcity of the time' and would withdraw from the Dutch and French congregations. In December 1630 a deputation from the Dutch church, led by its minister John Elison, came to the Mayor's Court to ask for help with their petition to the House of Lords about the continuance of the Dutch congregation in Norwich. The Court asked them to promise they would try and continue in their church 'in such sort as the Walloon Congregation is ordered'. At the same time the deputation agreed not to prevent Matthew Boyes from withdrawing from the Dutch congregation. The deputation included Peter van Hove. Just two years later, van Hove and John Vannixon were accused of failing to pay the rates due to the Dutch congregation. They appeared before the Mayor's Court and repeated their refusal. They were ordered to appear before the court again on the following Wednesday, but there is no further record of the case.

No doubt less wealthy and important immigrant families simply voted with their feet and left the incomer churches without fuss or court action.

Conclusion

In 1637 the two pastors (John Elison for the Dutch and Pierre de Laune for the Walloons) addressed a petition to archbishop of Canterbury, William Laud, who wanted members of the immigrant communities to attend their local Anglican parish churches. As the historian Robert Wyndham Ketton-Cremer explains,

> his somewhat peremptory reply contained one important modification, that only 'native-born subjects of the second degree' – the second generation born on English soil – were required to attend their parish churches. This reply was read by the pastors from their pulpits, 'with thanks to his Majesty for granting the continuance of their congregation, and allowing those of the first descent to remain members'.[90]

From the second decade of the seventeenth century onwards, many English Protestants went to the Netherlands to escape religious persecution in England. Some became members of the English church in Rotterdam. Religious freedom and economic gain – Norwich people were leaving for the Low Counties for the same reasons as the Strangers from the Low Countries had come to Norwich 70 years earlier.

---

90 R. W. Ketton-Cremer, *Norfolk in the Civil War* (1969), p. 74. The quotation is from Moens (1887–8), pp. 93–5.

Chapter 4

Life and leisure

Where they lived

There are several forms of document that indicate in which wards or parishes the immigrants lived. The census of 1571 lists the numbers in each ward, the return of 1622 names the incomers living in each ward, the taxation records give the names of aliens in each parish paying tax, some wills and probate inventories name the parish of the deceased, and many of the entries in the Dutch baptism register name the parish in which the child was born (no entries in the Walloon church baptism register do this).

Some 342 of the 827 baptisms in the Dutch church register name the parish in Norwich in which the child was born. Using these 342 families as a sample, we can see where young Dutch families were living in the first two decades of the seventeenth century. The parishes with the highest number of baptisms were St Margaret 53, St Laurence 39, St Michael Coslany 33 (and probably more as there are 15 cases which just record 'St Michael' without specifying which), St Mary Coslany 27, St Andrew 27 and St Gregory 22. Four parishes had no recorded baptisms of incomers; All Saints, St John Timberhill, St Etheldreda and SS Simon and Jude. Parishes with only one or two such baptisms were St Augustine, St George Tombland, St Helen, St John Sepulchre, St Julian, St Michael at Plea, St Michael at Thorn and St Peter Hungate. It is clear that these families were very much concentrated south of the river, from St Andrew's to St Benedict's street, and across the water in Coslany ward.

Incomers could not buy land in the city: the very fact that van Kurnbeck owned land in the city convinces me that he was not technically an incomer. One way around the restrictions was to purchase the freedom of the city. De Solemne did this in 1570, and this enabled him to purchase property in September 1571. This was at the corner of Pottergate and Holtor Lane (now Lower Goat Lane), so that we can pinpoint exactly where in the city the first-ever printing took place. A plaque now marks the spot. After this, I have found no incomers purchasing property in the city until the seventeenth century. Peter Verbeck bought a property in St Michael (Coslany) in 1612, and Jaques de Hem (another immigrant who purchased his freedom) bought property from 1616. Generally, however, it was the second generation, perhaps even the third, who began to appear in the city court rolls as purchasers of land: John van Rockeghem (land in Lakenham) 1632, Charles Verkin (land in St Michael Coslany) 1633, and Peter Vertegans (land in St Giles) 1635 are examples of this. Others occur in the 1626 landgable tax, such as Peter van Hove in St Laurence, Lewis de Hage and James Favarques both in St Martin at Oak, and John van den Abeale, 'merchant' (he is the only one whose occupation appears in the document) in St Andrew.

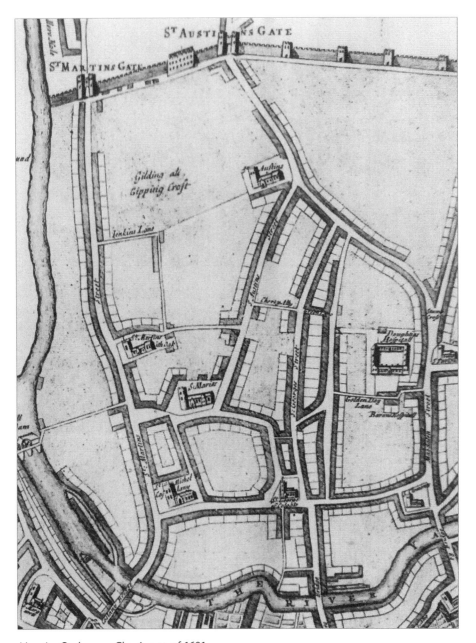

Map 4   Coslany on Cleer's map of 1691

The first incomers therefore rented from the English. Tawsen Verdyer, alien, rented a house and grounds in Pockthorpe from its owner Leonard Candler from the Annunciation (25 March) 1574 for a year: the rent for a year was £7 10s. They obviously got on well at first, as Candler asked Verdyer to stay on until Michaelmas, when he planned

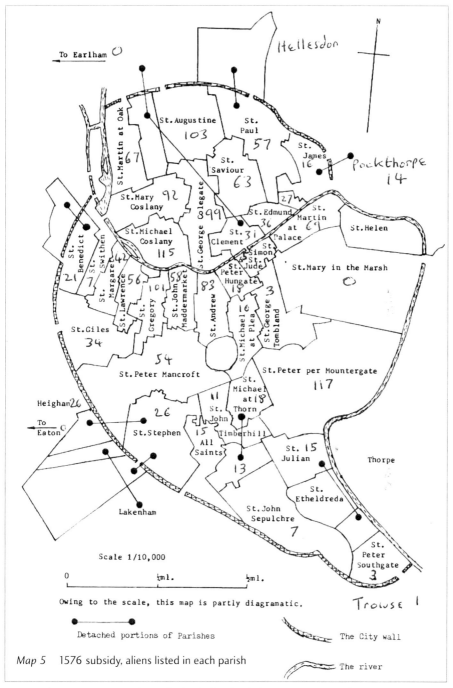

To Earlham

Hellesdon

N

St. Martin at Oak 67

St. Augustine 103

St. Paul 57

St. James 16

Pockthorpe 14

St. Saviour 63

St. Mary Coslany 92

St. George Colegate 99

St. Edmund 36

St. Martin at Palace 69

St. Helen

St. Michael Coslany 115

St. Clement 31

St. Simon & St. Jude 13

St. Peter Hungate 19

St. Mary in the Marsh

St. Benedict 21

St. Swithen 7

St. Margaret 42

St. Lawrence 56

St. Gregory 101

St. John Maddermarket 58

St. Andrew 83

St. Michael at Plea 16

St. George Tombland 3

St. Giles 34

St. Peter Mancroft 54

St. Peter per Mountergate 117

Heigham 26

To Eaton

St. Stephen 26

St. Michael at Thorn 18

St. John Timberhill 15

All Saints 13

St. Julian 15

Thorpe

Lakenham

St. Etheldreda

St. John Sepulchre 7

St. Peter Southgate 3

Scale 1/10,000

0   ¼ml.   ½ml.

Owing to the scale, this map is partly diagramatic.

Trowse 1

Detached portions of Parishes

The City wall

Map 5   1576 subsidy, aliens listed in each parish

The river

Notes: 1 There are no separate figures for St Etheldreda, which is treated as part of St Peter Southgate in the subsidy. 2 St Michael at Thorn is shown in two parts on the map. The subsidy treats the northern part under its older name of St Martin at Bailey. 3 St Martin at Palace had a separate part on the north side of the river: these are the figures given between St Edmund and St James.

Base map drawn by John F. Fone for his *Index to Norwich Marriages 1813–1837* (1982).

Figure 32 Church of St Mary Coslany, one of the parishes most associated with the immigrants. Photo by the author.

to sell the house. A dispute about this extension of the original lease then led to a court case.[91]

This must have been a large property: rents on parish houses were much lower. In 1608 an unnamed Dutchwoman was paying 15s a quarter rent (£3 a year) on one of the houses belonging to St Benedict's church. When Jaques de Hem rented a church-owned house in St Mary Coslany in 1623, he paid £2 a year rent: the sum was paid successively by him, his son Tobias and Tobias's executors down to at least 1640.[92]

Other incomers rented directly from the city authorities. When the city purchased Appleyard's house for a Bridewell in 1585, they let out the houses and shops around the edge of the property. In 1585 three of these were being rented by immigrants, at rents of between 18s and 60s a year. These tended to be transitory tenants: five years later, only one was still renting his property but four other aliens were now on the rent roll. One of these, Daniel de Hoo, was probably among the poorest members of the incomer community. He paid 5s for a half-year's rent on one of the rooms previously let to John Morley. In the previous entry these were said to be 'two little cellars in great decay', presumably the Bridewell undercrofts. Perhaps unsurprisingly, his name does not appear in the next rent roll.

After 1590 the word 'alien' is no longer used on the rental, but names like Nelke Deleve, widow (rent 18s a year) and Matthew Gan and Katherine van Lehaye (who rented part of a messuage together for 24s a year) in the 1596 rent roll suggest the continuing presence of immigrants in these properties. The occasional expenditure on maintenance is also recorded in the Bridewell accounts, for example in December

91   NRO NCR 12a/4.
92   NRO PD 191/23; COL 3/4.

Figure 33 Impression of Tudor Norwich by Colman Green (NRO MS 177)

1584 when a small sum is spent 'for 3 windows where the Strangers dwell', suggesting they occupied a particular part of the complex. The Bridewell is now a craft museum, and holds much material relating to the Strangers in the city.

Because the incomers had to contribute to their local parish church, there are frequent references to them in churchwardens' accounts. These are often very generalised, like these entries in the St Mary Coslany accounts:

> 1598: Of the Strangers of the same parish £3 2s 9d.
>
> 1596: For the Strangers alient £3 15s 8d.

The English paid £6 14s 9d. in the same year, so the incomers were paying approximately a third of the churchwardens' income – and receiving no benefit, apart from a place of burial.[93]

Some church rates do give more detail about where the immigrants lived. St Margaret's churchwardens' accounts are a good example. As early as 1567, 'a Dutchman in Mr Skinner's house' was paying church rates. The accounts list the Dutchmen contributing to the rate in 1590–1: 'Francis Fendick in Spurling's; the Stranger in Mr Johnson's house; Nicholas Fyrby in Mr Lynnes's house; Oliver Vittery in Mr Osborne's house; the tenant in Mr Johnson's tenantry next the street-side; the tenants within the yard the house being void; the Stranger in Thrymblyng's house; more from the Strangers in the same house'.[94]

Similar lists occur in the churchwardens' accounts for St John Maddermarket. In

---

93   NRO COL 3/4.
94   NRO PD 153/42.

1571, 'money received of the Strangers' included those living in Mr Winter's house, Peter Danell in John Plomerton's corner house, Simon Johnson in Mr Martin's house, and others in Sellard's house, Hothe's house and Ross's house. Anthony de Solemne, as a property-owner, paid for 16 quarters for his house (that is, he paid his rates for four whole years in one payment), and he had immigrant tenants, who also paid rates. Most significant is the entry in the list of payments by strangers: 'Mr Sotherton's tenants, Vinsont de Gren' who paid rates for five quarters: this entry is discussed in the section on Strangers Hall.

In 1602 'Francis the Dutch baker' was in arrears for his rates to the churchwardens of his parish: he was living at Mr Bush's house in St Peter Mancroft – conveniently near to the Market Place for selling his wares. An entry in the St Laurence parish register records the birth of a Dutch child in 'widow Myles' house' in 1571. A systematic search through other parish registers and churchwardens' accounts might well show up similar references.

These examples suggest that the immigrants were very commonly living in large houses, owned by aldermen or those of similar status, a pattern of life replicating that of the English poor and described by John Pound in his analysis of the 1570 census of the poor (which, it should be stressed, does *not* include any aliens, as these were not the responsibility of the city authorities). One entry in the burial register for St Julian is significant in this context: 'A Frenchman's child at Mr Gleane's house buried Holy Thursday 1590'. Thomas Gleane was alderman for Ber Street ward from 1571 to 1602, and served as mayor three times. The Mr Winter mentioned above could well be Alderman Thomas Winter, who had three English paupers in his property in St John Maddermarket parish at the time of the Norwich Census of the Poor in 1570.[95]

These entries naturally do not say what the rent payments were, but a case before the Mayor's Court indicates how incomers at the lower end of the economic scale lived. In 1586, a young immigrant named Katherine Verbeck lived in the house of an English widow, Margaret Elwyn, when there was a dispute about money. The court decided that a fair rent would be 3d a week, and that Katherine could keep the rest of her earnings (we are not told what work she was doing, perhaps she was Margaret's servant). This would work out at 13s a year, 3s more than Daniel de Hoo was paying for his cellar room, but might well include food.[96]

In 1583 Alderman Layer calculated that the Strangers paid for the rent on their houses a total of £292 15s 4d (presumably per year) in Colegate ward alone. As they were paying this to English house owners, it was clearly an impressive figure. Blomefield points out that many of the houses would have been empty before the immigrants came, providing no income at all for their owners.[97]

95   John Pound, *The Norwich Census of the Poor, 1570*, Norfolk Record Society, vol. 40 (1971), *passim*, especially pp. 14, 15.
96   Meeres (2012), p. 52.
97   Blomefield (1806), vol. 3, p. 294.

Strangers' Hall, a very fine princely dwelling?

There are a few mysterious places of birth in the Dutch Church baptism register. Two births, in 1605 and 1610, are said to have taken place in the 'Dutch house' in St James Pockthorpe parish, and another in 'George's Hospital' (no parish given). One has caused a great deal of speculation ever since it was transcribed by Walter Rye: the birth of Abigail Degrant, daughter of Tobias and Jannemin on 6 July 1604 in 'Xendochio'. This word means a lodging for Strangers, but it is not known to what building it refers. Rye was convinced it referred to the building in Norwich now known as Strangers' Hall, and that it provided early proof of its being linked with the incomers. His reasoning was that the name Degrant is very similar to de Gryn, the name of a man who paid rates on tenements on the west side of Strangers' Hall from 1567 onwards. Leonard Bolingbroke, the man who gave Strangers' Hall to the city, knew of this man, but claimed there was no evidence that he was a Stranger. Rye found the reference among the parish rate books that shows he was indeed an incomer.

The same couple had another child in 1611, and the place of birth is this time given as 'the Hospital parish'. Rye thinks this is another reference to Strangers' Hall, but this seems improbable. Another birth took place there, and in that instance Rye speculated that it meant the parish of St Helen, where the parish church was also the church of the Great Hospital. It seems unlikely that the family would have lived in two ambiguously named places, so probably the word Xendochio also refers to the parish of the Great Hospital.

There are several references in the city records of the early seventeenth century to 'Strangers'

Figure 34 Coloured postcard of the entrance to Strangers' Hall, early 20th century

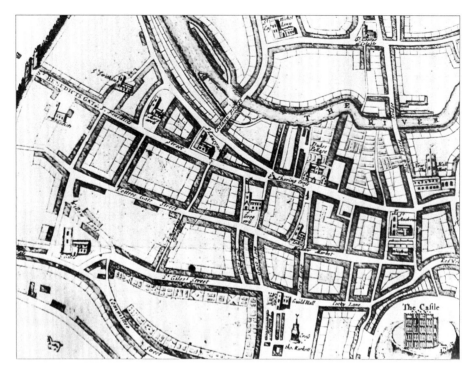

Map 6   St Benedict's on Cleer's map: many immigrant families lived in the parishes along this street

Hall'. However in each case it is clear that the reference is to the sealing hall of the Strangers, the building we now call St Mary the Less. As it is not likely that there would be two buildings of the same name, it would seem that the name of Strangers' Hall was not then attached to the present building of that name. Indeed, Boling-broke speculated that the name referred to Strangers who settled there at a much later period, refugees from the French Revolution at the end of the eighteenth century.

However, there clearly are links between the present Strangers' Hall and the incomers of the sixteenth century: the Hall was owned by the Sotherton family, and as we have seen Thomas Sotherton was instrumental in bringing the first Strangers into the city, so it would be very natural for him to let rooms in the Strangers' Hall complex to the incomers. If Rye is correct, de Gryn would be one of these, and he *is* right: I have seen the entry in the churchwardens' accounts where de Gryn is described as a Stranger living as a tenant in the house of Mr Sotherton. So there is no doubt that there were Strangers living in the house by 1571, even if it was not given the name 'Strangers' Hall' until much later.

A further possible link is in one of the Ypres letters, which refers to a refugee living in the 'High Street'. It is not certain that the letter was written by a man living in Norwich, and Norwich now has no street called High Street. However, the street on which Strangers' Hall stands *was* sometimes called High Street. In the 1626 landgable tax assessment, the house of John Alldriche, late Thomas Sotherton alderman abuts

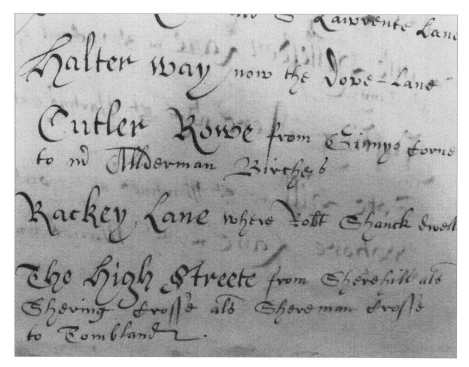

Figure 35 Entry from the 1623 landgable book, showing the location of 'the High Street' in Norwich. (NRO NCR 18d/4)

'upon the High Street north' (that is, lies to the south of the High Street). A contemporary street index at the back of the volume is even clearer: 'The High Street from Sherehill alias Shering Crosse alias Shereman Crosse to Tombland'.[98]

With that in mind, it can be seen how well the house described in the letter fits with Strangers' Hall. The house is referred to as 'the house of Master Thomas': it was Christopher Joby who first suggested this could be Thomas Sotherton. It was clearly a very grand house. The writer describes 'a very fine princely dwelling. I am quite on my own here in the best part of the house, with a fine furnished room and two small rooms to the side as closets for our room and a fine pleasing garden for me, a fine cellar.' Clearly, *very* few of the refugees anywhere in England would have lived in such a high-quality dwelling, and Strangers' Hall does indeed have fine cellars or undercrofts. Very probably this is a description of the building now called Strangers' Hall written in a letter sent back to Ypres by an immigrant living in the building 450 years ago. Unfortunately the name of the writer is not known. He signs himself 'Typer' but this is probably an alias, intended to keep his identity secret if the letter passed to the authorities – as indeed it did. From the details in the letter, it is evident that his wife was with him, but their daughter Kallekin was still back in Ypres.

A set of depositions before the mayor in 1577 give an insight into daily life in the

98   NRO NCR 18d/4 pp. 41d, 80.

Norwich Walloon community, people living at a much lower social scale than those resident in Strangers' Hall. When Margaret le Mahiew married Raynold le Maire, she sold a lot of household stuff – which Anthony de Lisle claimed really belonged to him (he had presumably lived in the house, whether as a lodger or a lover is not known). Three witnesses, all Walloons, were called – William Ployart, John Cachyn and Mary Southenare. Mary gave a list of the items sold: two pairs of black hose went for 6s 6d, a cloth jerkin for 4s 5d, and a doublet of linen cloth went for 21d (Ployart said that he had heard that the doublet was sold for 6d!). The unsold items were one old bed filled with straw, one old pair of sheets, 14 pieces of pewter (seven salt cellars, three small platters, four small pots) and one 'glassing bottle': these were being kept at Mary's house. Did this list make up the worldly goods of Anthony de Lisle?[99]

Archaeological evidence for the houses of immigrants appears to be meagre: 'Not a single 16th-century Stranger household has been recognised in the city.' In contrast, documents like probate inventories are a very useful source for showing what possessions immigrant householders had. In a couple of cases at least, they are actually lists of goods that were sold, with the values that they fetched. At the Mayor's Court of 20 February 1580, Strangers were licensed to sell goods of their deceased under certain conditions. They were to be sold within the houses where the goods lie and not elsewhere, not in any other house, the open street, or church yard, and not on Market Day or any Sunday or holy day.[100]

Probate inventories occasionally list the contents of a house room by room, giving us an idea of what each individual room was used for. Only two of the inventories of immigrants do this, both of properties with a workshop, a couple of other downstairs rooms and a single chamber above. These men were Martin Balden and William Vandercamme. Balden lived in St Clement's parish, and just paid the 4d poll tax in the 1581 subsidy. He made a nuncupative will on 29 April 1594, leaving everything to his son Mark. The will was proved by Martin's wife, Jane Balden, on 4 May. Vandercamme, a hosier living in St Peter Hungate parish, was better off: he paid tax on wealth of 20s in 1599. Vandercamme died in 1606: his will shows that he had a wife, Marie, and an unspecified number of children, presumably young as Marie was entrusted with their upbringing.

The different valuations of the contents of each room were:

	Balden	Vandercamme
parlour	£1	£8 14s 2d
shop	£1 10s 10d	£44 3s 2d
chamber	£1 10s 8d	£20 and more (inventory incomplete)
buttery	5s 6d	…
kitchen	…	£4 13s 3d

The contents of Balden's parlour included working equipment – an iron beam, troy

99   NRO NCR 12a/4.
100   D. H. Evans and Malcolm Atkin, *East Anglian Archaeology*, 100, p. 242; NRO NCR 16a/9.

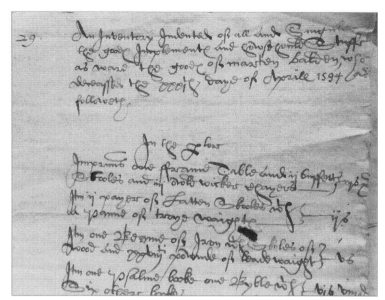

Figure
36 Probate inventory, Martin Balden (NRO DN/INV 11/29)

weights, lathes. The fireplace was in this room and was used for cooking, as shown by the presence of bellows, tongs, roasting irons, a spit, a trivet and a plate with a handle. The family books were also in the parlour – one psalm book, a Bible and six others. Probably daily or weekly prayers were held here. Vandercamme's parlour contents were worth eight times as much, and included silver cups and other silver items worth £4 5s. He also had bedsteads, three green curtains and a valence, a looking glass, cushions including six mockado cushions, 'a thing to hang a clock on' and a warming pan.

Both men had a 'shop', but here the contrast was even more striking. The contents of Balden's shop included a shop board and trestles, shears, a shoeing horn, pressing irons, as well as crepes, yarn cloth and two boxes with pieces of twist. The total value came to £1 10s 10d. Vandercamme's shop contents had a total value of over £44, made up almost entirely of products to be sold – 414 pairs of knit hose, (£21 8s) and 110 pounds of yarn (£18 6s 8d). It also contained a hose press, 50 press boards and 100 pairs of leg boards. Of course, the contents of each shop are those at the time of death, so that the values can depend on the stage in the trading cycle at that particular moment.

Each house had a third room: Balden a buttery, Vandercamme a kitchen. The contents of Balden's buttery came to a mere 5s 6d, including four dishes of pewter, two porringers and six 'other small pieces of pewter', altogether worth 2s 6d. He also possessed a mortar of latten, a kettle pot of brass, one iron pot and frying pan. Vandercamme had 64 pieces of pewter (plates, porringers, pots and salts) worth £1 6s 8d. He had three brass kettles, two brass pots and two iron pots, two dozen red trenchers, frying pans, children's chairs, a great brass kettle, seven tubs and firkins, and a kneading trough. Balden only had a little pot of brass, an iron pot and a frying pan.

Each house also had a chamber or upper room. Balden's had a poster bed, two old feather beds, one old pillow and two old blankets. Vandercamme had a coverlet of tapestry worth £5 10s, as well as a feather bed and a trundle bed. Balden's clothing consisted of one old gown, one cloak, one pair of breeches, one cloth jerkin and one leather jerkin. The total value of his clothing was 10s. Vandercamme had superior-quality clothing. One black cloak alone was valued at £1 10s, and another, a 'French cloak', at £1. The inventory is incomplete, so we don't know about all his clothing. He also had 15 Dutch books in his chamber, as well as a fowling piece and an 'old map'. Whereas Balden had little more than earthly necessities, Vandercamme clearly enjoyed some of life's luxuries.

Inventories reveal details of furniture, bedding and kitchen equipment, as well as any little luxuries that might be in the house. The furniture is usually pretty simple: chairs (William Powells had 'six Dutch chairs' but they cannot have been anything special as their total value was reckoned at just 1s), tables and cupboards of various kinds, some perhaps imported. One of the largest alien cargoes attracting duty was in 1584: Willem Vanscore paid 'for cupboards, chests and other things' valued at £69.

A typical list of kitchen equipment was that of Francis van Dyke – 22 pieces of pewter; five kettles, one skillet and chafing dish; brass pot and copper pail; one latchpanne; hake, spite, roosterer; two iron spoons and other implements. Matthew Ployart's kitchen equipment included six trenchers, six earthen platters, 12 pewter dishes, two quart pots, three iron pots, a frying pan, two little kettles, a spit and roasting pan, a gridiron and pair of tongs, two hakes, one fire pan and a pair of bellows. At the poorest level, Giles Tettart's kitchen stuff consisted of an iron pot, two pairs of bellows, a spit, a kettle, a little candlestick, a pewter pint pot, an earthen pot, two old sacks and a pewter goblet. Jacob le Poultre possessed seven trenchers, five wooden dishes, three drinking pots, two pewter pots, a gridiron and a trivet, a frying pan and a pair of pot hangers. The trenchers may also have come from the Low Countries: Jacob de Horne imported a load into Norwich in 1585.

Beds might be mentioned in wills. John Decock left his grandson his 'best bed, with the bedstead and all other things belonging thereunto as two head pillows, four pillowbeares, two pairs of sheets, two best coverlets and one undercoverlett'. Peter van Monsey left his wife the 'best bed furnished with bolster and pillows, two pair of sheets and two Spanish coverlets the one green the other white, the bedstead with the curtains'. Probate inventories give values to bedding. By far the most valuable was a feather bed, bolster and two pillows belonging to Matthew Ployart and assessed at £20. One of the poorest men for whom an inventory was compiled, Jacob le Poultre, had one old feather bed, one old flocked bed, three old bedsteads, nine bolsters, four old blankets, one bedstead and its curtains, altogether only worth £1.

Some incomers had a great deal of disposable wealth, as did Jooris de Vos, called George Fox in English documents. His bequests included £50 and a silver cup worth 50s to his wife Sara; £50 to John Hendrick (Sara's son by her first husband); £100 to his own son Peter on his wedding day, as well as a silver cup and a gold ring; and another gold ring to his younger son David.

Indeed, there was plenty of 'bling' among the richer elements of the incomer community. Susanne Backowe possessed a gold ring, an emerald set in silver, a gilt sixpence, two silver spoons and a 'great silver spoon'. William Powells' inventory includes £1 9s in gold, £7 in silver, one gold ring, one silver ring and one gold ring. John Decock's will mentions three silver spoons, and his probate inventory includes a gold ring and a silver goblet. Others had cash: when Adrian Coesse died in 1595, he left behind him £50 cash in a coffer and 'a piece of gold of unknown coin'. Altogether, his possessions were valued at a very healthy £189 8s 11d.

In contrast, some of the incomers had very few possessions, even those for whom probate inventories were made. The inventory of Jacob le Poultre reveals life at a much lower economic level: no gold or silver, just two candlesticks, three bushels of charcoal, 12 faggots, flags for burning, one warming-pan, and one old sword (worth only 10d). George Debucker's goods, valued at £7 10s 11d, included items like 'old cloak', 'two old hats', 'one old copper kettle', 'one tin platter and six tin spoons', 'one old little hammer' and a walking stick. John Boij's possessions were valued at £7 11s, his most valuable possession being his feather bed and bolster worth 26s; utensils included two brass pots, a pewter bowl and three pewter platters. His six shirts were together valued at only 20s. Jacob van Dicken's probate inventory valued his clothing at £3, and he owned nothing else – but he was owed a legacy of £89 18s 6d due to him because of the recent death of his mother. He must have been looking forward to receiving this, but death overtook him before he received his inheritance.

Women

Quite a number of women in the immigrant community left wills, or had probate inventories made of their possessions after their deaths. These were all single women or widows, of course: a married woman could not own property in her own right, since everything was treated as the property of her husband. I have looked at the wills or inventories of immigrant women living in Norwich, ranging from a servant to wealthy women with many possessions.

Prudens de Rijcke was a servant to George Mey (who does not appear in the 1567 census or 1576 subsidy, so was probably a later immigrant). She made her will in 1587, lovingly passing on her cash and her small collection of possessions, mainly clothing – she seems to have had no furniture of her own – to her master's children and to family and friends. She left no bequest to the poor of her community. Her bequests were:

> To the children of George Mey my master (by name John, James, Prester and Elizabeth) the sum of £5 between them. If any die, the money to go to the survivors, if all of them die, to go instead to the children of Lewes van Berghe,
> To Susanne, my god-daughter, the daughter William van Honcke: 20s.
> To Susanne's mother: two smocks, one red waistcoat, three neckerchers and three kerchers and blue apron.
> To Jane Drents: my best red petticoat, one saye waistcoat.

To Jane Puyell: my best hat, one linen apron, two neckerchers and two kerchers.

To Peter the son of Cornelis van Buchaghe: 10s and one piece of money to the value of 5s to hang about his neck.

To Peter's wife: one red waistcoat and one black saveguard.

To the said Cornelis: two bands of long ruffes.

To Mary the wife of Thomas Gaffar: one petticoat cloth.

To Augustine Joones' son: one band and a handkercher.

To Shilwaert Coster: two handkerchers.

To his child: two bands.

To his wife: one blue apron, one table napkin of damask.

To Anna Spiegel: the great damask table napkin.

To Debora van Berghe: one damask table napkin.

To the two children of Thomas de Mey: two kerchiefs apiece, of the very best.

To 'Bernardine': two kerchers and two neckerchers.

To Abraham van Sande: two white aprons.

To his wife: one blue apron.

To Prudens van Morchassche my kinswoman dwelling at Leiden in Holland: one tanye petticoat, one purple coat and one frisado [linen] petticoat. There was a condition: 'if my kinswoman shall walk inordinately' (I am not clear what is implied by this) then the sister of Peter Priem was to have the best of these three petticoats.

To Peter Priem: one pair of knit stockings.

To Francis Priem: one other pair of knit stockings.

To Prudens my kinswoman: my black waistcoat laid with lace and my coffer.

Prudens de Rijke did not die for many years after the will had been made. It was proved on 25 October 1598, with her master as one of the executors.

Lowysken van Rokeghem made her will on 26 October 1603: she could not write and made her mark instead. She was clearly proud of her possessions and gave very detailed instructions for who was to receive them. Her trade is shown in that she left her shuttle, 'to make says with', to her (unnamed) brother, together with a candlestick for the loom. Her brother's children were to have a box and a cushion of green say to sew on, together with the contents of the box. Marie was to have a little chest and its contents, Debora a box with all that it contained (although it is not said, these are probably two of her nieces). Likewise someone known only as Bartholomew, who received her psalter, was probably her nephew. Lowysken's sister Kaat was to have a pair of knitted hose.

She detailed her clothing and who was to receive it, as well as other possessions:

Waistcoats: 'my crimson waistcoat'; 'a blue waistcoat'.

Aprons: 'one linen blue apron my best save one'.

Knit hose: three pairs of 'knit hose dyed in black' were given to different women.

Kerchiefs: 'one of my best red kerchiefs'; four other women each receive a pair of kerchiefs, one pair described as being 'with single bands'.

2 saye thrumms.

John van Rokeghem, her cousin, a bloodstone.

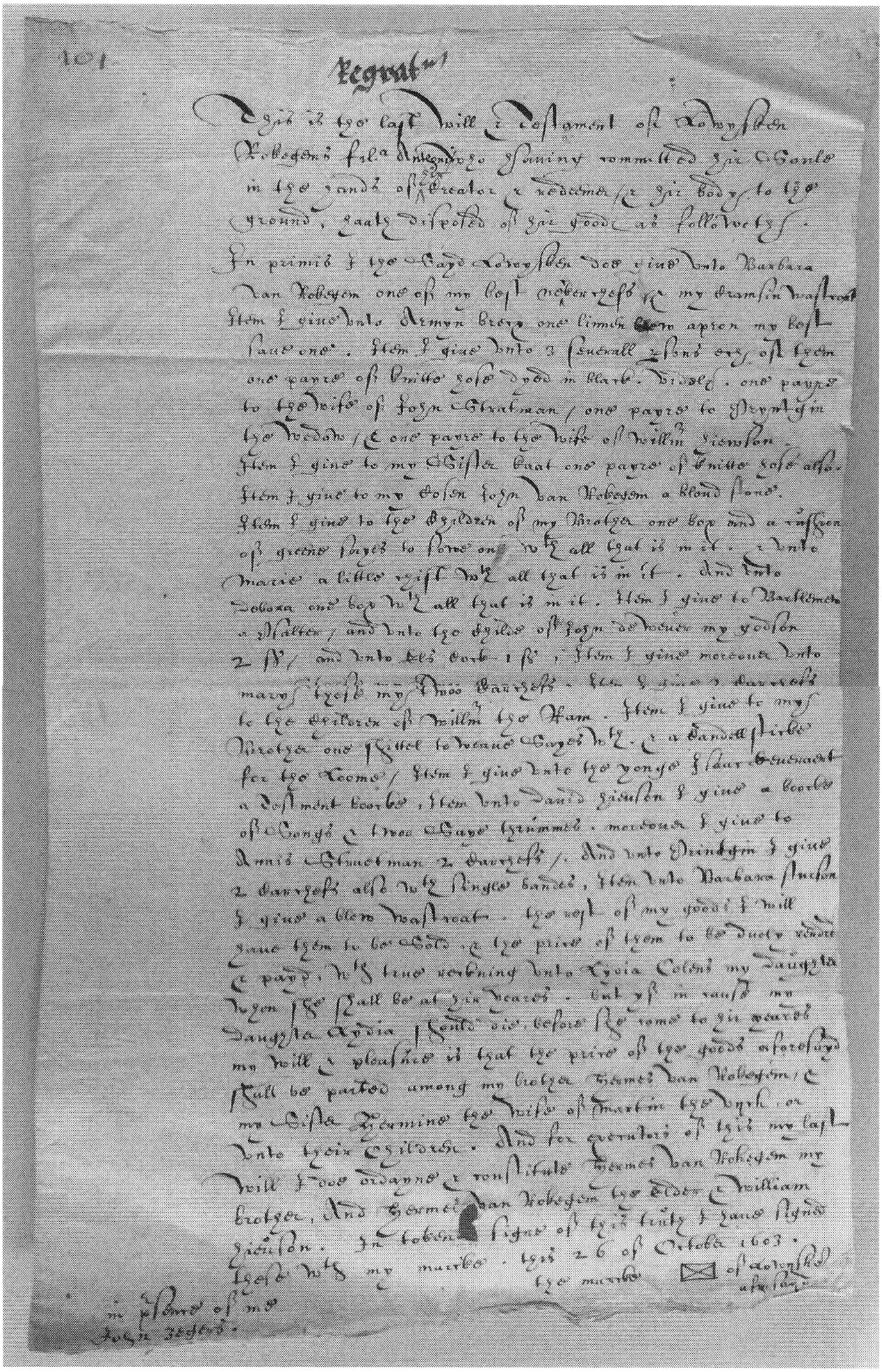

Figure 37 Will of Loweskyn Rokeghem: she has 'signed' with her mark at the bottom of the will (NRO NCC WILLS)

A testament book; a book of songs.
Sums of money: 2s to her godson, 12d to another child.

After these bequests, the remainder of her possessions were to be sold, the money to go to her daughter Lidia Colens if she reached full age. If she died earlier, the money was to be divided between Lowysken's brother and sister, who are named as Hermes van Rokeghem and Hermine the wife of Martin the Wych, or to their descendants. It is not made clear whether these are the same relatives as the unnamed brother and 'Kaat' mentioned earlier in the will or other siblings.

Lowysken was probably aware that she was dying when she made this will, and certainly she died very soon after: just over three weeks later, on 22 November 1603, it was being proved in the courts.

Was Lowysken a single mother? She does not actually use the term spinster in her will, but she describes herself as 'daughter of Anthony' [Rokeghem], which strongly suggests she was never married. Lidia *might* have been adopted, but she is described simply as Lowysken's daughter both in the will, and again when her case came before the politic men. In 1607, Michiel Colens accused Remeus van Rockeghem junior, who had been appointed tutor of 'his [Michiel's] daughter Lidia', of dealing unlawfully with Lidia's inheritance from her deceased mother. The case dragged on for eight years: when the politic man wanted to examine Rockeghem's accounts, they were told that Colens could go to the Continent and examine them, proof that he, like several other Norwich immigrants, retained business links abroad. In 1615, Rockeghem was fined 20s for his obstructive behaviour. He refused to pay, and the case went to the Mayor's Court, which upheld the fine and added an additional 12s fine for Rockeghem's disobedience. He finally paid up on 18 July 1615. The obvious question the case raises is why Michiel Colens did not look after his own daughter. Perhaps it was a moral judgement by the politic men, or possibly he was a single man, whereas Remeus (presumably, from his name, a relation of Lowysken) had a wife and family of his own (his son John is mentioned in Chapter 6).

Even more immediate, as being almost direct speech, is the will made by **Jane Jakemine Begots,** a single woman living in St Mary Coslany, who had been born in Antwerp. It is *nuncupative*, that is, not written down but spoken. She made it on her deathbed on 3 September 1603, in the presence of two witnesses, friends of hers in the Dutch community, Peter de Vos and Peter Demerle. These wills naturally tended to be short: Jane's was in fact rather longer than the usual. Like most members of the community, she left money for its poor, in her case 20s. She thought of members of her family. She had no husband or children, so made bequests to other relatives, leaving £10 to her brother Nicholas and another £10 to his (unnamed) daughter. She left another £10 to a nephew, Nicholas son of her brother John. This branch of the family was still in the Low Countries: she asked that their money be taken not out of her English goods but from those she still had in Flanders.

She then turned her thoughts to other friends in the Dutch community, especially children. She had a godson, the son of William Gilles: he was given 5s. Another child, the son or daughter of Jacob Bratseart, received the same. The six sons and one daughter of Christian Verkine each were given £7. One member of the community, Oliver Sandes, owed her money: she renounced the debt, so that the loan became a gift. Finally, her thoughts turned to her possessions. Her 'great cauldron or copper' was also to go to the Verkine children, either to be used by them or 'to do their pleasure', so they could presumably sell it if they did not want to use it. Marie Vermacus was to have her great chest, the unnamed daughter of Jacob Mergel her tippot [scarf or wrap].

Six weeks later, Jane's will was proved in the Bishop's Court in Norwich. An inventory was made of her possessions, which were put up for sale. The inventory starts with stuff that has been sold, mainly parcels of wool and white iron, fetching almost £10. Unsold stuff comprises in the main her personal goods, including a feather bed, valued at £1 and three pillows. Dining ware included five pewter dishes, three saucers and three wooden dishes. Her three gowns were valued at 15, 10 and 5s each, the most valuable being of broadcloth. Four pairs of her old hose were valued at just 2d.

Susan Backowe, of St Gregory's, made her will in 1598: her husband Peter, a hosier, had died earlier in the same year without leaving a will. She began her will with a confession of faith: 'I leave my soul into the hand and tuition of the immortal, omnipotent and super-essential God, my creator, Jesus Christ the anointed and lamb immaculate my sole and only redeemer, the Holy Ghost or Spirit my comforter and sanctifier, three persons in Trinity but one in Unity.' She was the only immigrant who said where she wanted to be buried, asking for her body to be buried in the church-yard of St Gregory's, or 'in the churchyard wherever she dies'. She left £5 for the poor of the Dutch congregation, and made many personal bequests:

Meynkien van Dole and Joan her servant: each to have 10s and two best kerchiefs.
John Wittewrongle: Peter Backowe's best cloak.
John his son: one gold ring.
Jacob his other son: a currall [child's teething ring] set in silver with certain things thereunto attached.
Gabriel Byshopp: 20s and two of Peter Backowe's best shirts.
William Tyranoe and Mary Backowe: £10 each.
Susanne van de Walle: my best bed for a remembrance.
Maudelin de Teowre: crimson petticoat, six neckerchiefs and six kerchiefs not imbarring her thereby from the parting of my goods and chattels.
Judith the daughter of William Tyranoe: a gilt sixpence.
Debora de Maye: two silver spoons.
John Wittewrongle the elder: the great silver spoon.
Pawlus de Windle: two of Peter Backowe's shirts, his best hat and his black cloak.
Marie Wittewrongle the elder: best apron for a remembrance.
Jacob de Boyse; a pair of hose, a pair of shoes and a cloak.
Then, a half of what is left of goods and chattels to be divided equally between Peter de Teowere, Maudlin de Teowere and James de Teowere (these three are referred to as 'children'); the other half between Giles de Teowere, Prudence his sister and Susan van der Walle, after them 'to the next of my blood lineally descended'.
Executors: John Wittewrongle, Giles de Teowere

She made this will on 14 September 1598, and must have died very soon afterwards, as it was proved on 19 September 1598.

A sworn statement by Maudlin recorded what Wittewrongle had done in his role as executor. He appeared to have carried on the business, as we have seen, and to have paid Maudlin wages as servant of the house (although a child, she was clearly old enough to do housework). The statement also gave valuations to various items that Wittewrongle removed from the house before the probate inventory was taken, including a feather bed worth about £15, a parcel of feathers, sold for 7s, various items of clothing and one pair of shoes. It may have been common for items to be removed before a probate inventory was made: we know about it in this case because of the scrupulous honesty of Wittewrongle as executor.

The probate inventory of **Vincentiana Heijtes**, widow of Francis van Beke, is the record of an actual sale of her possessions rather than a valuation. The heading says an inventory of goods 'sold in the very mansion house 5 and 6 March 1590', and halfway though the list is a heading, 'The second days sale'. Several of her clothes are specifically those of an incomer: a Dutch cloak (sold for £1 4s 8d), two Dutch hats (6s 11d), a Dutch hood (£2 1s 6d), a 'Flemish cloak for a woman' (£1 7s). Two gowns sold for £3 each: the entire goods of some of the poorer incomers amounted to little more than the price of one of these gowns. A silk petticoat also fetched £3; however,

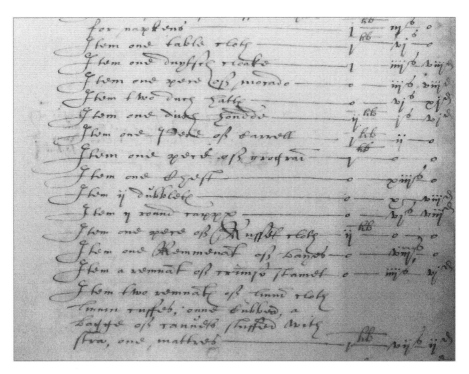

Figure 38 Probate inventory, Vincentiana Heijtes; Dutch cloak, hood and hats, in her inventory (NRO DN/INV 6/30)

another gown described as 'of the old fashion' was worth only £1 10s. The grand total of the sale came to £92 9s 8d: this was an immigrant with plenty of high-quality possessions.

The men

The earliest wills survive only in register copies made at the time, such as the will of **Joos de Ram**, a book-binder who died in 1577: 'I Joos ye Ram son of William, born at Chelbeck in Flawnders and now into England, being married with Margaret the daughter of James Bec and Elizabeth parents of Meteren in Flawnders.' In common with most other members of the Dutch and French communities, he left money to the poor: 'I bequeath and give unto the poore of our Dutch church within Norwich ten shillings.' Other bequests included those to Peter Wbeijnootz alias Rams, 'the son of my said wife' – a goblet of silver, which had Peter's name engraved underneath, 25 'pounds Flemish', 'all my garments as well woollen as lyninge' and several parcels of books 'as well Lattyn as Dutch'. He left the books for 'the advancement and furthering of his study, charging him diligently to study'.

Another early will was that of **John Smallbone**, who died in 1580 leaving a nuncupative will. A refugee from Flanders, he was already a widower when he arrived in Norwich with a maidservant in about 1567. In the 1576 subsidy, he paid tax on goods worth £1 in St Peter Parmentergate. Smallbone is described in the will as 'Stranger': he reveals his origins in bequests to the poor of the Dutch congregation and to the minister of the Dutch church.

From the beginning of the seventeenth century, the original wills sometimes survive, such as that of **John Hovenagle**, made 19 January 1603: he describes himself as 'Drapier; inhabitant and allient within the cittie of Nortwhich in the kingdom of Inglornd'. Hovenagle, a draper 'by vocation' as he says in his will, was clearly a wealthy man: he left the very large sum of £20 to the poor of the Dutch congregation, and made monetary bequests of £25 to various people. He was presumably a widower as he bequeathed his wife's best petticoat and best waistcoat to a Martha Vliegers. He left another petticoat and waistcoat to his sister Jemima Hovenhagle. All the rest of his goods were to be divided between Jacob Wormvoke, the testator's brother-in-law, and his own sister Jemima; she was probably under age as her share was 'to be put into the hands of the politic men to assist and advise her'.

In general, the men were less specific than the women about gifts of personal possessions. One exception was **James le Mulier**, who made his will on 21 October 1603, and in several cases these were actually his wife's property: although not explicitly stated, the impression is given that she had died a short while before he made the will – perhaps from the plague then raging through the city. He made the usual donation for the poor of the Dutch community, and made several monetary bequests. He then requested that three smocks that his wife had given to three women be delivered, and bequeathed a fourth smock to someone else. Three of his wife's best kerchiefs went to another woman. He also made bequests of some of his own property – his best kerchief went to Taneke Penninol and a shirt to Philip Taolor. He left John Cooper a garment he described as 'my worst cloak'. All his other possessions (presumably including better cloaks) were to be divided between the children of Michael le Mulier 'of Newport', a relation, and to the children of his wife's sister, Leonora Jeris. The reference is to Nieuwpoort, so this is another example of an immigrant to Norwich who still has connections with family in the Low Countries.

Francis van Beke was buried in St Michael Coslany church. In his will, made in July 1586, he described himself as the son of Hubert de Claring. Like almost all the immigrants, he left money to support the poor of his church group in Norwich, in his case £6 English to the Dutch church. He appears to have had close links to his home town of Ypres – he is the only Dutch or Walloon refugee in Norwich whose will recorded a gift to the poor of his home town, £6 Flemish. His two bequests of money were also in Flemish pounds: he left £12 Flemish to the children of William Damme, and £120 Flemish to one individual, Elizabeth the wife of Adam Kyndt. This was declared to be in order to make a total gift of £200, the same that her brothers and sisters had already had as their wedding portions. This sounds as if they were related to him, but the relationship is not stated in the will. The use of a Flemish currency might suggest that the beneficiaries were abroad, but this was not the case with the Kyndts who lived in Norwich and later at Cley in North Norfolk.

Van Beke then turned to his wife Vincentiana Heijtes, whose inventory has already been mentioned. Since they had no children, he left everything else to her – but only provided she remained unmarried. If she did marry again, whatever remained of the bequest at that date was to be taken from her. If she remained unmarried, she could enjoy the goods until she died, when what was left was to go to the couple's heirs – this is said to be 'according to the custom of the city of Ipres'.

Joos de Ram, who had possessions in England and Flanders, noted the difference between probate customs in the two countries. In England, it was 'a law and also a custom' that every man had power 'to dispose and give his goods as it pleaseth him': after specific bequests, he left the residue to his wife Margaret. However, his goods in Flanders went to Margaret in 'her right of widowhood and usufruct … according to the right and usage of that place', which equates to the situation described by Van Beke, that she did not acquire them in full and free ownership.

Walloon wills

Members of the Walloon community also made wills, naturally leaving money to the poor of the French congregation, and in a number of cases written in French. One of the simplest was that of **Giles Tettart**, made in 1585, and translated from French by Godfrid Burman. He left 10s to the French church, and made only one bequest: his brother Anthony received 10s and 'the cloke which I wear every day'. Everything else went to his (unnamed) wife and to their son John, with provision for £5 to go to his nephew Cornelius (Anthony's son) if John died young.

Another Walloon will was that of **Adrian de la Mee**, made 28 September 1603, and proved 9 December 1603. He wrote that he was born at Nomayn, was now 54 years old, and sick. He left £2 to the poor of the French church, and a further £1 to the church

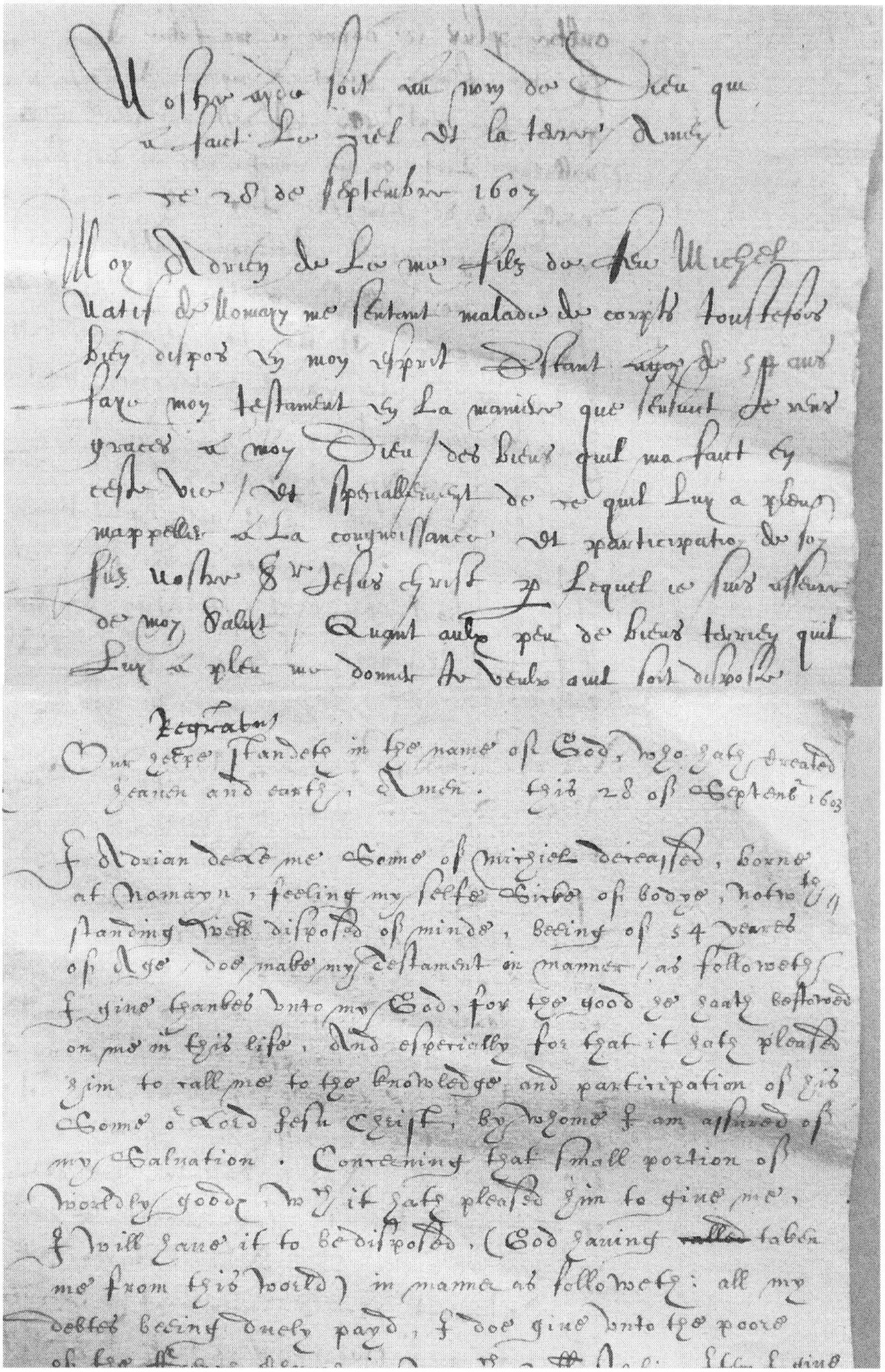
Nostre ayde soit au nom de Dieu qui a fait Le ciel et la terre Amen

ce 28 de Septembre 1603

Moy Adrien de Le me filz de feu Michel natif de Nomain me sentant malade de corps toutesfois bien dispos en mon esprit estant agé de 54 ans faiz mon testament en la maniere que s'ensuit. Je rens graces a mon Dieu des biens qu'il m'a fait en ceste vie / et specialement de ce qu'il luy a pleu m'appeller a la congnoissance et participation de son filz nostre Sr Jesus Christ par lequel je suis asseuré de mon salut. Quant aux peu de biens terriens qu'il luy a pleu me donner Je veulx qu'ils soit disposé

Legratus

Our helpe standeth in the name of God, who hath created heaven and earth, Amen. this 28 of Septemb. 1603

I Adrian de le me sonne of Michiel deceassed, borne at Nomayn, feeling my selfe sicke of bodye, notwithstanding well disposed of minde, beeing of 54 yeares of Age, doe make my testament in manner as followeth. I give thankes unto my God, for the good he hath bestowed on me in this life, And especially for that it hath pleased him to call me to the knowledge and participation of his sonne o Lord Jesu Christ, by whome I am assured of my Salvation. Concerning that small portion of worldly goods wch it hath pleased him to give me, I will have it to be disposed, (God having ~~ville~~ taken me from this world) in manner as followeth: all my debtes beeing duely payd, I doe give unto the poore

Figure 39 Will of Adrian de le Mee, in French, with contemporary English translation (NRO NCC WILLS)

itself. Six children received bequests. His wife Margaret was also ill (this was a plague year), and further provisions were made if she were to die before him. His clothes were divided among his sons, his best cloak, hose, dublett of grogryn and best hat going to Peter, his second-best cloak, pair of breeches, cloth jerkin, one waist dublett and one hat lined with velvet to James. Daughter Anne received 'our best bed whereon my wife and I do lie', with two pillows, two pairs of sheets, the bed coverings and curtains – presumably they would first have been disinfected if the couple did die of plague in the bed!

The record for speed in proving a will probably belonged to the executors of Walloon **Peter Tibaut**. The will was made on 30 December 1603, and proved on 2 January 1604: Peter was obviously on his deathbed when he made his very short will. The poor of the Walloon church were bequeathed £6, and also the three parts of a musket, caliver and rapier, presumably his contribution to the musters. The ministry was also remembered (£4). The only other beneficiaries were Peter's wife, named as Margaret de la Montaigne, and the children of Michael Favarq and his wife Marie Tibaut, presumably family members.

Growing up

A volume at the Norfolk Record Office, confusingly known as the Norwich Strangers' Book, is really a register of activities of the 'politic men', the governors of the Strangers community in the city. The volume is in Dutch where the Dutch 'politijcke mannen' are involved, in French when it is the turn of the French 'hommes politiques'. It runs from April 1583 to June 1590, with additional notes down to 1600. This volume is mainly concerned with one particular aspect of their work, the care of orphans in the community. The names in the volume have been transcribed by Raingard Esser.[101]

In each entry, the volume records the names of the politic men involved, the orphan(s), the tutors assigned to the child, the deceased parent(s), and guarantors. In all about 650 names occur, the great majority being male: females occur only as orphans or as deceased parents. In a few cases an extra detail is given for female orphans, but never for the males: the date they married, and thus ceased to be the responsibility of the authorities.

Although simply a register of names, the volume has many stories to tell, and raises many questions. To take one example, Hendrick Gheerart occurs several times in 1583 and 1584 as a politic man. By March 1586 he was dead, his wife having presumably died earlier. His five children – Gerson, Eliasar, Susanne, Hendrick and Abigail – were themselves assigned tutors by the politic men. In 1588 they appear once more and an extra tutor is assigned to them, but their names are not the same: there is no Susanne, the fifth child instead being named as Immanuel. Is this a scribal error? Or is something more complex going on in this family group? Each family history is told in a small number of formal entries in the register: we can only guess at full details of the interlocking relationships of those involved.

---

101 Raingard Esser, *Norwich Strangers Book 1583–1600* (Norfolk and Norwich Genealogical Society, 1990).

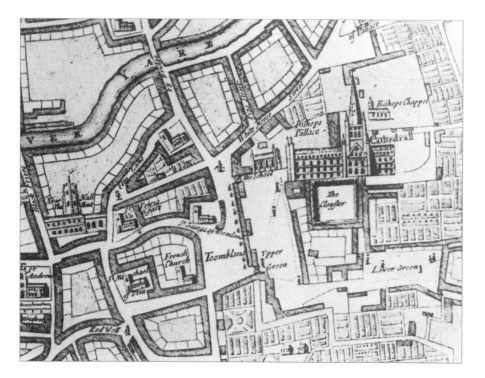

Map 7 The heart of incomer Norwich: bishop's chapel, French church and New Hall
(St Andrew's Hall) on Cleer's map of 1691

Some wills also reflect concern for the young children of the testator. **John de Pute** was a hosier of St Mary, Norwich with a pregnant wife, Mary. In 1633, just after Christmas (actually on 28 December) he realised that he was dying. His father-in-law Peter Hasbert, Peter Verbeck (a relative) and two women were called to his bedside and he made his will verbally. He left all he had to Mary and the unborn child. He must have died that same day or the next, as on 30 December the will was proved.

Mary duly gave birth and called her child John after her late husband. Less than two years later, it was her turn to feel the approach of death. On 2 October 1635 she made her will: everything was to go to her son John, then one year old. Her father was to look after the child. Three weeks later Mary too was dead: the will was proved on 26 October. Nothing more is known of John de Pute's story.

Some men may have been concerned at the power of the politic men to break up families. When **Malliart Browne** died in 1619, his will contained the instruction that his daughter Anna was to be brought up by her stepmother Suzanna, 'and nobody shall take her away from my wife unless they be both willing to depart the one from the other'.

In the case of **John Decock** it was the welfare of his grandson that was of concern. Decock left the boy the very large sum of £80, together with his own best bed, the cloth that his grandmother had given to him on her death bed, and three silver spoons.

However the boy's father, Decock's son-in-law, was clearly not to be trusted: Decock insisted that he was to have no dealings with the bequest. Instead it was to be looked after by another family member until the boy was of age.

Nicholas de Toict, a wealthy Walloon (his total bequests came to £350) may have had similar concerns. He left £25 to his niece Elizabeth Temberman; his son Toby was to hold the money until Elizabeth got married, or had need of the money.

As children grew up, it was natural that they should be chosen as apprentices by older men, often relatives, in their community. I have found several examples of these in the city archives, with Jaques de Hem, his son Tobias, John van Rockingham (the English version of Rokeghem), Peter van Hove and Peter Verbeck all taking on Dutch boys, sometimes their own children, as apprentices. These were usually from local families, although van Rockingham took on a boy (Isaac Evered) from the immigrant community at Colchester in 1628. I have seen no example in the documents of a Dutch or Walloon *girl* becoming an apprentice.

A Dutch boy might be apprenticed to an English master, for example Paule de Man who in 1631 complained to the politic men about the way he was being treated by English master Gilbert Gilman. The politic men took the case to the Mayor's Court, which ordered Gilman to treat his apprentice properly.

Baptism, marriage and burial records

Registers of baptisms, marriages and burials began in every parish church in England in 1538. As there were no other churches, or any other places at all, where people could be legally baptised, married or buried, and as people were compelled to attend their parish church, these should include all people in the country (there were no noncon-formist churches in England for another century or more). However, an exception was made in favour of the incomers, whose two congregations each maintained a register of baptisms and marriages, presumably from their inception. Unfortunately many of these registers have been lost.

Baptisms

A baptism register for the Dutch church for the period 1598 to 1619 is in the British Library: the entries were transcribed in *East Anglian Notes and Queries* new series vols 12 and 13. There are a total of 827 baptisms in the register, which ends in October 1619. A register of baptisms, marriages and burials for 1676–1879 is in the Guildhall Library, London; there is a xerox copy of this in the Norfolk Record Office.

The baptism register for the French church survives for the period from June 1595 down to June 1752: it is held at the National Archives. It contains a total of 1,075 baptisms (there are only 32 for the period after 1670). The entries were transcribed (and rearranged in alphabetical order) in Moens.

There are thus baptisms registers for both incomer communities for the period 1598 to 1619. The figures show that the Walloon community was rather larger than the Dutch over this period, or at least it had more babies, so presumably there were more young people. Both communities showed a decline in the number of baptisms.

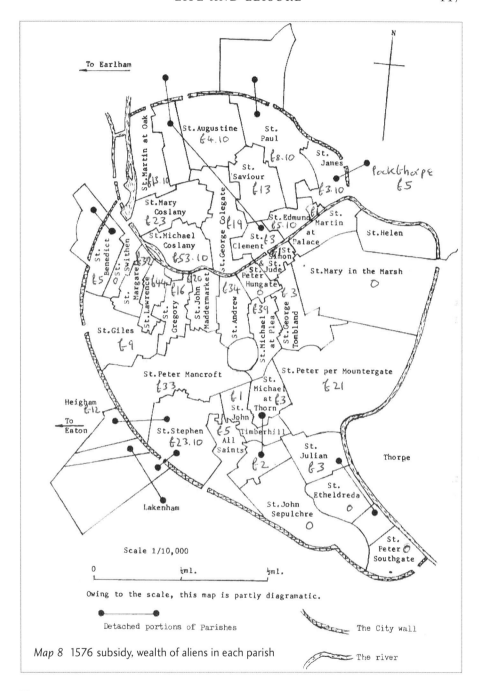

Map 8 1576 subsidy, wealth of aliens in each parish

Notes: 1 There are no separate figures for St Etheldreda, which is treated as part of St Peter Southgate in the subsidy. 2 St Michael at Thorn is shown in two parts on the map. The subsidy treats the northern part under its older name of St Martin at Bailey. 3 St Martin at Palace had a separate part on the north side of the river: these are the figures given between St Edmund and St James.
Source: base map drawn by John F. Fone for his *Index to Norwich Marriages 1813–1837* (1982).

In the years immediately before and after 1600 there were an average of 80 Walloon baptisms and 75 Dutch baptisms each year. This declined to 70 Walloon and 40 Dutch baptisms in the 1600s and 40 Dutch and 28 Walloon baptisms in the next decade.

Norwich had about 35 parish churches, each keeping a register of baptisms: as has been said, these recorded each baptism, and therefore each birth, in that parish. The immigrants in each parish were the only exceptions, and some parishes made efforts to record the births of these immigrants. In the case of St Laurence, uniquely, the parish church appears even to have baptised some of them.

St Laurence has a number of very unusual entries for the period 1569–71. These entries are not on a separate page but mixed in with the English baptisms, marriages and burials:

> 1569, 22 July: Abraham, son to Peter Wolfe, Dutchman, baptised.
> 1570, 20 May: Danyell Vanderbridgen son to John Vanderbridgen, Dutchman, baptised.
> 1570, 1 Sep: David Vandeiise son to Barnard Vandiiuse, Dutchman, baptised.
> 1570/1, 1 Jan: Nathanyell Ryckwart son to Theophilus Rickwart, alien, baptised.
> 1570/1, 19 Feb: Zacharius Rutnincke son to John Rutnincke born.
> 1571, 1 Jun: Tobias Vervinct son to Giles Vervinct, Dutchman, born in widow Myles house.

The first four entries state that the children were actually *baptised* in the Anglican church; I have not come across this in any other parish. The last two simply record the *births* of children within the parish; presumably they were *baptised* by Dutch or Walloon ministers in their churches. This is not uncommon. Several Anglican parish registers contain records of such births. They are especially important in the years for which the Dutch and Walloon baptism registers do not survive, as they are the only surviving record of these children.

There seems to have been an attempt by the parish of **St Peter Hungate** in Norwich to keep a register of those incomers born within the parish. There are eight entries inside the front cover, five relating to members of the Desturmewe family born in the parish and baptised in the Walloon church. The other three entries relate to Dutch people. One entry has been deliberately crossed through so severely as to be illegible. The other two are Peter Haibant and Elias Spillebote: the latter was the son of Lewis Spillebote, one of the original 30 invited to Norwich.

In **St John Maddermarket**, the parish clerk started a page at the back of the book headed 'Strangers aliants [aliens] born in St John Maddermarket', and recorded one name: James Lyburd, son of Charles Lyburd, born 9 March 1610/11. (The Dutch register gives the Dutch or Latin forms of the name, as is usual, corrects the date of birth, and gives the wife's name and those of witnesses: Jacobus, son of Carels Liebaert and his wife Anneken. James was born 8 March, baptized 17 March, and the witnesses included Jaques de Hem.) No more entries were made to the page in the St John Maddermarket register for 40 years, after which two were added in relatively quick succession: Martha, daughter of Jeremie Gose, baptised 4 March 1650, and

Richard, son of Richard Browne, baptised 31 December 1651. The first of these three entries was a record of a *birth*, the last two of *baptisms*: incomers or their descendants choosing baptism in the local Anglican parish church rather than the churches of the Dutch or Walloon congregations.

The clerk at **St Peter Parmentergate** also began a record of baptisms of immigrants in his parish. In this case there are just two entries, in the back of the register and also recorded in the main body of the text (which is very disorganised: frequently entries occur out of order). The two entries are:

> Zacharius Tewchyn son of Peter Tewchyn of Ypres 'dwelling in my parish' in St Vedast Lane baptised by the Dutch preacher in the church within the Black Friars 8 February 1567/8.

> Jacobus Vanderpeere son of John Vanderpetre of the town of Mydelborowe born 'within my parish' 5 November 1567.

The parish register for **St Michael Coslany** records the *birth* of John Rockingham, son of 'a Stranger', Remeus Rockingham, in the parish on 16 May 1577; the register notes that John was actually baptized in the Dutch church.

Apart from such entries in parish registers, a few births/baptisms of incomers were recorded in the Mayor's Court Book. Four families did this, beginning with Marthin More. In 1600, he registered in the Mayor's Court that his son John, born in Norwich, had been baptised in the 'Ecclesia Belgica' on 9 March 1597. In 1602, the Mayor's Court recorded that John Sente, the son of Peter Sente and his wife Christiana, had been baptised in the 'Ecclesia Belgica' on 1 December 1580. John was aged 21 at the time, suggesting that these registrations were for legal purposes, providing proof that the children were born in England. The other two were the Cruso family in 1601 and the de Hem family.

Marriages

No marriage register survives for the Norwich Dutch community before the general register already mentioned that begins in 1676. Two Walloon marriage registers for the Norwich Walloon community do survive at the National Archives. They cover the years 1599 to 1611 only, and about 100 marriages are recorded.[102]

Many of the entries in the Walloon church marriage register fail to record places of birth, but enough do so to show a pattern, with grooms and brides born abroad giving way to an increasing number born in Norwich as the years pass. Of those born abroad, six were born in Antwerp, four each in Lille and Armentières, and three in Tournai. By the early seventeenth century, both bride and groom are often Norwich-born, second-generation immigrants, choosing to be married at the Walloon church.

After 1611, members of the Walloon church had their banns recorded in the Walloon Church Book, but the actual marriages took place in Anglican parish

---

102 TNA RG 4/4149.

churches. Clearly, not everyone did register the banns: for example, John Vanhooute married Ester Verbeck in St Stephen's church in 1631, but no banns had been registered with the Walloon church.

I have found just two examples of marriages between two immigrants occurring in Anglican parish churches in the last 30 years of the sixteenth century:

> St Laurence: Charles Punisher and Frances Laumes, being both of the Dutch congregation, were married 30 October 1571.
>
> St Peter Parmentergate, 23 September 1585: Andrew Claribut married Maria [surname left blank], Strangers.

Andrew may have been a son of Pascal, one of the original invitees in 1566 (we know he had two children).

Marriages between immigrants and local people are discussed in Chapter 8.

Burials

The two communities had no facilities for burials, which took place in the church-yards of Anglican parish churches. In 1585, the Mayor's Court ordered that when an incomer 'old as well as young' died, the 'least bell in the steeple' of the local parish church should be 'knelled' by the clerk or sexton – who was to be paid 2d 'and not above' for this service. The 1589 French Book of Discipline laid down rules, which had no doubt existed from the beginning: burials should be in parish churchyards, should be simple, and be within 12 and 24 hours of the death. Deaths were to be registered by the elders and deacons – however, if this was ever done, no such record survives.[103]

These burial entries can be found in many of the Norwich parish churches, but many of the earlier entries do not even bother to record the names of the dead, and it is almost certain that they are far from complete. This is especially likely to be true during the years of plague, 1579 and 1603: these are discussed in Chapter 5. I have looked at the registers of most parishes for which they survive.

St Peter Parmentergate was one parish where names of the dead were always recorded. Burials begin as early as 1566, the first four being:

> 1566, 29 July: Joanne Dotelburge, stranger, was ----------------- [left blank, but is in the 'burials' section of the register].
> 1567, 22 July: Peter Lanser of Ypres buried.
> 1568, 18 July: Katherine Begell, Stranger, buried.
> 1570, 19 July: Judith Suees, the daughter of Joesse Suees of Ypres in Flanders, dwelling in this parish was buried.

Stranger burials in **St Peter Mancroft** are recorded from 1570, and the deceased were

---

103 Lucy Toulmin Smith, 'The Walloon church in Norwich in 1589', *The Norfolk Antiquarian Miscellany,* vol. 2 (1883), pp. 130–1.

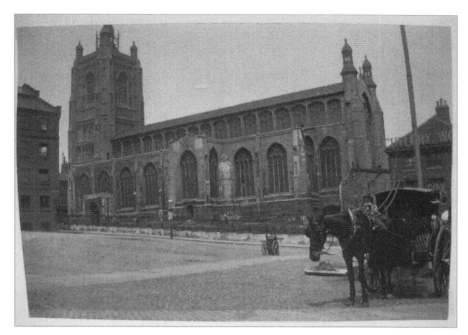

Figure 40 St Peter Mancroft church in a late Victorian photograph: there are many references to 'Strangers' in the church registers (NRO MC 2678/3)

always accorded the dignity of their names. The incomers here were relatively few and also relatively wealthy. However, in **St James Pockthorpe**, where immigrants were more common, and poorer, individual names were never given, the register using phrases like 'a Dutch woman and her daughter', 'a Dutch child of a Wallooner', 'a Wallooner's daughter'. **St Michael Coslany** does include some named incomers, such as Francis van Beke, buried on 22 March 1578/9. However, at the end of entries for 1592/3 the clerk has written:

> Buryed more in this year of Strangers whose names are not written, to the number of 15.

I suspect there were many cases like this, where the burials of immigrants went unrecorded. However, by the early years of the seventeenth century, the dead were almost always named, and often it was not even stated that they were incomers, as at **St Michael at Plea**:

> 1605, Vanbarton, Andrew, son of Jaques, buried 30 August.
> 1606, Van Barton, Katherine, daughter of Jaques, buried 12 May.

There are very few memorials in Norwich parish churches to incomers, and these naturally tend to be of wealthy ones. I discussed the van Kurnbeck memorial in St Mary Coslany in Chapter 1. The text of this is in Latin. Another monument was actually written in Dutch, that to Francis van Beke in St Michael Coslany (apparently no longer surviving). One of the earliest memorials that does survive is to Anna de Hem in St Michael at Plea: she died in 1603 while giving birth to her tenth child. The writing is very faded now but the pictures are clearer. You can see the whole family kneeling at prayer, and also some symbols representing death: the skull, the cross-bones and the hourglass. These have a very amateur look, and were perhaps added later.

The language of wills and probate inventories

The wills and probate inventories provide a rich source of documentation for the immigrant community, and survive in four languages. A small number of the most highly educated incomers might leave a will in Latin. This had been the usual language of wills in England in the Middle Ages, but by the mid-sixteenth century only a few clerics and people of similar education were doing this. However, the language served as a *lingua franca* for educated men throughout Europe. I have only seen two wills of immigrants in Latin, those of Antony de la Roque and Henry van Beuren. The probate copy of Beuren's will in English was compared with the original by Giles Langhelett on 4 January 1580.

However, quite a number of the incomers found their knowledge of English inadequate for the purpose, and made their wills in their own language, either Dutch or French. These were then translated into English for probate, usually by the politic men, and most commonly by their clerk Langhelett.

Examples of wills in Dutch are those of Abraham van Ixem, George Fenne, Francis Michaels, Andreas Priem and Peter van Hove. The wills are in English in the probate register, sometimes noted as being 'out of the Dutch original'. The probate copy of Fenne's will tells us that the translation was made, and compared with the Dutch original, by Peter Weynoote, but the Dutch text was not preserved among the probate records and is lost.

Examples in French are those of Giles Tettart, Thomas Choquetu and Hugh Herbert in 1602. These were all proved in the Norwich Consistory court. At least one will of a Norwich man proved in the Prerogative Court of Canterbury in London was in French, that of Isaie de Hovigneau. This is interesting as he was a second-generation incomer, having been born in Norwich. The will of Hugh Herbert was written on 7 November 1602, and proved on 13 April 1603. The original will was in French, and the probate entry records that it was translated into English and exhibited by Jan Cruso (a member of the Dutch, not the French community, he was presumably fluent in three languages – Dutch, French and English).

The will of Abraham van Ixem survives in three forms in the Norwich probate registry. There is a double page of notes in Dutch, headed by a religious thought or quotation, and then listing the bequests. This was drawn up by van Ixem on 3 August 1601, and has his signature and his 'mark'. The date 26 March 1602 has been added to the paper, probably the date he died. A formal will was then drawn up in English from the notes: this was done by Langhelett, who described himself as 'scribe of the politic men'. The will was proved in the Norwich Consistory court on 19 April 1602, and a formal copy of the will was then entered into the court register. The religious heading, which is present in all three versions (in Dutch, naturally, in the first version) reads, in its English translation: 'Our help standeth in the name of the Lord who hath made heaven and earth. Amen.'

I have looked at 14 of the 32 wills of incomers made in 1603 and where the original will survives. Six of the 14 original wills were written in English (John Bonkenelle, William Moens, Loweskyn van Rokeghem, John Hovenagle, Jane Jakemine Begots and Samuel Ployart). Six were written in Dutch and translated for probate purposes. In four of the six cases the original Dutch will survives (John Decock, Peter van Monsey, Andries Priem and Mark Moens), in two cases it has been lost (William Powells and James Hallynck). The other two wills were originally written in French and translated for the probate: the French will survives in both cases (Hugh Herbert and Adrian de la Mee). These examples suggest that there is a considerable body of original Dutch and French text among the probate records in Norwich, even allowing for many losses to the series of original wills over the centuries.

Probate inventories were drawn up by friends, usually within their own community, and although the great majority were in English, a few were written in Dutch (such as that of Elizabeth van de Sande) or in French (such as those of Everard Farvaque, for which copies survive in both French and English, and Elizabeth Cuvellir, only surviving in French).

Of course, the incomers might have spoken their own tongues among themselves. A 1573 dispute before the mayor between two Dutchmen, Thomas Hodgeson and Thomas Bateman (one of the first 30 to be invited to the city) turned on a written contract between them, which naturally enough was in Dutch.

Books

Many probate inventories of incomers mention books, usually a Bible and/or a testament, and often a book of psalms. Two men, John Battaile and Adrian Coesse, possessed Calvin's *Institutes*, and Coesse also had a commentary on the catechism. Preacher John Elison naturally possessed books, mentioned in his will. Another immigrant, Hubrecht Wiltens, bequeathed *Calvin on the Epistles* to his brother Simon Wiltens, and left (or returned) to John Elison 'what he did give me' – a *Book of Martirs* – and two handkerchiefs. The bequests of Lowysken Rokeghem included a psalter, a testament and a 'book of Songs'.

Walloon Adrian de la Mee also possessed Calvin's *Institutes*, which he left to his younger son Philip, along with his 'Great Bible', and the *Decades* of Heinrich Bullinger. Most other Walloons also possessed Bibles; in the case of Jacob le Poultre, they were particularly mentioned in his probate inventory as *French* Bibles. Rowland Nutt left a book to Mr Bonngins, the French preacher – Mullens upon the Psalms. (Nutt was *not* an immigrant, but the rector of St Michael at Plea until he was deprived in 1589, and the preacher at St Andrew until his death.)

Some immigrants had other books as well. As we have seen, Joos de Ram, a bookbinder by profession, mentioned books in Latin and Dutch in his will. Philip Andries, a hosier, left all his books to his son Samuel Andries 'if he give himself to the profession of a scholar'. William Vandercamme had 15 Dutch books in the chamber over his shop. Jacob Vanburton paid import duty on 'certain books' valued at £7 in 1585.

On 3 May 1608, the Assembly Book ordered that three of the sword-bearers' rooms in the porch be fitted up for a new library. This was the first municipal library in England. It was intended for visiting preachers: an adjacent room had bedding and linen for them. Two members of the Dutch community gave books – John Cropp gave four volumes in 1614, and Pastor Pierre de Laune gave a Bible concordance, and also a liturgy of the French church in England, the latter written by himself and published in 1616.

A couple of immigrants had maps, and a few had paintings. John Decock possessed a 'Map of the seventeen provinces' (of the Spanish Netherlands), while William Powells' probate inventory included a map of the world, and a picture of Adam and Eve.

A few of the immigrants went on to write books themselves. Nathaniel de Laune, the son of Peter de Laune, minister of the French congregation, went to Cambridge in 1618, and translated Peter du Moulin's *Elements of Logic* in 1624. Janus Gruter went on to become a well-known philosopher at Heidelberg University. Jan Cruso wrote two books in English on military subjects (perhaps based on his time as a captain in the Norwich militia?), and also poetry in Dutch, including one extolling the virtues of his new homeland:

> And in green dales
> I walk beside the Yare
> To take a little air
> And to the city
> Through thick woods do turn
> How I am there regaled
> By the choir of nightingales![104]

---

104 William Woods, 'Publications connected with the Dutch church in Norwich', in Norma Virgoe and Tom Williamson (eds), *Religious Dissent in East Anglia* (1993), pp. 31–5.

Chapter 5

Health and welfare

In the twenty-first century, people who do not like immigrants often complain that incomers are taking 'our' jobs and taking up 'our' places in hospitals and in the benefits system. The first claim was occasionally made in the sixteenth century as well, but the other claims could not possibly be: it was made very clear, at both a national and a local level, that the immigrant communities were entirely responsible for looking after their own poor and sick. One proof of that is the Norwich Census of the Poor of 1570: none of the poor named in the census is an immigrant. In fact, the incomers had a double burden placed on them: they had to pay for the care of their own needy, and also to contribute to the poor rates raised in the parish in which they lived.

The money was raised by a weekly contribution made in church, and there were other sources of income. One of the trading Orders laid down that all new baize workers – English as well as Dutch and Walloon – had to contribute 6d for the benefit of the poor of the Dutch church. In addition, most of the immigrant community wealthy enough to leave wills made a bequest for the care of the poor of their community. According to Esser, 57 per cent of Strangers' wills mentioned donations to the poor and/or the church of their community. Twenty-two of the 32 wills made in 1603 by incomers left money to their churches. Even as late as 1634, three in four wills were leaving money for their Congregation's poor, or their minister.[105]

In the late 1580s both communities ran into difficulties. In December 1587 the elders of the Dutch community complained to the Mayor's Court that many of their community were refusing to pay their rates to the Dutch church because of their own poverty owing to the hard winter and the decline in their trades. The city chamberlain gave them £10 out of the money the city had raised from its fees for sealing of aliens' commodities, the money being paid to George Fenne 'and the rest of the elders'. Two years later, in November 1589, the Walloons were said to be in great poverty because of the decay of their trades. Two local preachers, one of them Rowland Nutt, raised £28 for them, and this was handed over to the ministers of the Walloon church. The Corporation gave them a further £10.

In a random sample of 20 Dutch wills, 15 left money to the poor of the Dutch congregation. John Bonkenelle was by far the most generous with his bequest of £40; however, this only applied if his wife and daughter left no heirs. John Hovenagle left £20. Most people left between 10s and £4. Even people making verbal wills on their death-beds usually remembered the poor, such as Philip Andries who left £5 to the Dutch poor in his nuncupative will in 1625. Perhaps the most generous in terms of her very small wealth was Anne Vanderweigh, who by her nuncupative will of 1611

---

105   Esser (1995), p. 147.

left 20s to the Dutch minister and the same to the Dutch poor. After making small bequests totalling 45s, she left half of the residue of her goods for the poor, probably not a large sum but one revealing a generosity of spirit.

After about 1600, Dutch testators often showed their involvement in their local community by leaving money to the poor of the parish in which they lived as well as to the Dutch poor. For example, Abraham van Ixem left money to the poor of Gregory's, Peter Trewe to the poor of St Laurence and Jaques de Hem to the poor of St Michael at Plea. Adam Kyndt left 40s to the poor of the Dutch church in Norwich, but also bequeathed £3 to the poor in Cley, where he was living at the time he made his will. These sums would have been handled by the overseers of the poor of the parish. Trewe and de Hem also left money to the city authorities, who had to deal with the problem of poverty on a city-wide basis.

Most Walloons also left money to the poor of their congregation, though none was in the Bonkenelle class. The most generous was Nicholas de Toict with a bequest of £10, with others leaving between 30s and £5. Walloons too might leave money for the English poor of their local parish, like Hugh Herbert who left £3 to the poor of St Saviour's.

It was extremely rare for an Englishman to leave money to support the immigrant communities. One who did was Thomas Layer, who was mayor three times and was known for his support for the Strangers. He died in 1614 at the age of 86, and in his will he left 40s to each of the congregations. Another alderman, Henry Fawcett, who made many bequests that benefited the city, left £20 to the French poor and the same sum to the Dutch poor, in his will of 1619.

The incomer congregations continued to support their poor throughout the seventeenth century, with the Mayor's Court acting as court of arbitration. In November 1632 Francis Emperor, on behalf of the Dutch congregation, told the Mayor's Court they would allow 12d a week to the widow and three children of Daniel Pute, deceased. However, the Court thought they should have18d a week. In 1682 Gideon Cochadee of St Paul's parish fell into need. The Mayor's Court met on 9 September 1682 and decided that he was in the French congregation, and was 'of third descent from a Walloon or Frenchman': presumably he was a descendant of the Noah Cochadee, woolcomber, described in the 1622 Return of Strangers as born overseas. The French church was ordered to care for him and his family.

In 1712 the City obtained an Act of Parliament saying that the city should be treated as single parish under poor law rules: this was so that they could build a city workhouse paid for from poor rates. The Walloons managed to obtain a clause opting out of this: members of the French and Dutch congregations were to 'continue to provide for and maintain the poor of their own respective congregation as has been heretofore accustomed, so that such poor do not or shall not be or become chargeable to the respective parishes where they dwell'. This, of course, applied to that relatively small number of people who were *members* of the two congregations, not the many hundreds in the city who had incomer ancestry.[106]

---

106 NRO MC 29/17.

Plague and the immigrant community

The year 1579 saw a major outbreak of plague in Norwich. The effect on the city must, like the plague of 1349, have had almost the impact of a nuclear strike upon the city: Carole Rawcliffe estimates that 40 per cent of the population died in the outbreak. John Pound called the 1579 outbreak 'the worst outbreak of plague to afflict an English town in the sixteenth and seventeenth centuries'. Blomefield calculated that between 20 August 1578 and 19 February 1579, 2,335 English people and 2,482 Strangers died.[107]

As Blomefield indicated, plague had a particularly devastating effect on the immigrant community, as we can see from its inception. On 31 March 1579 the City Assembly noted that plague had broken out, starting in St Stephen's and All Saints parishes. Some people were already blaming the incomers, on three grounds:

1 They scoured their bays in the river.
2 They combed wool in open shops and poured the wash in the gutters, where it remained.
3 They did not keep their 'necessaries' [toilets] in good order.

The mayor sent letters to the Dutch and Walloon communities ordering them to remedy these issues. No Stranger was to scour bays in the river between New Mills and Whitefriars Bridge; they were to use water to flush down the gutters into the steams; they were to keep their necessaries dry. Of course, these issues were not in fact relevant to the plague scare, which was spread by rat fleas: the plague continued to ravage the city unchecked.

From the last week in June the Mayor's Court kept a weekly record of the number of burials in the city: there were well over 200 a week throughout August, September and October, peaking at 352 burials in the week ending 15 August. In the last week of October a further refinement was introduced: the number of Strangers being buried was recorded. The figures show that the Strangers suffered an extremely high rate of mortality, in some weeks making up two-thirds of those dying in the city. If the same level of mortality applied in the months before separate records of deaths among the Strangers were kept, as seems to have been the case, then well over 2,000 must indeed have died in this epidemic.

Any look at the Norwich parish registers for 1579 raises an obvious question: where are the bodies? Only a very small number of incomers were recorded as being buried in this time of plague. I have looked at the surviving burial registers for 1579 to see just what is recorded.

St Michael at Plea does record some Stranger burials in 1579:

Judith Bartringham, daughter of William the painter, Dutchman, buried 7 August.
David Bartringham, son of William the painter, Dutchman, buried 26 August.

---

107 Carole Rawcliffe, 'Sickness and health', in Rawcliffe and Wilson (2004a), p. 318; John Pound, 'Government to 1660' in Rawcliffe and Wilson (2004b), p. 36.

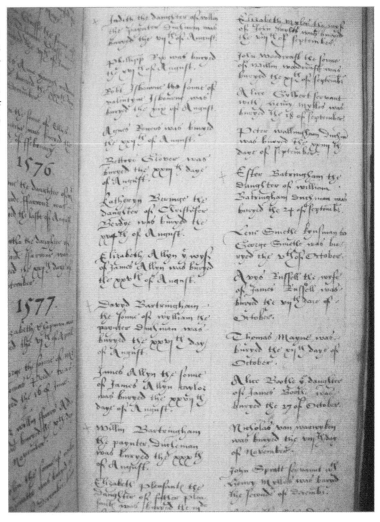

Figure 41
Bartringham family burials in the register for St Michael at Plea in the plague year of 1579 (NRO PD 66/1)

William Bartringham, the painter, Dutch, 30 August.
Ester Bartringham, daughter of William Bartringham, Dutchman, buried
   24 September.
Peter Wallingham, Dutchman, buried 24 September.
Father Israell the Dutch preacher buried 11 December.

Nothing more is known of Bartringham, whose family was so grievously hit – was he an artist? Nor indeed is anything known of Father Israell.

St James Pockthorpe records 36 unnamed incomers buried between July 1579 and the end of the year (27 'French', seven 'Dutch', two 'Strangers'). At **St Laurence,** between 18 July and the end of the year, 80 burials were recorded of unnamed people described as either Dutch or Strangers, sometimes several at a time. Four Dutch children were buried together on 20 August. **St Peter Mancroft** had 246 burials in

1579, compared with average of under 30 in a usual year, but just one was said to of an incomer: 'October 2; one John, a stranger'. **St Stephen** has almost 250 burials, about eight Strangers among them. **St John Timberhill** had about 70 burials, which included just two entries for Dutch people; however, five other burials had the word 'stranger' added in the margin in a contemporary hand. The dozen other parishes I have looked at all show an enormous increase in the number of burials in 1579 compared with earlier and later years, but no burials were recorded for any Strangers.[108]

The burial register for 1579 does not survive for nine parishes, but it seems most unlikely that the 2,000 'missing' Stranger' burials would all have been in these parishes. It seems most probable that they were buried in the Anglican churches, but in most cases without any record being preserved in the register.[109]

The reasons that Strangers died of plague are not really known. No doubt the poorer members of the community lived in crowded conditions which encouraged the spread. John Pound pointed out that people who worked with cloth and wool could be especially vulnerable as the fleas (originally from rats) lived in these materials, and indeed they could live in bundles of cloth away from their parent rats for several months.[110]

The plague did have a disastrous effect on at least one aspect of the weaving industry. Figures for the Bay Hall and the Camiant Hall show no falling-off for the period 1579–80, but the story at the Dyers' Hall was very different. The normal income was only £2 a year or so, and after the account was settled at Midsummer 1579 (at only 14s 6d), the accountant noted:

This account the tyme of the sycknes for want of following ceased and nothing collected for one whole year and half

When payments resumed from September 1581, they were at a much lower rate than before.[111]

There were many later outbreaks of plague in Norwich, some of which were severe. Armstrong recorded that 'in 1583, the plague broke out again and eight or nine hundred persons died of it, the principal part of which were strangers .... In [1588] the plague broke out here again, but did not rage violently.'[112]

There was a further severe outbreak in 1603. Blomefield said that 3,076 people died in the 1603 plague, while according to John Pound, the alien death rate in the 1603 plague was twice as high as that of the English.[113]

108 SS Clement, Peter Parmentergate, Benedict, Edmund, George Colegate, Simon and Jude, Peter Southgate, Gregory, Saviour, John Maddermarket, Martin at Palace, Giles, George Tombland.
109 Burial registers for 1579 do not survive for Sts Peter Hungate, Etheldreda, Helen, John Sepulchre, Julian, Mary in the Marsh, Swithin, Martin at Thorn, Paul.
110 Pound, in Rawcliffe and Wilson (2004b), p. 44.
111 NRO NCR 17d/10.
112 Armstrong, *History and Antiquities of the county of Norfolk* (1781), vol. 10, p. 157.
113 Pound, in Rawcliffe and Wilson (2004b), p. 44.

Once again, a very small number of these burials were recorded in the city's parish registers. St Laurence does record that three Dutch children were buried on 28 May 1603. Between that date and the end of December 1603, the register recorded a total of 40 incomer burials, all without individual names (23 Dutch children, four Dutch women, three Dutch men, nine Strangers, one Frenchman). During the same period 43 English people were buried, so incomers made up about half of all the burials in this parish in 1603/4. St James Pockthorpe is known to have had many immigrants. However, only 14 burials for 1603/4 were noted as being of incomers: six French children, three French boys, two French maids, just one Dutch child, and two adults – an unnamed Stranger and 'Martin Sowar, a Stranger'. As there were 98 burials in this church in this plague year, this is a much lower proportion than at St Laurence.

Other church registers, such as those for SS Augustine, Clement, George Colegate, Martin at Palace, Giles, Simon and Jude, and Peter Parmentergate had no mention of any Stranger burials at all in 1603/4. None of the 448 burials that I have counted in these parishes in the year were so described, and none had obviously Dutch or French names. Something is clearly missing.

The plague of 1603 differs from that of 1579 in that about 30 Strangers, aware of the possible imminence of death, made wills. Some were specific about the danger. Peter van Monsey wrote, 'if my wife Peeronel should chance to die of this sickness then is my daughter Easter van Monsy to have all that which we both leave behind us', and Matthew Ployart wrote, 'if it please God to call me out of this world by this sickness'. Andreas Priem also showed his awareness of mortality, writing 'considering that men are suddenly overtaken by death', and 'if it shall please God to take us all into His kingdom by this sickness'. John Decock wrote his will because 'I have felt myself weakened with the hand of God.'

There was another outbreak of plague in 1625, but it was much less severe, and did not have such a drastic effect on the Dutch and Walloon communities: burials in the city peaked at 90 a week during September, but only a dozen or so of these weekly deaths were of Strangers. The normal precautions were taken in the Stranger communities. Tobias de Hem told the Mayor's Court that the Dutch congregation had chosen Peter Heybaud to look after the infected poor. He had to carry a red wand 1½ yards long to warn people that he could be carrying the plague. The Dutch had their own pest-house too – in July 1630 they were given permission to take it down and stop paying the rent on it.

If they did so, it was at just the wrong time: plague broke out once more in 1631. This was a much smaller outbreak, perhaps mainly affecting the Walloon community. In April plague was found in two houses in St Augustine's parish – five people died. As was customary, the houses were locked, and the remaining members of the family were forced to stay inside until they either died of the plague or the danger of infection had passed. Food and water was supplied to them. A Walloon named Adrian Latrye broke these rules: leaving his wife and two children in one of the infected houses, in which two people had died, he placed another child elsewhere and himself moved into the house of Joseph Latrye, no doubt a relative. The Mayor's court ordered the whole family back into their own house, and they were locked in. They were lucky: none of them caught the plague and after nine weeks the house was duly opened up on 8 June.

Jaqueline Mansay was appointed a searcher and keeper of the infected among the French congregation, and John Denew and Peter Hawtoy were ordered to make sure that she did not go out except when she was being employed as a searcher (which involved searching a corpse for signs of plague). The same two men were told to provide a pest house in case it was thought desirable to remove the infected from their own houses. Elias Philippo was asked to provide necessaries for the inhabitants of the pest houses, both alien and native. When 'the widow Leskany', also a Walloon, was confined in their pest house after her husband had died of plague, Elias was told to provide necessaries for 'them', which could mean her children or other Walloon inhabitants of the pest house. It seems clear that this particular outbreak was mainly among the Walloons: only one plague death was reported to the court of 23 April, and that was a 'Frenchman'.

In the summer of 1631, each parish in the city was asked to donate money to help the infected poor of Wymondham, and the Dutch and Walloon congregations contributed too. The total raised was £103 5s 7d. The Dutch congregation contributed £5 12s 2d, a sum exceeded by only three of the 35 city parishes. The Walloons were less generous, or less wealthy, contributing only £1 16s 2d: perhaps plague within their own community inhibited their charitable giving.

Chapter 6

Some Dutch and Walloon families

This chapter uses a variety of original sources to tell the stories of some of the families coming to Norwich in the second half of the seventeenth century. Similar stories could be told of many other families, although as always it is the richer families who are best recorded.

Some Dutch families

The Cropp family

The Cropps were one of the few families with a continual presence in Norwich throughout the period from the 1568 census to the rate book of 1633–4, with successive generations providing medical service to incomers and natives alike. The entry in the 1568 census reads: 'Johannes Cropp, surgeon, Flanders, 1567, with his sister'. He must have married and had children fairly soon: one son, also named John, was born in 1572.

John Cropp I paid tax in Michael at Plea on wealth of £2 in 1576 and of £5 in 1581. In 1589–90 he paid duty for 'certain topnettes' of figs, valued at £12, and on sack and white wine valued at £40: were these imports purely medicinal? In 1595 he was one of only five members of the Dutch community to possess a musket. Both father and son were practising medicine in 1597 – according to Bishop Redman's visitation 'they practise surgery but whether licensed or no they know not.'[114]

John Cropp I died in July 1597 and was buried in the church of St Michael at Plea. He was rightly described in the burial register as a 'Dutchman', the last member of the family so designated. The family of his son, John Cropp II, were regularly using their local parish church – St Michael at Plea – rather than the Dutch church at least from 1601, when his son, also John (the third generation to bear that name), was baptised there, to be followed by four more children in the next 12 years: Jacob, William, Anne and Martha.

John Cropp II became a freeman in 1607, and a warden of the Norwich Barber-Surgeons Company in the same year. He donated four books to Norwich City Library in 1614. He was listed in the Return of Strangers of 1622, as living in Middle Wymer ward, and as born in England. However, he does not appear to have been a property owner: he did not appear in the 1626 landgable, for example. He was mentioned in a Paston family letter of 1625, Lady Katherine Paston writing to William Paston on 1 April informing him that John Cropp was to attend to the arm of Thomas Hartstong, a family friend: 'on Monday Mr Crope

---

114 J. F. Williams, *Bishop Redman's Visitation 1597*, Norfolk Record Society, vol. 17 (1946), p. 34.

I think will take it in hand, first by physic and after by applying strengthy things to it'. John's wife Anne died in the same year, and was buried in St Michael at Plea.[115]

In 1630, John Cropp was before the magistrates in a dispute with Adrian Parmenter, a grocer and part of the city establishment (he was later mayor): the details of the case and its outcome are not known. In 1633–4 he paid rates on property in St Michael at Plea, while a Mrs Cropp, widow, paid on a property in St Peter Hungate.

William Cropp paid £2 to the King's 'voluntary aid' in 1662, and paid hearth tax on property in St Michael at Plea in 1673. He died in 1680, by which time the family had become part of the Norwich community, with nothing to recall their descent from a refugee 60 years earlier.

The Verbeck/Beck family

The Verbecks are an example of a family who were part of the 'first rush' of incomers who remained in the city and who became anglicised over the generations: uncommonly one incomer took out an Act of Parliament to formally become an Englishman.

Giles Verbeck arrived in Norwich from Flanders in 1567, with a wife and four children. He was one of the arbitrators in a dispute in 1571. Nicholas (Clays) Verbeck was probably one of Giles's children. He paid tax in St John Maddermarket in 1581 and 1595, and in St Laurence in 1599. He died in 1604. His will, proved in London, called him a merchant stranger of St Andrew's Undershaft, London, so he presumably had property in London. His will was nuncupative: he died in the house of Abraham and Anne de Pute in London (they were relatives of his).

His wife Mary (Mayken), mentioned in the will, was living in Norwich in 1600 when she complained to the London consistory that a 'sister' within the church was slandering her. She died in 1604, and her will was also proved in London. She mentioned Peter Verbeck, 'now living in Leyden', his wife Katherine, 'now living in Norwich', and their son Peter. Katherine was the daughter of John de Pute and his (unnamed) wife, Marie's sister. Katherine had brothers Abraham, John and James, and an unmarried sister, Elizabeth.

Many of these people were residents of Norwich. Abraham Verbeck acted as a witness there in 1606. Peter himself was also living in Norwich by 1606, and four children of Peter and Katherine were baptised in the Norwich Dutch church:

Charles, born 7 July, baptised 13 July 1606.
Elizabeth, baptised 2 April 1608.
Marie, born 6 April, baptised 15 April 1610.
Peter, baptised 22 April 1613: Peter Verbeck senior was a witness to this baptism.

The first three children were born in St Michael Coslany parish, the fourth in St Mary Coslany parish. The next child, James, was not baptised in the Dutch church

---

115 Clive Wilkins-Jones, *Norwich City Library 1608–1737*, Norfolk Record Society, vol. 72 (2008), p. 195.

Figures 42 and 43 St Martin-at-Palace Plain and Bank Plain, use of a Dutch word in Norwich place names. Photos by the author.

but in the Anglican church of St Mary Coslany (on 8 October 1615), perhaps a significant moment in this family's move from Dutch incomer to Anglican parishioner status.

Peter Verbeck's wife was a witness in a court case in 1608, and Peter himself was a witness in 1611. In 1612 he bought property in St Mary Coslany from Daniel de Wylde, hosier, 'now in Rotterdam'. He presumably did the deal in Rotterdam, as the deed of title recorded that he paid 3,500 gilders of Flemish money for it, which, the deed helpfully informs us, amounted to about £350 of English money.[116]

Peter became a freeman, as a hosier, in 1614. He appeared in the muster lists of 1621 and paid tax as an alien on possessions in St Mary Coslany in 1622. He was listed as merchant and hosier of Coslany born 'beyond the seas' in the 1622 return. In some documents he was referred to as Peter Beck.

Peter Verbeck made a further decisive step in becoming English: he became naturalised in 1624, by Act of Parliament. A proviso was added that if he was convicted of 'colouring' Strangers' goods, then he was to lose the benefit of the Act. He was recorded in the 1626 landgable as owning properties in St Mary Coslany and St Michael Coslany.

---

116 NRO MC 1202 has the title deeds for the transactions, and the probate copy of Peter Verbeck's will.

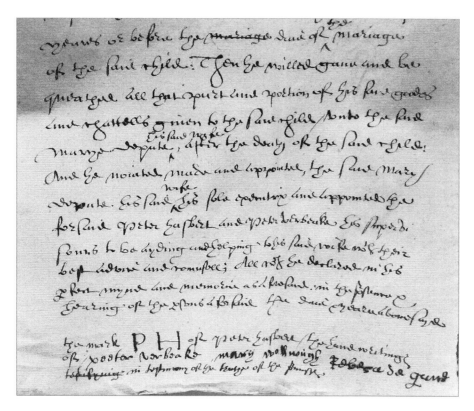

Figure 44 Signature of Peter Verbeck on a friend's will (NRO NCC WILLS)

Peter died in 1629. In his will, made in 1625, he described himself as a merchant. He left his property in St Mary Coslany and his household stuff to his wife Katherine for as long as she lived, or until she remarried. His son Peter was bequeathed the property after Katherine's death or remarriage, with 'my long drawing table, press and livery cupboards in the chamber next the street', and his father's apparel. Their children Elizabeth, Peter and James were each to receive £200 when they got married or reached 21: as executrix, Katherine kept the money until then. Peter gave £5 to John Elison the Dutch preacher, and £5 to the poor of the Dutch congregation. The will was proved at the Prerogative Court of Canterbury in London in 1629.

Peter's son James did not live to claim his inheritance: he died in 1633 at the age of 18, and was buried in St Mary Coslany church. Katherine Verbeck paid rates in St Mary Coslany in 1633–4 (the date of the city's first surviving rate book). She also witnessed a baptism in the French church in 1633, her name being given in the record as 'Catherine the widow of Peter Beque'. Charles Verbeck paid tax in St Mary Coslany in 1622, not as an alien but as native born. By 1633–4 he was living in St Michael Coslany and was recorded in the rate book as Charles Beake.

In 1634, Peter Verbeck II obtained a different property in St Mary Coslany, immediately to the north of that once owned by his father Peter, in which his mother

Katherine was currently living (clearly she had remained a widow). He bought it from an English merchant, Richard Dudley, paying £210 for it: the property had once been owned by John van Rokeghem, and previously by John's father Remeus, so the two incomer families had been next-door neighbours for a long time. Peter was now expanding his property portfolio.

Members of the family occurred as apprentices and freemen throughout the century.

A Peter Beake gave 30s in the 'voluntary aid' for King Charles II in 1662. One branch of the family seem to have come down in the world: Pieter Beek was listed as one of the 'poor members' of the Dutch church in a return of 1677.[117]

The link with Leiden makes it very likely that Nathaniel van der Beke was part of this family. Nathaniel became betrothed to Abigail Hogendorn there in 1623. Both were described in the Leiden register as 'from Norwich', presumably meaning that they were born in the city. At the time of the betrothal, Nathaniel was living in Haarlem in North Holland and Abigail in Vlissingeen in Zeeland. The family clearly retained links on both sides of the North Sea.

The De Hem family

The De Hems were later incomers, and one of the richest families in Norwich. Jaques de Hem did not appear in the 1577 subsidy, but was active in the city from 1587, trading with the Low Countries through Great Yarmouth. He paid for a letter of denization in 1590. He paid tax on goods in St Michael at Plea worth £8 in 1595, and purchased 300 quarters of rye in Amsterdam on behalf of Norwich Corporation in 1596. He bought his freedom for £50 in 1602, and in 1605 had seven children officially registered at the Mayor's Court:

Tobyas, born in St Andrew's parish on 8 March 1587.
John, born in St Michael at Plea parish, christened 15 September 1594.
Mary, born in St Andrew's parish, baptised 28 February 1585.
Anne, born in St Andrew's parish 30 March 1589.
Susan, born in St Michael at Plea parish, baptised 31 October 1591.
Hester, born in St Michael at Plea parish, baptised 6 March 1596.
Sara, born in St Michael at Plea parish, baptised 27 May 1599.

The only one of these baptised into the local Anglican parish church was Susan. The others were presumably baptised in the Dutch church, the registers for which only survive from 1599. All these were the children of Jaques and his first wife, Anna.

Anna died in 1603 giving birth to her tenth child (those not registered in the Mayor's Court had presumably died young). She was buried in St Michael at Plea, where her monument can still be seen: it tells us that she died at the age of 44. Jaques' second wife was Sara Derick, daughter of Abraham Derick, whom he married at St Michael at Plea (not in the Dutch church) on 4 November 1604. They went on to

---

117 *The East Anglian* new series vol. 1 (1885–6), pp. 58–60.

have five children between 1606 and 1622, two of whom were baptised in the Dutch church, two in St Michael at Plea, and one, Judith, who was recorded in *both* the Dutch church register and the St Michael at Plea register.

Jaques was recorded as an elder of the Dutch church in 1610 and 1615. Between 1616 and 1619 he bought four properties in the city, recorded on the City Court rolls (as a freeman he could do this, although 'alien born'). They were a tenement in St Michael at Plea, a messuage in St Andrew, a row of houses in St John Timberhill, and a messuage in St Mary Coslany, bought from Thomas Gooch. The property in St Michael at Plea was adjacent to the Red Well which gives its name to the present Redwell Street: from 1618–19 he paid the Corporation 4d a year for a piece of property on which he had built a wall 'next the street against the Red Well'. As his will showed, he also bought property in the country.

Jaques made his will on 2 March 1623/4, dying later in the same year. As a wealthy and responsible man, he made charitable bequests to the Dutch church, but also to both the Walloon and Anglican churches in the city. He left a donation to the Dutch preacher, a yearly rent for the Dutch ministry, and £4 for the poor of the Dutch congregation. Interestingly, he foresaw that the time would come when there would no longer be any need of a separate Dutch church in Norwich: his bequest to the Dutch preaching ministry was to continue 'during so long time as there shall continue a Dutch cong[reg]ation in Norwich'.

De Hem also made bequests to the English church – 40s to the minister of St Michael at Plea, 40s to John Payne, 'preacher of God's word and late minister of St John Ber St', and 40s to Ralph Furnes, the current minister there (Payne had been deprived of his living for nonconformity). He left £10 to poor of the city in general, and a further £3 for the poor in St Michael at Plea. He also left £3 to the Walloon poor and £3 to the Walloon ministry.

He left the family house in St Michael at Plea to his wife Sara 'as long as she remains a widow'. His main heir was his eldest son Tobias, who received the other properties. His other children also received money – except for his second son John, clearly the black sheep of the family:

> My son John Dehem to my great grief and loss and his own hurt and discredit hath had and gotten from me more than I am able to give any of my other children … yet I of a fatherly love and parent-like care for his good, hoping his reformation and amendment of life which to do I beseech God to give him grace.

John was to get £300 – an enormous sum for the 1620s – but only if he lived a life approved by his father's executors for one whole year.

Jaques left to his youngest son (not named for some reason, but clearly James) property in Foulsham and Wood Norton which Jaques had bought from William Hempstead: the refugee merchant had become a country landowner. All seven surviving daughters were mentioned: only one, Susan, was said to be married. He also made bequests to three godchildren, one of whom was Theophilus Elison. His servants were remembered as well – former servant Francis Ducket, present servant

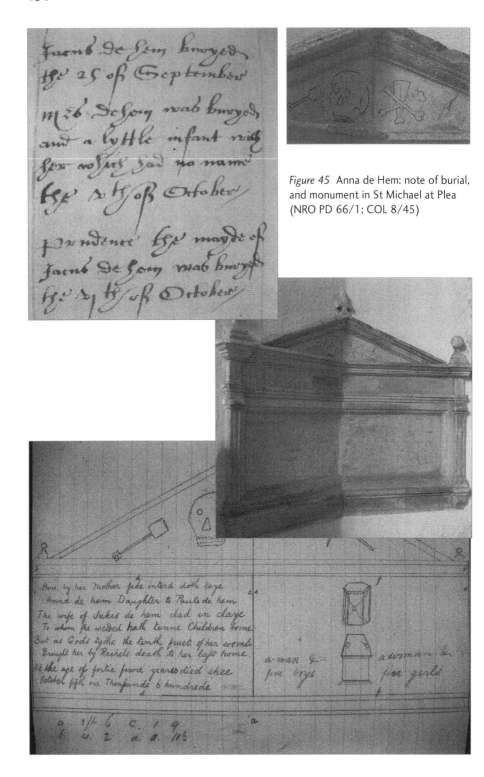

Figure 45 Anna de Hem: note of burial, and monument in St Michael at Plea (NRO PD 66/1; COL 8/45)

John Ruben, and an unnamed maidservant. He also left 300 guilders to nephews and nieces in Flanders.

Jaques was buried at St Michael at Plea on 31 May 1624: there is a brass in the nave in his memory, which records that he was 76 years old. His wife Sara did not long remain a widow. Less than eight months after Jaques' death, she married an Englishman, Donkin Barnet, widower, in St Michael at Plea on 13 January 1624.

Tobias de Hem

Tobias was born in Norwich, and went to Leiden University, matriculating in 1605. He married Susan Burnett, the daughter of an English doctor, in the Dutch church in London on 22 October 1611. She must have either been very pregnant, or have just given birth, as their first child, Sara, was baptised just eight days later! They had a second child, James in 1616, and a third, Tobias, was born 11 April 1619 in St Andrew's parish and baptised in the Norwich Dutch church on 25 November 1619. A fourth child, Abraham, was buried in St Michael at Plea in 1631, but it is not known when he was born or where he was baptised.

Tobias appeared in the musters lists and obviously enjoyed this aspect of his life, as he left £5 to set up a stock for the use of the Dutch company, and also left 40s for a supper.

At least one of Tobias's sisters, Susan, married an Englishman, Robert Buxton, and other siblings may well have done the same. Tobias bought part of a tenement in St Peter Southgate in 1618. He became constable of mid-Wymer ward in 1621, one of the first of the incomer community to achieve city office. In the 1626 landgable he was recorded as owning property in St Andrew and St Michael at Plea. In 1627 Tobias bought property in St Michael at Plea from his stepfather.

Tobias only outlived his father by five years, dying in 1629: he was buried in St Michael at Plea church on 3 August 1629. There is a memorial to him in the church, so there are three memorials there to this one incomer family: this is not matched in any other city church. Tobias left £10 to the preacher John Elison, and profits from his houses in St Mary Coslany to the ministry and poor of the Dutch congregation. He also made bequests to relatives and friends in Leiden and The Hague ('s-Gravenhage).

Tobias de Hem left a silver flagon to Norwich Corporation. On 31 March 1631 this was duly delivered to the Mayor's Court by James Lyberd, servant to the executors de Hem and Corselis. The flagon weighed 70 ounces, and Lyberd was given 5s for his trouble. It can still be seen today among the city regalia, evidence of the wealth and generosity of the immigrant community of four centuries ago. The Susan de Hem paying rates in St Andrew parish in 1633–4 was probably his widow, with another woman, called only 'Mrs de Hem', paying rates in St George Tombland.

The de Hems were one of the very richest of the Dutch families in Norwich, and quickly merged into the native community through several marriages.

The Van Ixem/VanNixon family

The Van Ixems represent one of the very few original 30 invitees whose line can be traced through several generations in Norwich to the time when they saw themselves as English rather than Dutch. Jooris van Ixem came to England with his wife and two children in 1561. They had three more children, born in England, and were in Norwich by the time of the 1568 census.

In 1583 Jooris van Ixem died, leaving two children, Abraham and Abigail, young enough to be assigned tutors, one of whom, Jan van Ixem, was their uncle. Abraham was probably almost grown up, as three years later, in 1586, he acted as guarantor for another orphan, along with a Wouter Casier. In 1588 Casier acted as a guarantor with Jan van Ixem on behalf of another orphan. The families were clearly closely linked, and become even more so: an undated entry in the book records Abigail van Ixem's marriage to Wouter.

Abraham van Ixem paid duty in 1589–90 on 114 pounds of liquorice, 30 pounds of ginger, 12 pounds of pepper and 3 pounds of white yarn. Both Abraham and another of the children, John, paid tax in St Gregory in 1595. In the same year he was in correspondence with the London Dutch Consistory court about an inheritance claim.

Abraham was married: his wife's name was Catherine, and they had a child, also Catherine, baptised in the Norwich Dutch church in 1598. Abraham died in 1602. Unusually, his will survives in three forms. There is a double page of notes in Dutch, headed by a religious thought or quotation and then listing the bequests: this was drawn up by Abraham on 3 August 1601, and has his signature and his 'mark'. The date 26 March 1602 was added to the paper, and this could well be the date of his death. A formal will was then drawn up in English from the notes: this was done by Giles Langhelett, as scribe of the politic men. The will was proved in the Norwich Consistory Court on 19 April 1602, and a formal copy of the will was then entered into the court register. The religious heading, which is present in all three versions (in Dutch, naturally, in the first version) reads, in its English translation, 'Our help standeth in the name of the Lord who hath made heaven and earth. Amen.'

Incidentally, the probate copy makes a curious error. It reads 'Abraham son of George Ham made ...'. However, the English original clearly reads 'Abraham son of George hath made...'. In this way a fictitious surname of Ham has crept into the will and the probate indexes. The father was of course George van Ixem, Jooris in the Dutch original.

Abraham bequeathed property to his wife, Mary Gelincx: he must have been widowed and remarried since 1598. Mary was to have £50 in ready money lying in the house – he was clearly a wealthy man. He also provided a servant/companion: Kargell du Boes was to have 20s if she stayed with Mary for a year, 40s if she stayed two years. He made provision for his children, including naming tutors – but he did not name the children. One of the tutors was to be his brother John. He left £3 for the poor of the Dutch congregation, and 10s for the poor of St Gregory's parish.

John van Ixem married Cornelia de Buckeres. Three of their children appear in the baptism register of the Dutch church, Catheryna in 1598, Abigail in 1600 and Hester in 1603. They must have had other children, born before the surviving baptism register starts. One daughter, Neelken, was a witness to a baptism in 1607, so was presumably at least 16 by then; the John junior in the 1622 Return is almost certainly a son.

John senior, who had been born in Flanders, obtained a letter of denization in 1603. In the 1620s John Van Ixem or Vannixon was a hosier, living in St Gregory's, and paying tax on property worth £6 (a figure only exceeded by one incomer). The 1626 landgable confirmed his ownership of property in St Gregory, and recorded that he also paid tax on a property in St Michael Coslany. John van Ixem junior, living in the same parish and born in England, was also wealthy, paying tax on property worth £4. John senior was one of a dozen hosiers (some English, some immigrant) who reassured the Norwich magistrates that they were providing work for all their workers, but warned that it was becoming hard to do so, as their stock was laid out and they could not get money for their wares.

John junior clearly saw himself as no longer part of the Dutch community, as he was one of those who refused to pay rates to the Dutch church. In December 1632 he and Peter van Hove were before the city magistrates where the letter from the Privy Council was read ordering them to pay; they continued to refuse to do so.

Both Johns paid rates on property in St Gregory's parish in 1633–4, and in the following year John senior was admonished by the city magistrates for receiving counterfeit tokens. In January 1635 John junior was appointed one of the collectors of ship money in St Gregory's: the family had merged in with the English community.

Some Walloon families

The Choquetu family

According to the 1568 census, Thomas Choqeteu was a wool-comber from Artois who had made the journey to England with his wife and his mother. He was living in St Augustine parish in 1576 when he paid tax on wealth assessed at £1. He made his will on 30 October 1579, one of the very few made by incomers during this year of plague. However he clearly survived, as he did not die until 1583. The original was written by him in French and translated by the politic men when he died. It is this translation which is recorded in the will register. It is clear that it is a translation as it uses phrases like 'he hath willed that …' rather than the direct 'I will that …' of the original will.

Choquetu made the usual bequests to the French-speaking community in Norwich, leaving 30s to the poor of the French congregation, and also 30 pounds of fine dressed wool to go to the Walloon community for maintaining their preacher and minister. He left the large sum of £120 to be divided among his six children (not named, and presumably all born in England as no children were recorded in his 1568 census entry). Other bequests went to two sisters, Elizabeth Schoctu, the wife of Steven Caudron, and Gene Schoctu, the wife of John van Roye. The remainder of his goods were bequeathed to Bartholomew le Roy, from his surname a relative, perhaps the son or brother of his brother-in-law John. Bartholomew was clearly in England, as he was a witness to the will, but it was not stated where the other beneficiaries were living.

One of Thomas's sons was also named Thomas: he married Jenne Desmarets, sister of Francois Desmarets the sworn clerk of the Walloon congregation in Norwich. He had at least two sons, Thomas and Jaques, but was dead by the time the latter was baptised in the Norwich French church in 1607. The third Thomas Choquetu went to Gonville and Caius College in Cambridge when he was 15 years old.

After that, the name disappears from the record: there are no marriages or baptisms in the Walloon church registers. Rye speculated that the men named Cookoe and Cucko paying rates in 1633–4 were descendants of the family, but these names occur in earlier lists of Englishmen in the city. Either the family had left the city, or they had become fully anglicised.

The Ployart or Ployer family

The Ployarts came from Armentières; we know because William gave the town as his birthplace when he married his second wife in the Norwich French church. William was born in about 1546: his age was given as 31 in a 1577 court case. The family were not in the 1568 census, but presumably arrived in Norwich in the next few years. William Ployart was the only man in St Pauls' parish to have wealth assessed at 30s in 1576 – seven others in the parish were assessed at £1 each, and 50 others, including Matthew, just paid the poll tax. Matthew's name immediately follows William, so he was probably his son. William 'Pleyer' and Matthew 'Player' also paid subsidy in 1581, by which time both were living in St Paul's parish.[118]

By the early 1580s William was an established member of the Walloon community in the city. He served as a tutor to five orphans or sets of orphans between 1583 and 1590, and served as guarantor for another pair of orphans in 1589–90. He was an elder of the French church in Norwich in the early 1590s, and was listed in the 1595 Walloon muster list. He must have moved to St Saviour's parish as he paid tax there in 1599, but by the time he wrote his will in 1603 he was described as of St Peter Hungate. This high mobility within the city seems typical of the immigrant community in the sixteenth century.

William was married twice and had several children. By his first wife (whose name is not known) he had at least one child, Samuel, and possibly more: I suspect that Matthew was another son. His wife was still alive in 1599, when she acted as a witness to a ceremony in the French church, but she must have died soon afterwards, as he then married again, to Elaine Carpreau, who had been born in Tournai. The couple had two children, Susan and Marie.

William Ployart made his will on 3 August 1603. After the customary bequests to the poor of the Walloon church (£6) and to the Walloon ministry (£4), he mentioned his wife and his daughters. He did not mention his sons by his first marriage, who

---

118   NRO NCR 12a/4.

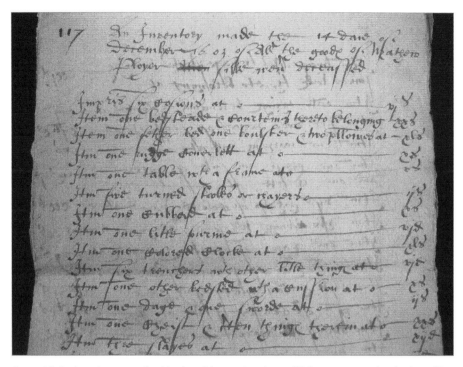

Figure 46 Probate inventory for Matthew Ployart , immigrant Walloon weaver, who died in 1603 (NRO DN/INV 19/117)

were adults. William must have died on the day he made the will or the day after: he was buried in St Peter Hungate churchyard on 4 August. His will was taken to the Archdeaconry Court in Norwich for probate on 16 August. (For some reason it was also proved in London on 16 March 1603/4. Several incomer wills were proved in both places, perhaps owing to their not fully understanding the English probate system.)

Matthew Ployart was probably one of William's sons. This is not absolutely certain, but he was certainly closely related: William, Samuel, Matthew and their wives appeared as witnesses to the baptisms of each other's children. He was a silk weaver by profession, living in St Martin at Oak in 1603. His wife was named Susan, and they had two daughters, Sarah and Susanne, baptised in the Norwich French church in 1599 and 1601 respectively.

On 13 September, it was Matthew's turn to make his will. He was specific about the reason, the plague, writing, 'if it please God to call me out of this world by this sickness'. He nominated Samuel Ployart, Joel Desormeaux and Thomas Choquetu as guardians for his young children. His fears were justified, as he was dead by 4 October when his widow had the will proved.

Samuel Ployart, who was definitely William's son, had three children baptised in the Norwich Walloon church between 1599 and 1602 – Samuel, Benjamin and Judict – and may have had others before the date of the surviving register. Two months after his father's death Samuel made his will, on 8 October. He left 40s to the poor of the French congregation and 20s to maintain the minister of the French church. His will stated that his father William and his sister Marie Ployart had both died so recently that he had not yet received the inheritance due to him from them. This was assigned, together with his own possessions, to his wife and children. This was another will made by a man close to death: the will was proved just 11 days after it was written.

In just two months three male and one female family members had died, and there may have been other deaths among the wives and children in the family. We only know of the deaths of those family members who left wills or were mentioned in them (like Marie). Elaine, William's widow, survived the plague, acting as a witness in 1607 and 1608, but the Ployart family then disappear from the record: perhaps plague had effectively wiped out the family. No one of the name occurred in the 1618 muster list or the 1622 return of 'Strangers', and no Ployart (or any name remotely like it) occurred in the 1633–4 rate book for the city. Some members of the family may have moved to Yarmouth: an Anne Ployart married there in 1657, and there were burial entries for Thomas and Elizabeth Ployart a few years later.

The Herbert family

Hugh Herbert told us in his will that he was born in Warlencourt in Artois. He did not appear in the 1576 or 1581 subsidies, but signed the Book of Discipline of the Norwich French church in 1590. He was clearly established as one of the wealthiest Walloons in the city by 1595, in which year he paid tax on wealth of £6 in St Saviour's parish. In the same year, he bore arms at his own expense at the musters.

Hugh married twice. His first wife was Sara de la Tombe, by whom he had two daughters, Ester and Sara. She died, leaving a 'portion' to each of her daughters, and their rights were preserved in the contract made for his second marriage, to Elizabeth Desbarbieux. He had two further daughters by her, Elizabeth who married Francis Desmarets, and Rachel, whose husband's name is not given, but who had a son called Michiel Castell. If he was the infant of that name baptised in the French church in 1601 his father's name was Jan Castell.

Herbert made the usual bequests to the Walloon community in Norwich, leaving £5 to the poor and £3 to maintaining the ministry. He also left money – 30s – to the English poor in the parish in which he lived, St Saviour's. He was one of the very few incomers I have found whose will made any conditions as to his burial – he wanted his 'body to be buried after the Christian simplicity of our Reformed church'. Herbert must have been ill for some time before his death: rather touchingly he left 30s to Lawrens Broquette for 'his assistance in my sickness' and a petticoat worth £3 to Judith Desbarbieux, no doubt a relative, 'for her good service in my sickness'. Herbert's executors and witnesses included many leading Walloons: Maximilan du Rieu, Pasquier Herbert, Thomas Bonnell, Thomas de la Tombe, and Francis Desmarets, described as 'sworn clerk of our Walloon congregation' – who was also Herbert's son-in-law.

After his death in 1603, his widow Elizabeth soon remarried, wedding Maximilian Durie in the French church on 19 November 1604.

Pasquier Herbert was probably Hugh's brother. A wealthy cloth merchant, he was born at Chattalon sur Somme. He did not figure in the 1577 subsidy, but appeared in the aulnage accounts for the first time in June 1585, when he paid duty on two barrels of butter (which was used to grease wool). Over the next decade he regularly imported butter – on one occasion specifically described as 'Friesland butter' – flax, cloth and yarn: his imports included 'Gentish cloth and linen yarn', and 'four pieces of Hollands'.

Pasquier's wife was called Barbara le Febre. She made her will in 1609, by which time she was the only member of the family in Norwich: she wrote perhaps the saddest will left by any of the incomers, describing herself as:

an ancient woman here in the city of Norwich where at the present I have no kindred.

She left money to her nephew Vincent Monson living in Middelburg, the son of William Monson living in Tourney. Other beneficiaries included Judith Herbert, the wife of Claude Leschise and presumably a relative of her late husband, and her own sister Laurentia, wife of Peter du Rieux, and Laurentia's daughter Jacqueline. She also left the poor of the Dutch community in Norwich all her smocks, as well as money.

Another Pasquier Herbert was born in Lecelle in Tornesy, and in 1602 married Marie du Pont in the French church in Norwich. Marie was born in Canterbury, no doubt the daughter of Walloon refugees who had settled in that city. Their four children were baptised in the French church between 1604 and 1609. A member of the Philippo family acted as witness in every case, so the two families were closely linked.

The Herberts then disappeared from city documents: no one of that name occurred in the 1622 Return, and none paid rates in 1633–4.

The Philippo family

No Philippo appeared in the 1576 or 1581 subsidy lists, so the family probably arrived in Norwich in the late 1580s or early 1590s. A Pierre Philippo appeared in the Walloon militia list for 1595: he had his two daughters, Sara and Marie, baptised in the Walloon/French church in Norwich in 1595 and 1608. The name of the children's mother was not given in the baptism register, which habitually names the fathers only. She was actually called Jenne Lambeys: we know this because she accompanied Sara to the Dutch Republic when Sara married a man born in the Ardennes in the Walloon church in Leiden in 1614.[119]

An Elias Philippo had a large number of children baptised in the French church in Norwich, starting with Anne in 1609. A son, Elias, was baptised in 1611, and by the 1630s there were two adults of that name in the city, sometimes distinguished by the words senior and junior. Elias Phillipo appeared in the 1618 Walloon muster lists, and he signed the Book of Discipline in 1625. The same man, or more probably his son, signed as elder in 1658.

---

119   Tammel (1989), p. 90.

The Elias born in 1611 had three brothers, including Onias, the youngest of the family, who was born in 1626. He also had six sisters, at least three of whom married other members of the Walloon community in England. Anne married Pierre Cateau in 1628: he was part of the Canterbury community, where he was born. Jenne married Jean L'Emperor, of the well-known Norwich family, and Elizabeth married James Cateau, probably Pierre's brother. Both Elias and Onias also married, and between them the three sisters and two brothers had more than 20 children baptised in the Walloon church in Norwich. The same forenames recur in the families: Elias, Onias and Pierre for the boys, Marie, Jenne and Sarah for the girls.

The Elias born in 1611 is also the man who rose to become an important local figure, being made High Sheriff of Norfolk in 1675, a great achievement for the son of an immigrant. A baker by profession, he married twice, his first wife Mary dying in 1650. His second wife Isbel died just a short while after Elias himself in 1678.

As we have seen, Elias was an active member of the both the Walloon and the city community, supplying the former with a pesthouse for use in time of plague in 1631. In December of the same year, the city authorities paid Elias to bake twopenny loaves for the city's poor, which would mean the English poor as Dutch and Walloon poor were not the responsibility of the city; he was allowed money out of the city's funds to do this.

Elias's brother Onias, whose links with the Huguenot community are described in Chapter 8, died in 1693. The family is commemorated with a plaque in St Saviour's church, where Mary is buried, but Elias, Isbel and Onias are all buried in St Augustine's churchyard.

The name Philippo also occurs in Canterbury, and illustrates once more how such families were connected, both in England and across the seas. Jan Philippo, born in Canterbury, became a husband in Leiden twice in 18 months. He married Susan Fauwerkes of Leiden there in June 1615. In February 1617, as a widower, he married a relation of his first wife, Pyrone Huys of Roux in Flanders. His brother Philip Philippo also married in Leiden in 1617. The Philippo family are an example of an incomer family with links to other immigrant communities in England, and who retained close connections with their homeland.

Chapter 7

Making connections

Links with 'home'

Raingard Esser estimates that there were about 200 Stranger wills between 1570 and 1640, 45 in the period up to 1603, and 32 in that year alone (a plague year). Thirty-three of the wills (16.5 per cent) mention family members or goods in the Low Countries, but only seven before 1603. Esser sees this as evidence for the poverty of the first generation of refugees.[120]

Certainly it was not uncommon for seventeenth-century wills to include bequests to friends and relatives across the Channel. John Decock, an aqua-vitae seller who died in 1603, left bequests to children of Peter Decock in Newkerche, and to Francis Decock in Leiden. George Hallewyck, a hosier, who died in 1625, left £34 to the six children of his cousin Lodewijk Hallewyck dwelling in Flanders, and £5 to Jacob de Jus, a preacher 'dwelling in Holland'. Jane Begots clearly still had assets abroad, as we have seen. When George Fenne made his will in 1592, he left to his wife (unnamed in the will, but known from other sources to be Winifrede) an annuity of 16 pounds Flemish out of houses in Utrecht. She did not return there, but remained in Norwich, presumably in receipt of her annuity, until her own death almost 30 years later, in 1621.

The will of Nicholas de Toict, a Walloon who died in Norwich in 1618, illustrates that there could be a network of family members stretching across England and into the Low Countries. Beneficiaries included his daughter-in-law Rachel, wife of Toby du Toict; his sister-in-law Jane Millome; her daughter Sara and his niece Elizabeth Temberman. These family members presumably lived in Norwich. However, Nicholas left a further £200 to his wife's 'kindred'. £100 went to Sara Deane, daughter of Giles, who lived at Sandwich. The other £100 went to John Layare and his sister Maria Layare, who were both living in Holland. Anne Vanderweighe, apparently one of the poorest people making a will, left 30s, by far her largest bequest, to her father, 'he dwelling beyond the seas'.

Anthony Clarebot acted for the family in dealings abroad – according to his father's will, he had sold the family's goods in Flanders and kept the money for himself! Paschier Clarebote, his father and one of the original 30 invitees, died in 1590. In bequeathing his property to his children and grandchildren, he excluded Anthony until he had rendered due account for this money.

---

120 Esser (1995), p. 147.

Trading links

A legal case shows that English merchants were still trading with the Netherlands. In 1573 there was a dispute between Ralph Owner, a Yarmouth merchant, and William Page, a London ironmonger, about a cargo that was at Emden, just over the Dutch border in Germany. The burgomaster of Emden, as was customary, chose six English merchants in the town to act as arbiters in the case. One of them was Nicholas Surrey, smith, of Norwich, perhaps surprisingly as in the Norwich tax records he is described as an alien. In any case, the incident shows that there were plenty of English merchants still engaged in trade with the Dutch. Emden indeed acted as the main port for the Low Countries in the periods when Antwerp was not available, for example in the decade 1564–74.[121]

Several cases heard before the mayor involved trade disputes, and some relate to members of the Dutch community; sometimes the evidence of witnesses survives. These depositions heard before the mayor can provide more or less direct speech from the incomers involved. The records consist of interrogatories (questions to be asked) and the recorded answers of the witness.

One such case concerned Cornelis de Ram. We know from the 1568 census that he had come from Zeeland in 1567 with his wife and two children, and that he was a *tabellarius,* or courier: the case presumably arose while he was acting in this role in England. In May 1571, four barrels of cochineal, worth the enormous sum of £360, disappeared from a Spanish ship called the *Flying Dragon*. Travelling from Cadiz to Antwerp, she had been captured by Sea Beggars and taken to Meadhole in the Isle of Wight, from where the cargo was dispersed throughout Britain by sale. Cochineal is a scarlet dye that derives from an insect found in Mexico and South America; it was one of the many products imported into Spain after the conquest of the Aztec Empire. The case which came before the mayor of Norwich in July 1573 concerned a packet of cochineal that Ram had brought to the city in the previous year, so it could have been part of that cargo. He carried it in a bag tied to his saddle. The case was important enough for John de Hoorne de Han, a London merchant, to come to Norwich to give evidence. We do not know the exact nature of the dispute or the result of the case, but it appears that one Francis Gwysten had attached the packet to Ram's horse and ordered him to carry it to Norwich, but that, whether through carelessness or criminal intent, it did not arrive in a complete state.

A similar case involved the carriage of goods from the Continent. In 1593 Mallyard Rickwarde, a Dutchman living in Norwich, brought a case concerning 'silk Cyprus', which he had purchased when he was in Rotterdam, but which was apparently not up to standard when it arrived in Norwich.

A case before the court in 1573 reveals many interesting details about life in the community. The case was bought by Tannekyn Boys, who had recently been widowed and wanted to ensure her rights in her late husband's property and business were

---

121 The case came before the mayor of Norwich in 1576: NRO NCR 12a/4; Robert Ashton, *Reformation and Revolution 1558–1660* (1985 edn), pp. 86–7.

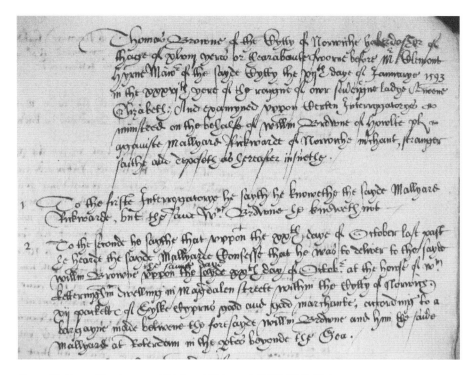

Figure 47 Deposition in case of Mallyard Rickwaert (NRO NCR 12a)

protected. His name was Dominic du Boys. The answers to the depositions show that he dealt in salt, had several business partners, some Dutch and some apparently English, and that both Tannekyn and her husband travelled abroad in connection with the business. Indeed her husband had property in Zeeland (it is not clear whether it was owned or rented), and appears to have died there.

Dominic appears to have been living abroad. He gave John de Vive (or van Vive; both versions of the name are used in the case), who lived in Norwich, the sums of £24 and 16 angels to be spent in Norwich in Dominic's interest, either in the provision of clothing for his children in Norwich or in securing an income for them. The matter came to a head when there was a row in the Dutch church when the community was assembled for service at Christmas in 1572. A man named Clays Vanvervykin confronted van Vive, saying that he had spent money on the children and so van Vive should hand over some of the cash. Van Vive produced a letter from Dominic saying that the money should be invested to make a profit for the children. When Vanvervykin asked him what profit had been made, he replied by claiming he had passed the money onto Tannekyn. This was apart from the sum of 1 angel, which everyone involved agreed had been used by Tannekyn on a voyage back to the Low Countries, presumably to visit her husband.

One disputed sum was £8, apparently in the hands of one Laurence Pitt (an alien, despite his English-sounding name: he lived in Nieuport) and allegedly owed to

Dominic for salt he had bought from him. Pitt also travelled freely: Vanvervykin recalled meeting him on Norwich Castle Hill, on which occasion Pitt claimed he had already passed the money on to Tannekyn.

There was also the question of whether there were any goods of Dominic's in the Low Countries at the time of his death. Once more Clays Vanvervykin was involved in the matter. A man named Adrian Bastien, alias Decker, gave evidence that he was at Dyryckeston in Sellonde [Zeeland] when he received a letter from Vanvervykin in Norwich asking him to go to Cawinfore and call at the Skowter's house (a local official; an English equivalent would be 'magistrate') where Dominic had stayed before his death. He was to ask if the Skowter knew anything about any money that had been sent to John Vivian in England for salt that had been sold. Bastien did go as requested, and he spoke to the Skowter's wife. She told him that about £20 had been sent to Vivian, and that Vivian had written to Tannekyn saying that he had received the money for her use.

We only have the evidence of the witnesses of the case, so it is not known if Tannekyn received her entitlements. It is perhaps a tribute to the legal processes in Norwich that a widow who had only been in Norwich for six years thought the case was worth bringing to court. If she is the same Tannekyn Boys, widow, paying tax in St Margaret's parish in 1625, she continued as a widow for half a century, but this could be another woman of the same name.

As these examples suggest, there was plenty of movement across the North Sea, on both a short and long-term basis. A document in the domestic State Papers for 1578 states that one of the benefits the Strangers brought to Norwich was money, as every time they went abroad they had to pay the city authorities 3s for a passport to travel (and they had to pay again at Yarmouth, showing that this was the usual route of travel).[122]

Links with other incomer communities

As we have seen, many of the first incomers to Norwich came from Sandwich or London, and there were close links between the Norwich communities and those elsewhere in England. In November 1569, for example, the Norwich community sent £5 8s 1d to Sandwich.[123]

The French churches held about 30 colloquies, from the first (in London) in 1581 down to 1660. At least one was held in Norwich, in April 1583. The French Book of Discipline of 1589 ordered that yearly meetings were to be held of all the French churches in the kingdom. The French churches at colloquies in the 1590s were those at London, Norwich, Canterbury, Rye, Winchelsea and Southampton.

The Dutch churches also held synods, those represented in a synod held in 1604 being London, Norwich, Colchester, Sandwich and Maidstone. The London Dutch

---

122 Walter Rye, 'The Dutch refugees in Norwich', *The Norfolk Antiquarian Miscellany*, vol. 3 (1887), p. 247.
123 Vane (1984), p. 137.

church was seen as the head of the immigrant churches, and was consulted by the Norwich community. These letters were often written by, or addressed to, the 'three colleges' – elders, deacons and politic men. For example, the Norwich politic men and Consistory wrote to London on 22 September 1574 complaining about the influx of Strangers at Norwich, who might cause unrest and disorder in the community. On 8 April 1577, the Consistory of the Norwich Dutch church told London that the three colleges had sat together and decided to refuse to pay towards the travel expenses of a messenger of the prince of Orange in England.

There were many personal links between the immigrant communities, and people frequently moved between them. Several wills illustrate this. Nicholas Verbeke, who died in London 1604, made a nuncupative will leaving everything to his wife Marie. She was living in Norwich by April 1606 when she made her own will. Isaie de Hovigneau, born in Norwich, lived in London and died there in 1603. The family had close links with Norwich – Isaie was present at Walloon weddings in Norwich in 1595 and 1598, Jan de Hovigneau was an elder of the Norwich French church in 1604, and Samson Hovigneau married Elsie Clarebote in Norwich January 1604/5

One family important in both the Norwich and London communities was that of John Ruytinck, from Ghent. A notary (according to Moens), he was involved in a dispute about the election of wardens for the drapers in 1571, and in reviewing the Book of Orders in 1574. He had at least two sons, Simeon and Zachary. Forster identifies him with the Johannes Fyntincke of the 1568 census who arrived in England in 1567 with his wife and one infant (whom Forster identifies as Simeon), while Zachary's birth is recorded in the St Laurence parish register. Simeon became a preacher of the Dutch church in London, and a historian: he describes Saint Bartholomew's Massacre as 'a frightful and bloody murder'. His widow, Marie, died in London in 1622. Her will mentions five children and two maidservants. Her brother-in-law Zachary was left her 'silver cup wherein the picture of Justice is engraven' and his wife received her best silk apron.[124]

Other links between the communities led to marriage. The Norwich Walloon church marriage register included two people born in other English communities – Jonas Cortenay born in Sandwich, and Marie du Pont born in Canterbury. Christopher Joby mentions a marriage in the Walloon church at Canterbury: Balthasar Verhulst, widower, born at Antwerp, and Elizabeth Destailleux, daughter of the late Joos, native of Norwich, on 10 August 1606. Joos Destailleux was an elder in the Norwich church in 1589. There are many similar instances.

Links with the English

Although the Dutch and Walloon communities were centred on their respective churches, there were many links with the native inhabitants of Norwich. One of the most beneficial to both parties was the hiring of apprentices. The Mayor's Court books and Norwich Quarter Sessions books contain many records of apprenticeships,

124 Forster (1967), p. 42.

showing how English people gained skills through contact with the incomers. To take just one example from 1573, John Halfebers, an immigrant silk weaver, took on two English apprentices who lived with him and learned the art of lace making. Thomas Bucke, son of Anne Bucke, was apprenticed to dwell with John Halfebers, a Stranger, for seven years to learn lace weaving. A Norfolk tailor, Richard Whitterel, had two sons, who both became apprentices of incomers, one to be trained as a bay weaver, the other as a pin maker. Girls benefited too – two female orphan sisters named Browne were found work in service with Dutchmen in the city.

The city authorities appreciated the skills brought in by the immigrants, and made good use of them. In 1576, they reached an agreement (the only surviving copy is in French) with Guy de Leuwalle, a Walloon, to serve the city in the manufacture of bays for a year. In 1581 the city authorities employed a Dutchman, Nicholas Beoscom, to teach pin making to their orphans housed in the Great Hospital. When the Norwich Bridewell authorities needed another 'twystering mill' in 1584, they bought one for 59s from an unnamed Dutchman. In 1595 Jaques de Hem was chosen by the city to buy up rye in Amsterdam for the city's grain reserves, and to transport it back. Other institutions also made use of the skills of the incomers: in 1586 the churchwardens at St Peter Mancroft paid Abraham Panvoorth to supply and repair glass for the church.

The Dutch brought many aspects of their culture with them, including the tulip, the Dutch gable – and the canary. Dutch sailors had brought the birds back from their voyages to the Canary Islands, and adopted them as their favourite pet. When they came to Norwich they brought their canaries with them. The hobby of canary breeding soon spread to the English in the city, and became extremely popular among Norwich people in subsequent centuries. We have seen that English weaver Anthony Tills had a birdcage beside his loom in his garret, and another example is Robert Rippin, a Norwich worsted weaver, who had three birdcages in his kitchen when he died in 1727. Norwich soon even produced its own breed, the Norwich plain-head, already recognised as a distinctive breed by the early eighteenth century.

The canary has become a symbol of the way in which the life of the city has been enriched by incomers, as well as the emblem of Norwich City Football Club. In the 1970s no less a figure than the Dalai Lama purchased some Norwich canaries. He bought them from local breeder Chris Goodall, who was also a 'Canary' himself – he was a former Norwich City player![125]

The immigrants were of course subject to English justice, and made use of local courts in civil cases, while those who committed crime might come before the local criminal courts. Two cases in the Mayor's Court illustrate the civil side. In March 1571, the wife of Charles Foiret took the wife of Cornelius Dierichsse to the Mayor's Court, claiming that she was owed 12 Flemish florins, or in English money 6s 8d, for a year's work as a servant. Mrs Dierichsse refused even to attend the court. On 11 April the court ordered the husband to pay the money, with an extra 6d for costs. The case also shows the variations in the way a name might be spelled. The offender's name is spelled Dierichsse in the writ in Dutch (which has been

125 Frank Meeres, *Norwich: A History and Celebration* (2004), p. 30.

pinned into the court book), Dulyson in the court book entry and Deryson in its heading.

People might turn to the English courts after having failed to get satisfactory results from the politic men. In June 1602 Willemyne Clyncket, the wife of James Demara, went to the Dutch politic men to complain that her daughter had been badly bitten by a dog owned by Pyrma, widow of Francis van Dyke. Willemyne had called in a surgeon, and the politic men decided that Pyrma would have to pay the surgeon's fee of £3. This was a large sum, and the court ordered her to pay in two instalments. However, because she 'obstinately refused' to pay, the matter came before the Mayor's Court, which sent her to prison. All the people involved in the case had come from the Spanish Netherlands; we are not told whether the dog had too!

Cases involving immigrants might also appear before the Norwich Quarter Sessions. As early as 1578 an immigrant was the sole witness in a legal case, a dispute between Norwich doctor William Fever and a patient, Robert Dingle. The witness was John Fleming, alien. He said that Dingle had taken medicine from Fever to cure sores on his face but was refusing to complete (and pay for!) the course of treatment as he was 'almost cured'.

Opposition and support

Two of the mayors were opposed to the incomers. Thomas Whalle, a grocer and mayor in 1567–8, tried to secure the agreement of a majority of the Assembly to turn out the foreigners, but failed. Thomas Green, a butcher, was mayor in 1571–2; he, together with the sheriffs and aldermen, signed and delivered a protest against the settlement of strangers in the city.[126]

In the first years of the coming of the Strangers, English worsted weavers, butchers, smiths and cordwainers all complained to the Mayor's Court and asked for relief from interference by Strangers. In case of the cordwainers, the court decided that eight Strangers could be admitted as cordwainers and no more. In fact they named only six: Bartholomew de Clerke, Gherade van de Walle, Victor Desvesyns, James Marrishall, Boose Gallaunte and Anthony Wylton. There were other disputes between the incomers and the citizens of Norwich, the Dutch taking their protests to the Privy Council. They said that because of the persecution in the Low Countries:

> many poor Christians which (rather than they would forsake Christ and his Gospel) left their houses, lands and friends, and took refuge in this your Majesty's realm. And many of them came to Norwich aforesaid, using all means to get their living in the sweat of their brows in the said sciences, rather than that should be chargeable to any man.

In the time of Mayor Robert Wood (1569–70) there were complaints about the incomers by some: they had done more harm than good to the city, and they took

---

126 Basil Cozens-Hardy and Ernest A. Kent, *The Mayors of Norwich 1403 to 1835* (1938), p. 60.

jobs in the city, sucking these away from the English. It was noted that 'by reason of the business in Flanders the city was very much replenished with strangers'. This was not unique to Norwich: in Sandwich, where the original group of immigrants in 1561 had been followed by a flood in 1567, there were also complaints from the English that the newcomers were taking English jobs.

Matters came to a head in 1570. On 16 May John Appleyard and other country gentry announced that they would beat the Strangers out of Norwich. They tried again several times over the next few months, but few people joined them. According to the evidence of the patent rolls, John Jerningham of Somerleyton was pardoned for supporting Appleyard when on 26 May he tried to raise a rebellion at Norwich. Appleyard said that 'if he could get but four faithful gentlemen in Norfolk to rake his part he would take in hand to expel and drive out the Dutch men and strangers out of Norwich'. Jerningham supported him then, and on the following days.

On 16 June Jerningham was again in support when Appleyard tried to raise a rebellion at Trowse, together with John Throgmorton of Norwich, George Redman of Cringleford and Thomas Brooke of Rollesby. They said that

> we will raise up the commons and levy a power and beat the strangers out of the city of Norwich, and also take Sir Christopher Heydon and Sir William Butts and put them in the Guildhall in Norwich and there keep them, for Norfolk men never had the like cause to rise, and after we have levied our power we will hang up all such as will not take our parts.

On 24 June the malcontents assembled in Harleston to march on to Norwich, but were easily rounded up before they entered the city. They were tried in the Assize Court in August, and the leaders executed. Others were sentenced to life imprisonment, but released after a few years. Brooke was hanged on 3 August 1570. A poem he wrote on the eve of his execution was printed by Anthony de Solemne. Redman was buried at St Peter Mancroft after his execution, as the parish burial register records: 1570, September 2: 'George Redmond for his offence suffered death'.

The historian R. Hindry Mason suggested that the expulsion of foreigners was just an excuse, the real aim of the rebellion being to release a local hero, the Roman Catholic duke of Norfolk, from imprisonment in the Tower of London and put him on the throne in the place of Queen Elizabeth. He quotes Eachard as saying that the plot was that 'at Harleston fair the people should be assembled by sound of trumpet under *pretence* of expelling the foreigners that had fled from the Duke of Alva'.[127]

According to Mason, 33 offenders were tried for 17 offences, of which the most important were plotting the Queen's death, and rescuing the duke of Norfolk from the Tower. Just one of the charges mentioned incomers, 'spoiling of making havoc of the strangers'. Thirteen of the accused were charge with this offence, although they did include all the main leaders – Appleyard, Throgmorton, Redman and Brooke.[128]

---

127 R. H. Mason, *History of Norfolk* (1884), p. 158.
128 Mason (1884), pp. 158–9, quoting State papers, Domestic: Elizabeth vol. lxxi, 61.

Figure 48 St Michael at Plea, in a mid-20th century photograph. Memorials to the de Hem family can still be seen in the church (NRO N/LM 2/11).

I have seen just two cases in the Mayor's Court of what might be termed racist attacks. On 6 June 1576 Robert Burman was imprisoned for railing against the Strangers, but released upon his humble submission. In 1582 an Englishman named Christopher Wheatley, a reeder by profession, was before the Mayor's Court charged with beating up two Dutchmen in the street. However, this was clearly not a random attack: there had been 'history' between Wheatley and the Dutchmen, who gave testimony as to his 'lewd life from time to time'. Wheatley was condemned to a public whipping with rods. One other man can be considered a generally unpleasant person rather than a racist. William Ugg of Norwich, a 'vile whoremonger and adulterer', among many other offences was 'a puller of Duitche women's kerchers openlie in the market at Yarmouth'.[129]

One Norwich opponent of the Strangers, Nicholas Wright, did write to the Privy Council in May 1583 accusing the incomers of breaking the rules – keeping more servants than was permitted, selling by retail, and defrauding customs officials. The mayor and aldermen rejected these accusations against the incomers, telling the Privy Council that the four incomers named by Wright – Gerard Vosse, Jaques Baskinge, Francis Tryon and Anthony de Sacke – were 'four of the chiefest master workmen' and condemning Wright as an informer.[130]

Blomefield describes a disturbance between the citizens and Dutch strangers in 1613. He says that the Dutch had begun to exercise the ancient trades of the city,

---

129 Forster (1967), p. 139 citing University Library, Cambridge MS Ee 2.34 fo 3.
130 Rye (1887), pp. 247–8.

unlike the Walloons who did no such thing. The Dutch persuaded King James to issue them a charter to this effect, but the mayor was able to get it cancelled.

These were very small difficulties. Most local people agreed with the praise showered upon the incomers by Queen Elizabeth, when she wrote to the city from Greenwich Palace on 19 March 1570/1:

> She reminded the citizens of Norwich of the advantages they had derived from the settlement amongst them of so many skilled workers who inhabited houses which previously had been standing empty, and who provided work for large numbers of people who would otherwise have been unemployed. She therefore entreated them to continue their favours 'to the poor men of the Dutch nation, who seeing the persecution lately begun in their country for the true religion, have fled into this realm for succour, and were now placed in the city of Norwich'.

To most observers, it was astonishing how good Norwich was to her incomers. Alexander Neville noted that Norwich was 'a city seated daintily, most fair built she is knowne, pleasing and kind to Strangers all, Delightful to her own'. Michael Drayton described Norwich as:

> That hospitable place to the industrious Dutch,
> Whose skill in making stuffs, and workmanship is such,
> (For refuge hither come) as they our aid deserve,
> By labour sore that live, whilst oft the English starve:
> On roots and pulse that feed, on beef and mutton spare,
> So frugally they live, not gluttons as we are.

In the last lines, he was making the sound ecological point that the incomers were content with a simple diet of roots and pulses, whereas the English, by insisting on the extravagance of roast beef, laid themselves open to starvation in bad years. The same point was made by Assize judges in Norwich in 1620/1: they recommended that the English poor be encouraged to learn from the immigrant community, and grow root crops.[131]

---

131 Joan Thirsk, *Alternative Agriculture: A History* (1997), p. 38.

Chapter 8

Merging in and moving on

Naturally, not every immigrant arriving in Norwich settled down and merged with the local community. Within ten years of the first rush of incomers, a few began to return 'home', or went to the northern provinces that were freeing themselves from the control of Catholic Spain. Moens lists 16 people mentioned in Ypres town records as returning there from Norwich between 1576 and 1578. They included Thomas Bateman, even though he had become a denizen of England in 1570: he and his brother Francis moved to Ypres in 1577. However, it does not follow that all those listed as returning to Ypres settled there. As Moens points out, they may simply have returned there to settle their affairs before a permanent move to England. Nevertheless, the fact that the Batemans appear in no tax lists for Norwich after 1576 make it fairly certain that they left the city for good at this date.[132]

There is nothing in Norwich that records people leaving, but records abroad sometimes show people from Norwich arriving. In 1577, Jan Teutons and Lodewick van Rijke moved to Leiden from Norwich, as did Jan and Marguerite van Braeckenal and their two children in August 1579. On 4 January 1590 two Flemish drapers, Adriaan Tarte and Joos de Heedere, were specifically asked by the city of Leiden to come over from Norwich and work in the city.[133]

Seven families or individuals are known to have moved from Norwich to Leiden in 1596, six in 1597 and two more in February 1598. A further 14 families made the same journey between April 1601 and October 1608, including three people whose occupations were recorded: Louwijs de Fosse and Pierter Cortijs were saymakers and Rogier Savijn a wool-comber. These returnees included Samuel Navegeer, perhaps a relative of the 1567 letter writer.

A more complete source is the *Registers of Betrothals and Marriages, Citizenship, and of Sentences in Leiden* for 1576–1640, which, with occasional later entries, has been edited by Johanna W. Tammel. This contains an enormous number of names of people from Norwich. The appendices list 597 names of 'Flemish/Walloon and other non-British names' of people described as coming from Norwich. As the title suggests, most of the people in the register are men and women about to get married. A total of 285 men and 203 women described as 'of Norwich' were betrothed in Leiden. No less than 129 of these grooms or brides are recorded as being 'of Norwich' but also as living in Leiden (the actual street or neighbourhood is usually, but not always, named). These

---

132 Esser (1995), p.143.

133 In 1973 W. Tillie, city archivist at Poperinge, sent to the Norfolk Record Office a list of people returning to Leiden from Norwich between 1579 and 1614. Tillie gives his source as: Centraal Bureau voor Genealogie, Nasssaulan 18, 's-Gravenhage (Holland). Other names come from personal information given by the Leiden city archivist.

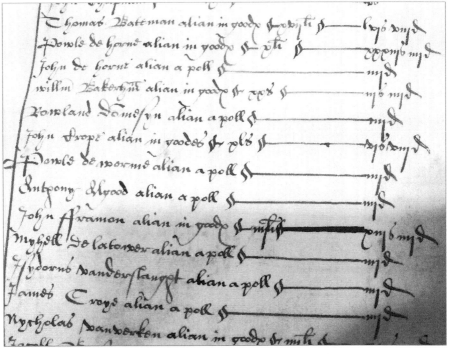

Figure 49 Thomas Bateman on the 1576 subsidy (NRO NCR 7i box 3)

people were presumably born in Norwich, but had moved to Leiden, and intended to get married there. The others recorded as 'of Norwich' but not as living in Leiden perhaps came to the town to get married. Where did they live afterwards?

The earliest marriages of Norwich people occur in the register in the 1590s, for example:

> 1590, Judit van der Bosse of Norwich betrothed to Pieter de Bruijne of Hontschote in Flanders.

> 1592, Moyses Draet of Norwich betrothed to Cathalina Coens of Hazebrock in Flanders.

Later examples include two sisters from the Norwich community who went to Leiden for their betrothals in 1615 and 1619. Susanna Bailgey was betrothed there to Isaac Giljon of Frankendael in 1615, Lijsbeth Bailliju to Jan Jacob Druiff of Leiden in 1619. Each was accompanied by their mother, Cathelijne de la Cluse.

Leiden was in the independent Dutch-speaking north. Indeed, the southern provinces, from where most Walloons came, were still controlled by the Spanish, and Calvinism was still not tolerated. However, many French-speaking people moved to Leiden from the south, and there was a Walloon church there. Fourteen people born in Norwich chose to get married in the Leiden Walloon church rather than the Dutch church favoured by all the others crossing the sea to get betrothed. These 14 marriages involved four partners from Leiden, and others originally from the southern provinces: three from Valenciennes, for example, and others from Carpy and Dyle in Artois, and Memen and Tourgoign in Flanders. These Walloon couples, with one partner from Norwich and the other from the southern provinces, presumably settled in Leiden.

Most of the people from Norwich in the Leiden register were either getting married or acting as witnesses to a marriage. Three other groups are included in the document people who became citizens, the victims of inquests, and criminals. All include a small number from Norwich.

Some 32 Norwich-born people chose to become citizens of Leiden between 1600 and 1629, and thus committed themselves to long-term residency. The 30 men had a wide range of occupations, with textile work, especially say drapery, predominating. Other occupations included one schoolmaster, two tobacco merchants, one glass maker and one mirror maker: occupations that, apart from the first, do not show up in any Norwich record. The records do not mention wives and children, but at least some of the men presumably had families. The two women who became citizens in their own right were Anna Couwen and Hester Creckels, who both became citizens of Leiden in 1601. One of Hester's guarantors was her brother Michael, presumably already a citizen. Anna married Claes Tevele of Ypres in Leiden the following year.

Two Norwich men were the subject of inquests, both being found dead from severe injuries. They were Daniel Poleij in 1611 and Aeron de Hoge in 1618. Both were presumably long-term residents of Leiden as both had married there several years before their deaths.

Eight people 'of Norwich' were convicted of crimes, usually theft, in Leiden between 1592 and 1637. They included two women, Debora Raes (smuggling and drawing beer on which no duty had been paid), and Elsje Thomas (giving shelter to beggars and suspicious persons). All eight were banished for terms varying from a year to life. It is not known whether any returned to Norwich after their banishment from Leiden.

Other places in the Dutch Republic

The Leiden records mention 13 people in the Stranger community who were born in Norwich but living in places in the Low Countries other than Leiden at the time they went to that city to get betrothed. These must just represent just a small sample of people whose parents had moved to Norwich, but who chose to return to their homeland. None of the 13 had moved to the southern provinces, still under Spanish control, but they were scattered through the northern provinces, now the Dutch Republic, where their form of religion was that of the state. Three were in Amsterdam, and two each in Rotterdam, Harlem in North Holland and Vlissingen in Zeeland. One person each came from Delft, Den Haag, Zutphen in Gilderland, and Langeraar and Korteraar in South Holland.

Burn quotes Roger Coke's *Second Discourse in Taste*, published in 1670:

Coke tells us that in 1636 or 1637, 140 families out of Norfolk and Suffolk settled in Leiden, Alkmaer and other parts of Holland and established woollen manufactories. They were welcomed by the Dutch, who exempted them from excise, and from payments of house rent for seven years.[134]

Ketton-Cremer thinks that about 500 people left the city of Norwich alone because of the persecutions of Archbishop Laud and Bishop Wren. However, he notes that these were not necessarily Dutch or Walloon immigrants or their descendants returning 'home' – 'in such lists as survive of those who left Norfolk for Holland or New England in these years, there are very few French or Dutch names'. Indeed, Wren when defending himself, claimed that most of the emigrants went for economic rather than religious reasons: 'it was generally reported in Norwich, that they could have fifteen shillings in Holland, for work which here yielded not ten shillings.[135]

Some no doubt were immigrants, or their descendants, going 'home', and there is some archaeological evidence in support of this. One pit on Botolph Street contained far more Low Country wares than would be expected – two dated vessels of 1614 and 1625, with other material down to about 1640. Perhaps these were discarded items of a family of Strangers who returned home in about 1640.[136]

Records of people applying for permission to travel to the Low Countries in the 1630s show how intermixed the populations of the two sides of the North Sea had become, as the following examples show. James Baxter, a 40-year-old weaver 'of Norwich', had been born and now lived in Leiden, and had come on a visit to Norwich to see friends. Sarah Walbanke of Norwich was the wife of William Walbanke, who was living in Rotterdam, and wanted to move to be with him. Rachel Gooch was making the opposite move – she wanted to go to Amsterdam and fetch her possessions as she and her husband now lived in Norwich. The prize for toughness must go to Margaret Vawe of Norwich, a widow apparently travelling alone, who wanted to move to Leiden. She was 80 years old.

Other places in Europe

Some of the Leiden betrothals involve one partner from Norwich and one from another European country:

Janetgen Leper of Norwich and Pierre Noyer, spinner, of Abbeville, France, 1605.

Mary Persy of Norwich and Pierre de Thotijs, shoemaker, of Spain, 1611.

Samuel Schoneclays of Norwich, twisterer, and Maertgen Honts of Emden, Germany, 1613.

Susanna Pieters of Norwich and Laurens Besoet of Bremen, Germany, 1621.

Judith Verschoore of Norwich and Wessel van Hulffet, fustian worker, of Wessel, Germany, 1624.

---

134 J. S. Burn, *History of the French Walloon, Dutch and other Protestant refugees settled in England* (1846), p. 71.

135 R. W. Ketton-Cremer, *Norfolk in the Civil War* (1969), pp. 73–9.

136 D. H. Evans and Malcolm Atkin, *East Anglian Archaeology*, vol. 100, pp. 244–5.

Figure 50 Norwich citizen enjoying his pet canaries, a hobby taken from the sixteenth-century immigrants (NRO N/LM 2)

These betrothals indicate that Leiden was at the heart of a European-wide diaspora of one-time refugees from the Spanish Netherlands, now able to return, thanks to regime change, to a free Dutch Republic.

The New World

For other people, even the move from Norwich to Leiden was just one stage in their life journey. François Cooke and Esther Mahieu were betrothed in Leiden in 1603. They lived in Norwich, moving back to Leiden in 1606: they were admitted to communion there on 1 January 1608. They had several children, but it is not known whether any of them were born in Norwich. In 1620 François and their eldest son John travelled to the New World on the *Mayflower*. Three years later Esther followed, bringing their other children. The Pilgrim Fathers – who sailed to America from Leiden – included at least two other people who had been born in Norwich and later moved to Leiden: Desire Minter and William Holbeck (although Desire appears to have returned to England after a year or two).

Jan Jehan, a brewer's mate from Norwich, was living in Rotterdam in 1614. In that year he became betrothed to and married Sara Kaire, also from England, in Leiden. The couple also moved to the New World, arriving in Plymouth in 1623.

Moving elsewhere in Britain

As we have seen there were close links between the communities within Britain, and a good deal of movement between them, some only temporary but some permanent. Many Norwich immigrant family had business interests, and in some cases owned property, in London, for example.

Returns of Strangers in London do not name people who have moved from Norwich as one stage in their journey, but they do record those aliens living in London but born in Norwich. The 1593 headcount mentions one family and two other individuals. The family is that of Jane Buskyn, with her five children aged between 11 and 24, all born in Norwich. Jane is said to have been born in Armentières, to be the widow of Jacob Buskyn, and to have lived in England for 25 years. Norwich documents add to our knowledge of this family. Jacob Buskyn is in the 1568 census: a wealthy man, he arrived in England in 1567 with his wife, two children, two servants and a maidservant. The family lived in St Mary Coslany. Buskyn paid tax on wealth of £8 in 1576, and clearly prospered in his new environment – his recorded wealth of £24 in 1581, three times that of any other alien. Clearly the family later moved to London; we do not know whether this was before or after Jacob's death.

The only two other Norwich-born aliens in London in 1593 were the 9-year-old son of box-maker Peter and Margaret Mansprey, Peter himself having been born in Bruges and having lived in England for 22 years, and Nathaniel Michelle, merchant, of whom no further details are given.

By 1635 there were many more second-generation incomers. Examples of Norwich-born aliens in London in returns of 1635 include Nathaniel Letten, working as a servant to Francis Sayon, merchant, and John Cocke and Elias Wacker, no occupations given, living on what is now Shoreditch High Street. Marriage would have been a common cause of movement among the immigrant community, as in the case of Elizabeth Morrelus, Norwich-born wife of London merchant Peter Morrelus, himself born in The Hague ('s-Gravenhage). The clerk making out the return wrote down her birthplace as she pronounced it, NORRIDGE. Was this because of a Norfolk accent or a Dutch intonation?

The London Dutch Church Book contains certificates from the Norwich congregation to the London congregation vouching for people moving to the capital. There were ten of these between 1611 and 1616, including Tobias de Hem in 1612 and his sister Esther four years later. Tobias came back to Norwich, so these moves were not always permanent, but Esther's might have been, as she moved with her husband, Jan Libaert. There are many other cases of movement between immigrant communities: for example, at least 77 Strangers are known to have gone from Sandwich to Norwich between 1565 and 1603.[137]

There are several marriages recorded in the Leiden registers where one partner is from Norwich and the other from one of the other English communities (not counting the 27 marriages where both parties are from Norwich): 23 marriages feature one party from Norwich and one from Colchester, and 20 marriages have one from Norwich and the other from Sandwich. There are smaller numbers for the other English communities – five from London, four from Canterbury and three from Great Yarmouth.

Other towns might also take an interest in the skills that the Norwich immigrants possessed. In 1601 the Royal Burghs of Scotland head-hunted three Walloon cloth-makers then living in Norwich, Gabriel Byshopp, Nicholas Wandebrok and Philip

---

137 Raingard Esser, *The Norwich Strangers and the Sandwich Connection: The second Pauline Leith lecture* (1992), pp. 67–81. There is a copy of this on the Norfolk Record Office bookshelves.

Wermont. They agreed to move to Edinburgh with their looms and their servants to make 'all sorts of stuffs'. They were to train master craftsmen in Edinburgh in these skills, for which they were paid 3,000 'Scottish pounds', and were to be free of rates and taxes for ten years from their arrival in Edinburgh.

Staying on and merging in

There are also plenty of examples of immigrants marrying English men and women, and settling down. Even in the 1568 census there are a small number of examples among the Walloons: Nicholas Carron had an English wife, and Jean Grand had a wife from London (nationality not stated).

As early as 19 November 1569 Joisus de Frese, otherwise Foiedham Defrese, stranger, married Norwich-born Mary Maynard in St George Tombland. He is not in the 1568 census, so presumably came to the city after May 1568. This could have been a whirlwind romance, but he might have lived in England before he came to Norwich. A few such marriages can be found in Church of England marriage registers in the last years of the sixteenth century, for example:

Samuel Dryebread 'son of a Dutchman' and Agnes Byrde, St Michael at Plea, 1589.

William Scot, English, and Christian Hoot, Dutch, All Saints, 1598.

George Balie and Ann Custinole 'a Dutch widow', All Saints, 1599.

Naturally some of these 'mixed' couples had children, such as Samuel and Anne Dryebread, baptised at St Michael at Plea in 1590 and 1592, and Ayla and Abraham Scot, baptised in All Saints church in 1599 and 1600. These children are among the earliest examples of that merging of the incomer community with the native-born community, which is often said to have given Norwich people their unique character.

Letters from the Norwich Dutch consistory to its London counterpart refer to other cases of marriage, or less regularised relationships. In 1579 Moddaert Trioen, a Norwich Dutch Stranger, was accused of abandoning his wife and being involved with other women including English women. In 1587 Charles van Werven married 'Jacqemyne N' in an English church; in 1589 a Dutch man married an English woman. Other Dutch were also said to be 'secretly' marrying English partners. Another irregular union was recorded in the Mayor's Court Book in February 1581: Dorothy Thornton, an English woman, confessed that she had had sex with Charles Heck, alien bay weaver, in Chapel Field on the previous Sunday. The court decided that were Dorothy to have a baby, then Heck would have to pay for its upbringing.

The 1622 Return of Strangers contains just one 'mixed race' entry: William Emperor was said to have a Stranger father and an English mother. By this time marriages between immigrants or their children and English people were common. They are best recorded among the richer elements in the city, such as Mallyard Ridoot's daughter Debora, who married Englishman Richard Puckle. Several members of the de Hem family married English partners, as we saw in Chapter 6.

Other signs of integration included the purchase of property in the city, already discussed, and the taking-up of civic office. One of the first was Peter van Hove, constable in 1619. Other second-generation immigrants holding office included John Vannixon, collector as early as 1609 and constable in 1628, and John Vanrockingham in 1628. Like several Englishmen, some members of the incomer community were prepared to pay *not* to have to serve, such as John Wittewrongle of St Michael Coslany, who paid 40s in 1642 rather than serve as constable.

Higher office came later – James Denewin was sheriff of Norwich in 1665, and Isaac Decele in 1668. The Philippos also held office at this date: Onias was collector in 1650, Elisha between 1650 and 1656. In 1665 (a plague year) he was granted dispensation from city offices in return for building a pest-yard, and in 1672 he paid the large sum of £100 for dispensation from all city offices. He also rose high in the county hierarchy, being appointed sheriff of Norfolk in 1675.

The de Hague family also achieved prominence in city life. Elisha de Hague was baptised in the Walloon church in 1677, at a time when few children were being baptised there. His father John was an active member of the congregation, serving as deacon in 1674 and politic man in the following year; his daughter married the French church minister Jaques le Franc. One of his sons, also Elisha, was speaker of the Common Council for 20 years and town clerk for 18 years. He died in 1792 aged 74. His son, yet another Elisha, succeeded his father as town clerk and held the post until 1826. There are portraits of both in the Castle Museum collections, and family monuments in St Augustine's church, where they worshipped by the later eighteenth century.

A very small number of immigrants chose to go all the way and make themselves English subjects. The most complete way of doing this was to have an Act of Parliament passed stating that the person was now an English subject, with full rights, and the rights descending to their children. This was a very expensive undertaking and not one often taken on. One Norwich incomer who did this was Peter Verbeck (see Chapter 6). It was much cheaper to obtain from the central authorities a letter of denization, which gave some rights, including that of owning property, but not the full rights of an English subject. One of the 30 original invitees who did this was Thomas Bateman, although it does not appear to have prevented him from returning to Ypres within a few years. The records do not usually show where those taking out such letters lived, but some of the denizations are of names familiar in Norwich, such as van Ixem, George Fenn and later Jaques de Hem. Joos de Ram obtained a letter of denization as early as 1566; five years later his position as a leader of the Dutch church in Norwich was challenged, and 'because he was a denizen, he was rejected'.[138]

Only those born abroad needed to take out letters to become denizens. This is why the various headcounts of incomers usually noted whether or not the children of incomers were abroad or in England. Those born in England of foreign parents had more rights, but even they did not enjoy all the rights of those born in the country 'of English blood'.

A more informal way of becoming part of the English community was in the

138 Stephen S. Slaughter, *The Dutch Church in Norwich* (1933), p. 26.

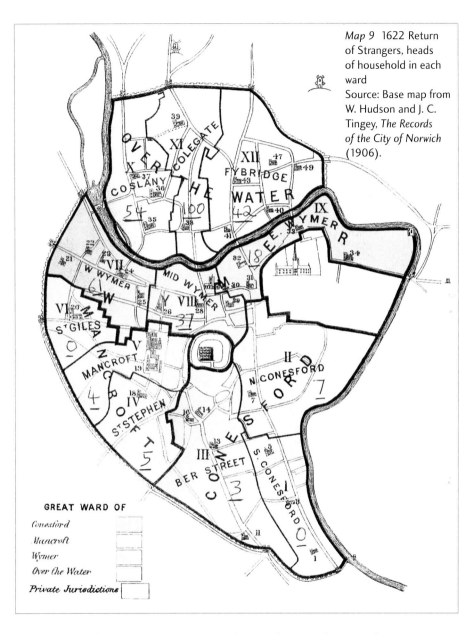

Map 9 1622 Return of Strangers, heads of household in each ward
Source: Base map from W. Hudson and J. C. Tingey, *The Records of the City of Norwich* (1906).

anglicisation of names. Some were simply translations; de Brune became Brown, Faber or Smedt became Smith, Pieter Vertegans became Peter Rottengoose. Other names were just made more English-sounding, Jansen becoming Johnson, Douvert becoming Dover. Two more examples are cited by Fell: Ten Heural became Hovell and Du Rieu became Durye.[139]

---

139 Fell (1975), p. 24.

The freemen's records also show how a name may become anglicised over the generations. Two aliens, William and Francis de Keyser, were admitted to the freedom as curriers in 1591 and 1598 respectively. They were probably descendants of the William and Jan Keyser who had come over from Brabant in 1567. A generation later the name has become Dekeyser alias Emperor: a son Francis was admitted to the freedom under this name in 1626. By 1635 the 'de Keyser' element of the name had been forgotten: a freeman employing an apprentice in that year is simply called William Emperor. By this date, very many Norwich families must already have had immigrants among them, and the opinion held by many Norwich people today that they have 'Stranger' ancestry is likely in many cases to be true.

Chapter 9

The Huguenots

The origins of the word Huguenot are not known, perhaps the most likely theory being that it comes from the German word Eidgenosse, meaning 'a confederate'. This became Eignot in Swiss German and Huguenot in French.[140]

As has been said, some authorities regard the French-speaking refugees from the Spanish Netherlands as Huguenots, in which case all the references to Walloons in earlier chapters can be taken to refer to Huguenots. One problem is the fluid nature of country boundaries. Many of the Walloons came from places like Lille and Armentières, which most readers would think of as being in France, as they have been since the French took them from Spain in the second half of the seventeenth century. Both the French and the Spanish persecuted Protestants. So a Calvinist fleeing from Spanish persecution in Lille in the 1560s would be called a Walloon, and his Calvinist great-grandson fleeing from French persecution in the same city a century later would be called a Huguenot.

Restricting the word Huguenot to mean refugees from the kingdom of France, the records show a small number of such incomers to Norwich. The 1568 census included Renatus Soneau from France, a wool-comber, who arrived in England with his wife and two children in 1568. The 1571 headcount included an unnamed French man from Dieppe who had arrived in Norwich between late March and October of that year. Marriages in the Norwich Walloon church in the early seventeenth century include that of Jacob Groma, who according to the church register was born at Tiny in France. The small trickle of new blood could have kept the Walloon church in Norwich fresher than the Dutch congregation: 'The fact that Walloons were joined by French emigres at different periods during the seventeenth century served to emphasise their continued separateness, the symbol of which was their membership of the Walloon church.'[141]

An edict of January 1562 offered Protestants the right to meet and worship, but violent reactions followed, as at Sens in April 1562 and Toulouse the following month. Then came the Massacre of St Bartholomew on 24 August 1572. About 8,000 Protestants were murdered in Paris, and at least that number in other towns. After the massacre, 'crowds of panic-stricken fugitives from Dieppe began to arrive at Rye on 27 August with harrowing details of their sufferings, and the news spread like wildfire through England'.[142]

---

140 Noel Currer-Briggs and Royston Gambier, *Huguenot Ancestry* (1985), p. 4 favours this derivation, but suggests other possibilities.
141 Vane (1984), p.138.
142 J. B. Black, *The Reign of Elizabeth 1558–1603* (1959 edn), p. 159.

There was civil war, with attempts at compromise like the Peace of Beaulieu in 1576, and the Peace of Bergerac in 1577, providing only temporary respite. In 1598 the Edict of Nantes was issued. This allowed both Protestants and Roman Catholics equal status and freedom of worship in France, and the Huguenots no longer needed to flee. However, the Catholics were always by far the larger group. and life became increasingly difficult for French Protestants in their home country throughout the seventeenth century. By 1600 the French Protestants made up only about 5 or 6 per cent of the total population, and were concentrated mainly in the south. They suffered further losses in a concentrated Catholic campaign, and La Rochelle was besieged from 1628. An Anglo-Dutch relief expedition failed, and the city fell in 1629, leading to more refugees. Persecutions included the *dragonnades*, mounted troops forcing the Protestants to accept the Roman Catholic religion or face death.

As with the Dutch and Walloon refugees, a Huguenot family might originally flee to England, most commonly London, and move to Norwich later, perhaps after many years, or even several generations. Ninham's Court in Norwich is named after a family of painters who lived there in the eighteenth and nineteenth centuries. The most famous of them was Henry Ninham, who was a member of the Norwich School of Art, and who painted very English pictures of Norwich, mainly of its buildings. Ninham was from a refugee family: his ancestor had fled from the St Bartholomew's Day Massacre. Another Norwich family with a similar tradition was the de Carles. The first known reference to the family is to John de Carle, apprenticed to a dyer in the city in 1629. The marquis de Carle is said to have been head of a Protestant family who owned a chateau not far from Bordeaux. He was murdered in the Massacre, but a nephew, François, escaped to England and reached Colchester in 1573. John could be his son or grandson. In view of the links between the Norwich and Colchester communities this not improbable, but it remains speculation.[143]

Several of the pastors at the Norwich Walloon church were Huguenot refugees. Jean Marie, pastor at Lion-sur-Mer in France, fled to England after the Massacre of St Bartholomew. He was sent to Norwich to be the minister there in about 1572. He died in about 1593. Nicholas Basnage, a native of Normandy and minister at Evreux, also fled to England at the time of St Bartholomew's Massacre, settling in London. He was sent to Norwich to assist Mare in 1585. When Marie died Basnage claimed he had the right to succeed him as minister, but this led to a dispute within the French church. Basnage was in Norwich until 1597, when he returned to Normandy. Pierre de Laune was minister from 1601 to 1656: his father William came from Normandy, having fled to England in or before 1582. Pierre himself was born at Latrie.

As pressures in France increased, one group of Huguenot refugees landed at Great Yarmouth in September 1681, and came to Norwich 'in a distressed condition', intending to make for London. There were 13 of them: Lewis Rossel, Simon St Amand, their wives and four children, James Gabert, Stephen le Fevre, Magdalen Meunie, Nicholl du Plessier and Susan Briand. On 17 September the Mayor's Court gave them £3 and sent them on their way.

---

143   NRO ETN 1/23/26, 28: notes on de Carle family history.

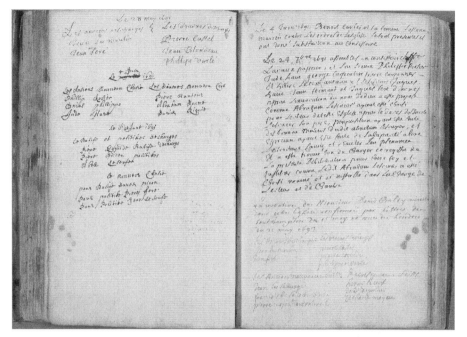

Figure 51 French Church book, with Martineau entries (NRO FC 29/17)

In 1685 Louis revoked the Edict of Nantes, while exiling all Protestant pastors and at the same time forbidding the laity to leave France. To the surprise of the government many did leave, often at great risk to themselves. Men who were caught, if not executed, were sent as galley slaves to the French fleet in the Mediterranean. Women were imprisoned, and their children sent to convents. About 300,000 Huguenots left France, settling in non-Catholic Europe: the Netherlands, Germany, especially Prussia, Switzerland, Scandinavia, and even as far away as Russia. About 50,000 came to England. There are many inhabitants of these islands who have Huguenot blood in their veins, whether or not they still bear one of the hundreds of French names of those who took refuge here.

Many thousands fled; how many came to Norwich is not known. Moens thought that only a few Huguenot families settled in Norwich; however, John James thought there were many. Penny Corfield sums up the situation: 'There is some uncertainty about the number of Huguenots that eventually settled in Norwich ... at a guess, they numbered some 100 to 200 individuals.'[144]

At least two of the exiled clergymen came to Norwich. **Pierre Chauvin**, former minister at Veillevigne near Nantes, took refuge in England, and was appointed to the Norwich French church on 21 January 1684. He was ordained in the Anglican church,

---

144 Penny Corfield, 'A provincial capital in the late seventeenth century: the case of Norwich', in Peter Clark (ed.), *The Early Modern Town* (1976), p. 239. She cites J. James, *History of the Worsted Manufacture in England* (1857), p. 166.

Figure 52
Memorial tablet to
the Boileau family in
Tacolneston church.
Source: *Norfolk
Archaeology* vol. 3
(1852) opp. p. 299.

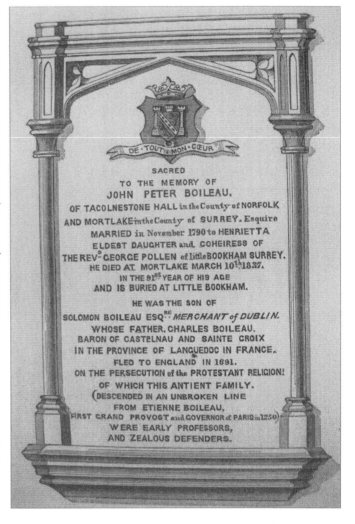

frequently attended Anglican services, and had four children baptised in the Anglican parish church of St Michael at Plea. In 1686 he wrote to the bishop of Norwich claiming that the Walloon church in Norwich had been in disarray for the past 60 years – they had no discipline, they allowed Quakers to attend their services – and the church leaders were depriving him of some of the income he had been promised when he was invited to Norwich to take up the position. **Pierre le Caux**, a refugee minister from Castre, was appointed to the Norwich church in 1689.

Huguenot families that did come to the city included the Colombine, Martineau and Boileau families. The first two are discussed in Chapter 10. The Boileaus are less well known. Charles Boileau, born in Nimes, fled from France to Holland in 1685, and took refuge in England in 1701. He met his wife while he was in Holland. Their descendants came to Norfolk in the nineteenth century, and John Peter Boileau (Charles' grandson) lived at Ketteringham Hall – and helped preserve the Roman fort at Burgh Castle for posterity. There is a Boileau Close in Tuckswood: how many of its residents know that the name is that of a refugee family welcomed into England over three centuries ago?

Other Huguenots included the le Noirs. Abraham le Noir was one of the politic

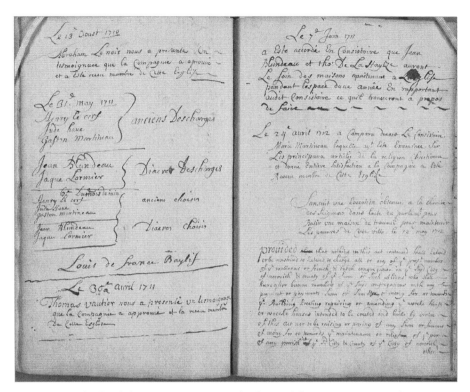

Figure 53 French Church book – appointments of elders and deacons (NRO FC 29/17)

men in 1707–9, and a city bailiff in 1713–14. He had seven children baptised in the French church between 1686 and 1702, including three called Jenne and two called Timothy. Jean le Monnier of Norwich married Francoise Pierre in Martin's Lane French church in London in 1703. Pierre le Monnier 'anglice Miller' was baptised in the Norwich French church in Norwich on 30 June 1752 (his is the last entry in the French church register). Names could soon become anglicised: Pierre and David le Monnier are described as 'le Monnier or Miller' when their children were baptised in the French church, and later generations simply became Miller.

Several watch or clock makers are known to have had Huguenot origins. Thomas Amyott came to Norwich at the revocation of the Edict of Nantes in 1685, settling in St Peter Mancroft parish. He was a watch and clock maker, as were several later members of the family. Lucas de Caux is said to have come to London from France in about 1693, and to have moved to Norwich in 1704. The family used both the French church and the Anglican parish church of St Michael at Plea, three family members being baptised in the former between 1704 and 1724, and one in the latter in 1707. The parish register records that Esther de Caux, widow, was buried in the French church on 24 January 1730/1, and Lucas de Caux on 8 March 1730/1. Matthew Juler, born 1756, clockmaker in Norwich, was the son of John Juler of North Walsham, born 1712, who was himself supposedly the son of a Huguenot refugee who had arrived in North Walsham in 1686.

Another Norwich family said to have Huguenot origins is the de Carles. We have seen that one branch traces its origin to the time of the Massacre of St Bartholomew. Another relates to the Revocation of the Edict of Nantes. Family tradition tells a romantic tale:

> 1685 having brought renewed persecution of the Protestants, the Dragonards pursued two young sons of the Comte de Carle of Castillion. They escaped to the sea, one was drowned, but the other was rescued by a London fishing boat and landed upon a London wharf. He was making a precarious living by standing outside a hotel, blacking shoes and running errands. One day, Robert Brettingham, a wealthy Norwich builder, who was staying at this hotel, noticed the boy and realised he was no ordinary lad. As he spoke French he learnt his history and offered to take him to Norwich and teach him his business. John de Carle was only too glad to accept, and his story had a romantic ending as he eventually married his master's daughter, Elizabeth.'[145]

Whatever the truth of this, the de Carles were working for several generations as stone-masons in St John Maddermarket in the later eighteenth and nineteen centuries: there is a family memorial in the parish church. Their work included church monuments, some of the Norwich bridges, and the Quaker Meeting House in Goat Lane in Norwich. Catherine de Carle married Joseph Smith in St John Maddermarket in 1810, and this family became prominent in the city, with one member becoming mayor in the later nineteenth century. Another branch of the family lived at Bury St Edmunds.

As we have already seen, several Huguenot families did not come directly to Norfolk after the Edict of Nantes, but later descendants did establish themselves in the area. They included Rochemont Barbauld: his grandfather Ezekiel had been smuggled out of France in a barrel in 1685. Ezekiel came to England, becoming minister to a chapel in Plymouth, and later serving several London churches. His son Theophilus was born in London, and later returned to Europe, when he became a palace chaplain in Cassel. Rochemont, his son, was born there in about 1750, moving to London in 1762 or 1763, and later to Warrington. Rochemont was a frequent visitor to Norwich in the 1770s: he founded a school at Palgrave in Suffolk, and preached at the Octagon Chapel.

The Barbaulds and the Martineaus were linked. When Guillaume Martineau joined the French church in Norwich in 1722, he brought with him a certificate from Ezekiel Barbauld, as one of the ministers of the Huguenot church of London. Thomas Martineau (later the father of James and Harriet Martineau) was one of the first pupils at Barbauld's Palgrave school.

Many of these refugees came through a very dangerous escape adventure, just like many refugees today, for example Paul Turquand and his wife Marie, a member of the Martineau family. Paul Turquand was born in Poitou and married Madelaine

---

145 NRO ETN 1/23/26, 28.

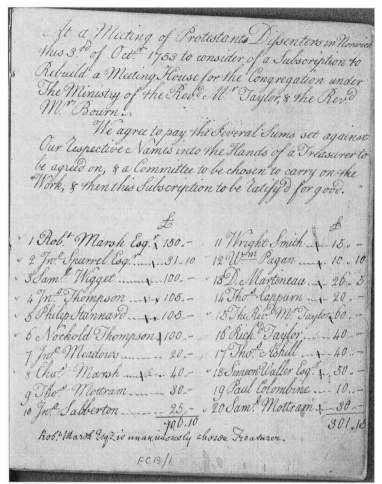

Figure 54
David
Martineau
and Paul
Colombine
contribute to
the building
of the
Octagon
Chapel
(NRO FC
13/1)

Martineau of Chauvigny. They decided to flee, placed their four children with friends and tried to reach a seaport. They travelled by night for three days, and then split up, Paul heading for Nantes and Madelaine for La Rochelle.

Madelaine took three weeks to reach La Rochelle. Once there, she managed to find an English captain to take her on board. The ship was searched but they did not find her. The ship then sailed for Plymouth, where Madelaine settled. While there she learned the art of making an article called 'shags'. Paul was apprehended at Nantes, imprisoned and tortured, and only released when he was unable to walk. It took him six months to recover from his beating. Eventually he managed to escape to Holland and from there he made his way to London. He hoped to find his wife there, but there was no trace of her. Neither knew what had happened to the other, and it was three years before they were reunited by pure chance: Paul met a traveller from Plymouth who knew his wife there. Eventually the couple were reunited in London, and their children were able to escape and join their parents. Paul died in Spitalfields in 1743, aged 76.

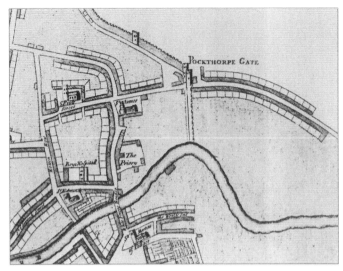

Map 10
The suburb of Pockthorpe, as shown on Cleer's map of 1696

Many Norwich people know that the Assembly House includes rooms named after the Noverre family: for many years there was a Noverre Cinema. Although not part of the diaspora of the 1680s, the Noverres were another family of Protestants from France. Augustin Noverre came from France to London in 1755, and later settled in Norwich. He first came to the city after he wrongly thought he had killed a man in an affray in London. He was able to go back to London later, but finally settled in Norwich in 1797. The family worshipped at St Stephen's church in Norwich, and three generations are remembered there: Augustin, died 1805, Francis, died 1840, and Frank, died 1878.

In terms of religion, the situation in Norwich for those of the Protestant faith had changed since the sixteenth century. There were now many churches of all kinds that the incomers could join. Language may have led some of the incomers to the French church for a while, but many found their spiritual homes in other Nonconformist, or even Anglican, churches in the city. The so-called French church in Norwich was very much the church of the French speakers from the Low Countries. A small number of Huguenot families did join their worship at least for a time, but it was never a Huguenot church in the way that 'French' churches in London were. The Martineau family and Colombine family both have plaques (put up by descendants) in St Mary the Less recording that they did worship there, but in fact they soon went elsewhere, some Martineaus and Colombines to the Unitarian Octagon Chapel (which both families helped pay for), other Colombines to the Anglican church of Saints Simon and Jude.

Even at the height of Huguenot immigration, numbers of worshippers at the French church remained small. Just a dozen men signed the Norwich Church Book of Discipline in the 1690s. Five of these signed in 1690: Jean de Moullin, Henry le Cerse (who actually made his mark rather than signing, the only one of the dozen who was unable to write his name), Jean Fere, Jean Fremoult and John de Cleve. Another seven signed in 1693 and the years immediately following: Francis Lacolombine, Gaston Martineau, Augustin de Cleve, Jaques Fere, Jean de la Haize, James Lorier and Thomas

Figure 55
Mulberry tree planted outside St Mary the Less to commemorate its links with the Huguenot community: sadly, the tree does not survive. Photo by the author.

de la Haize. Many of these were clearly recent incomers, but others may have been descendants of the Walloon incomers of the previous century.

Half a century later, by the middle of the eighteenth century, the French church was in terminal decline. Monsieur Vallotton became pastor in 1739, at which time, he recorded, the church had just 25 members. By 1750 death had reduced the number to 12, several of whom were elderly, as he noted. The 12 were 'The widow Miller, old; her sister Esther Miller, old; John de Cleve, old; Thomas Loquine, old, and his wife; Abraham Pigney and his wife; Peter Colombine and his wife; David Miller; Peter Miller; Paul Colombine'. Other descendants of the Huguenots had gone elsewhere to worship.

One link between the older Walloon community and the recent Huguenot incomers is supplied by Onias Philippo. In May 1682 he hired a house at Pockthorpe where he employed a company of Frenchmen, presumably Huguenots, who came to the city from Ipswich. However this aroused the local populace to anger, no doubt because they felt their jobs were being taken. They stormed the house and drove the French out. One Frenchwoman was so badly beaten that she died two or three days later. According to the report in the Calendar of State Papers, the English in Norwich thought the incomers were a troop of Papists masquerading as Protestants.[146]

Although these incomers were not welcome in Norwich, the French linen manufactory at Ipswich appears to have been quite large and to have lasted quite a long time. A letter to the bishop of Norwich in 1686 refers to a proposed fund to support it:

> a sum of 2 or 3 thousand pounds will settle the manufacture for ever, and employ not only the French that are now in Ipswich but any others who will come to work in the same manufacture, except some such cause be taken the French now in Ipswich will want work before the end of this summer and consequently will leave the town.

146 *Calendar of State Papers Domestic* 1683, p. 363.

Ipswich at least appreciated the worth of the incomers; some people in Norwich were not supportive. In 1690 the French weavers in the city complained to Parliament that they were being harassed by informers who claimed that they were breaking the rules on apprenticeships, just the same complaint that had been made against the Walloons and Dutch incomers 80 years earlier.[147]

The Huguenots are commonly said to have introduced silk weaving to England. If so, it was a revival, as we have seen references to silk among the sixteenth-century wave of immigrants. Keith Wrightson says that Huguenot refugees established silk weaving at London and Canterbury but does not mention Norwich. Burn wrote that 'they improved to a much higher degree of perfection the fabricating of silks', which is probably a correct assessment.[148]

It was an earlier Huguenot who brought the mulberry tree to Norwich. In 1609 Francois de Verton (known as the seigneur de La Foret) travelled through England selling mulberry trees from his tree nursery in the Languedoc. He was in Norwich for eight days, and certainly sold some trees while in the city, even if, as Joan Thirsk notes, he 'distributed a little more than half the number he hoped'.[149]

The Huguenots also introduced *crape*, a new type of very fine, twisted and crimped silk gauze designed specifically for mourning. This became so associated with the city that it was generally called 'Norwich crape'. Penny Corfield calls it 'the one new fabric developed in this period. It was made of worsted, or of mixed worsted and silk, and was a very light and fine material. It was retailed at under twenty-five shillings the piece. When first introduced, the crape had an immediate fashionable success.'[150]

Huguenots, like any immigrant group, enriched the community in which they settled by bringing their own ways of living and working. As well as silk weaving, they are said to have introduced oxtail soup to Britain, and to have enjoyed fine pastries and high-quality coffee and tea. The very word refugee, so often (sadly) heard on the news these days, is itself a Huguenot word!

The writer W. G. Sebald, himself an immigrant to Norwich, summed up the Huguenot achievement:

> Following the revocation of the Edict of Nantes by Louis XIV, more than fifty thousand Huguenots fled to England, many of whom, experienced in breeding silkworms as in the fabrication of silk stuffs – craftsman and merchant families such as the Lefevres and the Tilletes, the De Hagues, the Martineaus and the Columbines – settled in Norwich, at that time the second largest city in England, where since the early sixteenth century there had been a colony of about five thousand Flemish and Walloon weavers. By 1750, a bare two generations later, the Huguenot master weavers of Norwich had risen to become the wealthiest, most influential and cultivated class of entrepreneurs in the entire kingdom. In their factories, and those of their suppliers, there was the greatest

---

147 Quoted in *The East Anglian or Notes and Queries,* new series, vol. 11 (1905–6), pp. 21–2.
148 Keith Wrightson, *Earthly Necessities: Economic lives in early modern Britain* (2000), p. 167; Burn (1846), p. 17.
149 Thirsk (1997), p. 124.
150 Corfield (1976), p. 248.

imaginable commotion, day in, day out, and it is said in a history of silk manufacture in England that a traveller approaching Norwich under the black sky of a winter night would be amazed by the glare over the city, caused by light coming from the workshops, still busy at this late hour.[151]

---

151 W. G. Sebald, *The Rings of Saturn* (first trans. into English 1998).

Chapter 10

Some Huguenot families

The Martineau family

Gaston Martineau, from Bergeret, Perigord, France, was a surgeon who fled persecution in France. According to his (much later) memorial in St Mary the Less he left France in 1685. He was certainly living in London by 1693: he was made free denizen of England by warrant of 25 March 1693, and in that year married Marie Pierre in the French Protestant Church in Spitalfields. She was also a refugee, and had come from Dieppe, according to tradition escaping on the same boat as Gaston. He settled in Norwich in 1693, taking the oath necessary to practise as a doctor in the city in 1695. His sister Mary also came to Norwich, and married an Englishman, Edward Pope, in St Peter Hungate church in 1699.

Gaston's eldest daughter Marie, who had been born in London, married Pierre de

Figure 56
Gaston
Martineau
subscribes to
the 39 Articles
(NRO DN/
SUB 1/1)

Columbine, from another refugee family (see below). His third son David, born in Norwich and baptised at St Michael at Plea in 1697, married an Englishwoman, Elizabeth Finch. Gaston died in 1726, and was buried in the French Church. His son, grandson and eldest great-grandson were also surgeons in the city.

Another great-grandson, Thomas, was the father of the two most famous members of the family: Harriet and James Martineau. Harriet Martineau was born in

Norwich in 1802: a plaque on a house in Magdalen Street marks her birthplace. In her early life she was a devout Unitarian, worshipping at the Octagon, as did many members of the Martineau family. She was a writer on economics and politics, becoming famous in her 30s for the stories she published as *Illustrations of Political Economy*. *Punch* referred to 'those graceful graphic stories of our dear Miss Martineau'.[152]

Harriet was also a leading

Figure 58 James Martineau
(NRO MC 201/39-44)

152   *The East Anglian,* new series, vol. 1 (1885–6), p. 55.

advocate of the abolition of slavery. She took great pride in her Huguenot ancestry, writing:

> On the occasion of the Revocation of the edict of Nantes in 1688, a surgeon of the name of Martineau, and a family of the name of Pierre, crossed the Channel, and settled with other Huguenot refugees in England. My ancestor married a young lady of the Pierre family, and settled in Norwich, where his descendants afforded a succession of surgeons up to my day. My eminent uncle, Mr Philip Meadows Martineau, and my eldest brother, who died before the age of thirty, was the last Norwich surgeon of that name. My grandfather, who was one of that honourable series, died at the age of forty-two, of a fever caught among his poor patients. He left a large family, of whom my father was the youngest.'

Harriet left Norwich in 1845 and lived in the Lake District for the last 30 years of her life, dying in 1876.

Harriet's brother James was born in 1805, also in Norwich, and attended Norwich Grammar School. He was also a devout Unitarian, and principal of Manchester New College from 1869 to 1885. He retired at the age of 70, only to start a new career as an author, writing important works of theology. He died in 1900 at 95.

Some of the family retained links with the French church. Gaston was an elder for over 20 years in the early 1700s, and a century later Philip Meadows Martineau was a deacon from 1809. In 1828, as 'sole surviving Deacon and Trustee', he appointed Henry Martineau to serve with him.

The Martineau family have given their name to the road where the Norfolk Record Office is based. Kate, the duchess of Cambridge, wife of Prince William and probable future queen of England, has a Martineau among her direct ancestors.

The Colombine family

François Jacolumbine fled from France to Norwich in 1685. He worshipped at the French Church, and his name soon changed to the more English Francis Colombine. In his will he left money to poor people helped by the French Church, some of whom were no doubt themselves Huguenot refugees. Francois Colombine married Anne, one of the daughters of Pierre le Caux: they had four children. Francois died in 1699 and was buried in St Clement. Anne outlived her husband by more than 40 years, dying in 1741: she was buried in St Michael at Plea. A monument put up in the French church by his son says that Francis came from the province of Dauphiny, and that having taken a degree abroad in early life, he practised physic in Norwich. It gives his age at death as 85, describing him as 'a man of piety, probity and learning'.

François' son Peter was born in Norwich in 1697. He was a worsted weaver by trade. In 1719 he married Marie, daughter of Gaston Martineau, an example of how second-generation immigrants often find partners within their community. The marriage took place in St Luke's chapel, Norwich Cathedral. Peter was the first Huguenot to achieve civic office, becoming a city councillor from 1733, sheriff in

Figure 59 Will of Francis Colombine, Huguenot refugee to Norwich, made in 1698 (NRO NCC WILLS)

1751, alderman from 1752 and mayor in 1755. His rise showed that it was possible for the descendants of refugees to become assimilated into their new communities within a generation. This was a much more rapid rise than the Dutch and Walloons: the first descendant of that community to be mayor appears to have been Daniel Fromanteel, mayor in 1725–8. Peter died in 1770, and was buried in the French church. Peter's children included Francis, also a city councillor, who became sheriff in 1769 and mayor in 1776.

In 1757 Francis married an English girl, Susan Mason of Yarmouth, in the church of SS Simon and Jude in Norwich, and some of their children were baptised there: 1758, Francis; 1759, Susan; 1760, Peter; 1765, Mary; 1772, Charles. Several of their children were buried in the French church, and these prove that their first two children at least were not baptised in SS Simon and Jude: 1765, Mary, aged 8; 1766, Peter, aged 6; and 1772, Charles, aged 14. Of these, only Peter was among the children baptised at SS Simon and Jude. The family were clearly in the habit of naming their latest child after one who had died.

Francis's fortunes declined in later life, and he resigned his office as alderman in 1802 because of his poverty. The Corporation granted him and his daughter an annuity of £100. Francis died 17 February 1808, aged 83. Several other members of the Colombine family held city office from the mid-eighteenth century onwards. David Colombine was a councillor from 1752, and sheriff in 1772. Francis Colombine junior was a councillor between 1787 and 1789, Paul Colombine served as a constable in 1736 and as a poor guardian in 1747–8. In contrast, the Martineaus did not hold civic office until well into the nineteenth century, with Henry Martineau serving on the council between 1819 and 1829.

Francois Colombine had been an elder at the French church from 1693. Like the Martineaus, most later members of the family worshipped in other churches, but a few retained interests in the French church. David Colombine was a deacon in 1753 and an elder from 1770, and Paul Colombine was an elder for many years from 1753.

The Aufrère family

The Aufrères were another Norfolk family with Huguenot origins: Antoine Aufrère fled to Holland after the Revocation of the Edict of Nantes. Unlike many refugees he had foreseen persecution coming and had manged to transfer much of his wealth out of France. He had married and had two sons born in France. Antoine and his family moved to London, where he died in 1701.

Israel Aufrère, Antoine's son, was a preacher in the French churches in London. He married Sarah Amsincq in Holland. He died in London in 1758 at the age of 91.

Anthony Aufrère, one of Israel's sons, was the first of the family to settle in Norfolk. He had become an Anglican clergyman and was appointed rector of Heigham in 1728. In about the same year he married Marienne de Gastine in Holland; she was herself the daughter of a refugee from France. They had two children, Susan and Anthony. Marienne died soon after the birth of her son, and Anthony (senior) married a widow, Mary Smith, through whom he inherited property in Hoveton St Peter.

Anthony (junior), born in 1730, became a prominent Norfolk landowner and magistrate. He married Anna Norris and the couple had 15 children. Their eldest child, also Anthony, was born at Hoveton in 1756. He was an antiquary and translator of works written in French and Italian. He and his family were in France in 1802, when relations between France and England broke down: he was one of many detained in France by Napoleon and was forced to stay in France with his wife and children for 11 years, first in Verdun then later in Avignon. His luck turned in 1814: he was released and his father died, so he inherited Hoveton Hall, where he settled. He died in 1833.

Two of Anthony's brothers, George and Philip, went to Norwich Grammar School. Both went to Cambridge University and became Anglican clergymen. A later Aufrère, also an Anglican clergyman, created a local scandal when he shot his maidservant in 1835, an event that led to his imprisonment in Norwich Castle gaol.

Chapter 11

Conclusion

The legacy of the incomer is everywhere in Norwich. Dutch-style gables and pantiles are reminders of their influence. Why are open spaces in the city are called Plains rather than Squares? This is a word brought over by refugees, in this case the Dutch word 'plein'. Weavers' windows, unusually large windows in attics to allow more light onto the loom, are sometimes called 'lucams', deriving from the French word 'lucarne'.

The canary, originally brought by the Dutch, became a popular pet among Norwich people, as we have seen, and this history is reflected in the badge of the city's football team, frequently seen on television.

Over 350 years ago the city sent to the central authorities a letter explaining what the Strangers had done for Norwich. I have tabulated this for the convenience of the modern reader:

Figure 60
The legacy: long windows in attics, allowing light for weavers. These are known in Norwich as 'lucams', from the French word 'lucarne'. Photo by the author.

Figure 61
The legacy: Dutch-style gables and pantiles on a house in Norwich Cathedral Close.
Photo by the author.

Figure 62
The legacy: celebrating the success of Norwich Canaries.
Photo by the author.

They have brought a great commodity, namely the making of bays, moccados, grograynes, all sorts of tufts etc, which were not made here before. Whereby they do not set on work only their own people but do also set on work our people within the city, as also a great number twenty miles about the city, to the great relief of the poorer sort there.

By their means our city is well inhabited, and decayed houses rebuilt and repaired that were in ruin, and now good rents paid for the same.

The merchants by their commodities have and may have great trade as well within the realm as without the realm, being in good estimation in all places.

Where there are a larger number of people, people are bound to trade more with each other, both in the city and with men of the country.

They contribute to all sorts of payments – taxes, subsidies, watch money, ministers' wages etc.

English people have learned to make the products the incomers make, whereby the [English] youth are set to work and kept from idleness.

They dig the ground and sow flax, and make it out in linen cloth, which sets up many people in work.

They dig and delve a great quantity of ground for root crops, which is great succour and sustenance for the poor, both for the incomers themselves and for everyone in both city and country.

They live wholly of themselves without charge, and do beg from no man, and do sustain all their own poor people.

To conclude: they for the most part fear God, do their work diligently, obey the magistrates and all ordinances, live peaceably among themselves and with all men – and we think our city happy to enjoy them.[153]

Ten things for which to thank these immigrants. Norwich has benefited – and continues to benefit – from an enormous range of incomers over the centuries. They are one of the key strands in the uniqueness of the city – the Welcome Stranger!

---

153 Domestic Papers, Eliz. Vol. 20 no. 49, cited in Rye (1887), p. 196; Moens (1887–8), p. 262. Rye says that the date 1561 has been added in pencil in a modern hand, but as he notes, this is clearly wrong – it must date from about 1577 because of its reference to the Strangers having been in Norwich for ten years.

Appendix

Tables

Table 1 1568 census totals, as given and corrected

	Dutch	Walloons
Married persons	314	64
Single, over 17	193	19
Single, under 17	461	95
Widows and widowers	52	19 ('widows')
Children born in England	112	40
Servants over 17		9
Servants under 17		3
Total as given	1,132	339
Correct total	1,480	v339

Table 2 Where the 1567–8 Dutch refugees came from

Province	Number of families
Flanders	309
Brabant	45
North Brabant	4
Zeeland	26
Holland	5
Friesland	2
Picardy	1
Not said	26

Table 3 Where the 1567–8 Walloon refugees came from

Province or town	Number of families	Province or town	Number of families
Flanders	23	Namur	2
Lille	23	Antwerp	2
Artois	9	Cambrai	1
Hainault	5	St Pol	1
Armentieres	5	Denison	1
East Flanders	6	Moselle in Lotharingia	1
Valenciennes	4	Utrecht	1
Liege	2	France	1
Brabant	2	Mons in Hainault	1
Not said	9		

Table 4 Occupations, 1568 census

	Dutch	Walloons
All occupations with five or more workers		
Woolcombers	152	18
Weavers	52	10
Merchants	23	9
Tailors	18	2
Fullers	10	1
Smiths	13	0
Carpenters	11	0
Fringemakers	0	8
Drapers	0	5
Dyers	4	1
Ministers	5	1
Shoemakers	1	5
A selection of other groups with less than five workers		
Booksellers	4	0
Schoolmasters	2	2
Printers	2	0
Gardeners	2	0
Medical	2	0
Potters	1	0
Silk weavers	1	1
Hemp spinners	0	2
Glass makers	0	1
Bakers	0	1
Locksmiths	0	2

Table 5 Numbers of Strangers in the wards of Norwich, 1571, and a comparison with the
estimated English population in 1569

Ward	Strangers 1571	English 1569
South Conesford	151	472
North Conesford	235	508
Ber Street	207	1,012
St Stephens	125	862
St Peter Mancroft	126	963
St Giles	62	167
West Wymer	827	1,417
Middle Wymer	567	967
East Wymer	316	1,196
Coslany	412	1,058
Colegate	471	800
Fyebridge	462	1,203
Totals	3,993	10,625

Table 6 Alien taxpayers in 1576, by ward and parish. Source: 1576 subsidy

Ward	Parish	Total number of aliens	Tax-paying aliens	Wealth
Con	John Sepulchre	7	0	0
Con	Michael Ber Street	13	2	£2
Con	John Timberhill	11	1	£1
Con	All Saints Ber Street	15	5	£5
Con	Peter Parmountergate and George	117	12	£21
Con	Peter Southgate and Etheldreda	3	0	0
Con	Martin [at bailey]	18	3	£3
Con	Julian and Edward	15	2	£3
Con	Carrow	0	0	0
Con	Lakenham and Bracondale	0	0	0
Con	Trowse	1	0	0
	Totals, Conesford ward	201	25	£35
Man	Peter Mancroft	54	12	£33
Man	Stephen	26	7	£23 10s
Man	Giles	34	8	£9
Man	Eaton	0	0	0
	Totals, Mancroft ward	114	27	£65 10s
Wym	Earlham	0	0	0
Wym	Heigham	26	4	£12
Wym	Benedict	21	1	£5
Wym	Swithin	7	0	0
Wym	Margaret	42	7	£32
Wym	Laurence	56	10	£44
Wym	Gregory	101	8	£16
Wym	John Maddermarket	58	8	£20
Wym	Andrew	83	17	£34
Wym	Michael Muspool [at Plea]	16	7	£39
Wym	Peter Hungate	18	0	0
Wym	Simon	5	1	£1
Wym	George [Tombland]	3	1	£3
Wym	Martin [at Palace]	69	11	£20
Wym	Christchurch	0	0	0
	Totals, Wymer ward	505	74	£226

continued overleaf

Table 6 continued

Ward	Parish	Total number of aliens	Tax-paying aliens	Wealth
OtW	Michael Coslany	115	21	£53 10s
OtW	Mary Coslany	92	10	£23
OtW	Martin at Oak	67	13	£13 10s
OtW	Augustine	103	4	£4 10s
OtW	George [Colegate]	99	6	£19
OtW	Clement	31	2	£3
OtW	Saviour	63	10	£13
OtW	Edmund	36	3	£5 10s
OtW	Martin [at Palace] that part north of the river	27	1	£1
OtW	Paul	57	8	£8 10s
OtW	James	16	3	£3 10s
OtW	Pockthorpe	14	2	£5
OtW	Hellesdon	1	1	0
	Totals, Over the Water ward	711	84	£153
	Totals for the city	1,531	210	£479 10s

Table 7 Taxation of 1576, aliens paying the most tax. Source: 1576 subsidy.

Name	Ward	Parish	Wealth
Thomas Bateman	Wym	Michael [at Plea]	£17
Walter de Gryter	Wym	Andrew	£12
Oliver Corboll	OtW	George [Colegate]	£10
Jasper Mathias	OtW	Margaret	£10
Philip Andrews [Andreis]	WYM	Laurence	£10
Anthony Bullard	OtW	Michael [Coslany]	£10
Powle de Horne	Wym	Michael [at Plea]	£10
Jacob Buskyn	OtW	Mary [Coslany]	£8
Nicholas Surrey	Man	Peter Mancroft	£8
Anthony Paston	Wym	John [Maddermarket]	£8
Adrian Wallone	OtW	Michael [Coslany]	£8
George Vanderkese	OtW	Michael [Coslany]	£8
John Haling	Man	Stephen	£7
Jacob Rubyn	Wym	Laurence	£6
Leonard Tarlyn	Wym	Laurence	£6
John Bunnewell	Wym	Margaret	£6
Francis Trian	Wym	Margaret	£6
Hosen de Foxe	Wym	Laurence	£6
Jacob Kepapas	Con	Peter Parmentergate	£5
Philip Metsen	Con	Peter Parmentergate	£5
Francis Allen	Man	Peter Mancroft	£5
George Drewery	Man	Peter Mancroft	£5
Peter Powle	Wym	Heigham	£5
Victor Krekel	Man	Stephen	£5
John Waterlye	Wym	Benedict	£5
Mr Dr Martin	OtW	Mary [Coslany]	£5
Jacob Gryngole	OtW	George [Colegate]	£5

Table 8   Incomers paying most tax, 1595. Source: 1595 subsidy.

Name	Parish	Ward	Wealth
Jaques de Hem	Michael at Plea	Wym	£8
Frauncis Mychael	Martin at Palace	Wym	£8
Abraham van Ixem	Gregory	Wym	£6
Hugh Herbert	Saviour	OtW	£6
Peter de Wylde	Saviour	OtW	£6
Adrian Wallwyn	Peter Mancroft	Man	£5
Bastien van Burren	Andrew	Wym	£5
William Vertegose	Stephen	Man	£4
Prudence van Dika	Margaret	Wym	£4
Philip Andries	Peter Hungate	Wym	£4
Thomas Bunnell	Martin at Palace	Wym	£4
Peter Wallwyn	Michael Coslany	OtW	£4
John Letten	Mary Coslany	OtW	£4
John Williamson	George Colegate	OtW	£4
John Myner	Peter Parmountergate	Con	£3
James Odett	Peter Parmountergate	Con	£3
John Lynnett	Stephen	Man	£3
Gerard Fansine	Giles	Man	£3
John van Ixem	Gregory	Wym	£3
Gerard Vervincke	Gregory	Wym	£3
Katherine de Seccy	John Maddermarket	Wym	£3
Nicholas Verbeake	John Maddermarket	Wym	£3
Charles Powell	Peter Hungate	Wym	£3
Richard Decall	Martin at Oak	OtW	£3
John vander Puse	George Colegate	OtW	£3
Christian Cornelis	Saviour	OtW	£3
William Player [Ployart]	Saviour	OtW	£3

Table 9 Return of Strangers, 1622

Ward	Born of parent Strangers	Born beyond the seas	Totals
South Conesford	0	0	0
North Conesford	3	4	7
Ber Street	0	3	3
St Stephens	1	4	5
St Peter Mancroft	2	2	4
St Giles	0	0	0
West Wymer	37	24	61
Middle Wymer	18	19	37
East Wymer	10	8	18
Coslany	24	30	54
Colegate	52	48	100
Fyebridge	21	21	42
Totals	168	163	331

Table 10 Wealthiest incomers, 1620s

Name	Walloon or Dutch	Parish	Occupation	Wealth
Malliard Widoote	D	Trowse/Carrow	Husbandman and gardener	£7
John Van Ixem (Vannixon)	D	St Gregory	Hosier	£6
Martin Moonen	D	St Mary Coslany	Hosier	£6
Peter Verbeck (Beck)	D	St Mary Coslany	Merchant and hosier	£6
Giles Sandeville	W	St Gregory	Hosier	£5
James Depute	D	St Andrew	Hosier	£5
Tobias de Hem	D	St Andrew	Merchant	£5
Matthew Deboyse	W	St Andrew	Merchant and draper	£5
Elias des Bonny	W	St Benedict	Weaver	£4
Peter Verdegans (Rottengoose)	D	St Benedict	Gardener and hosier	£4
Abraham Appart	D	St Laurence	Dyer	£4
John Vannnixon junior	D	St Gregory	Hosier	£4
John Deboyse	W	St Peter Hungate	?	£4
John Cruso	D	St Andrew	Merchant and hosier	£4
Daniel Lettany	W	Over the Water ward	Hosier	£4
John Favarck	W	St Martin at Oak	Weaver	£4

Table 11 Weekly burials from the Mayor's Court Books: June 1579 to February 1580. From the last week in October, the numbers of Strangers among the dead are noted.

	Died	Of which, Strangers		Died	Of which, Strangers
1579, 27, June	56		31 October	89	62
4 July	66		7 November	94	69
11 July	98		14 November	45	31
18 July	133		21 November	40	22
25 July	167		28 November	53	41
1 August	244		5 December	58	blank
8 August	268		12 December	63	48
15 August	352		19 December	48	35
22 August	226		26 December	29	24
29 August	331		1580, 2 January	27	23
5 September	298		9 January	44	35
12 September	288		16 January	34	27
19 September	208		23 January	35	28
26 September	275		30 January	38	29
3 October	230		6 February	29	20
10 October	241		13 February	30	24
17 October	249		20 February	29	24
24 October	144		27 February	41	26

Bibliography

M. J. Armstrong, *History and Antiquities of the County of Norfolk* (Norwich, 1781), vol. 10.

Robert Ashton, *Reformation and Revolution 1558–1660* (1985 edn, London).

Brian Ayers, *The German Ocean: Medieval Europe and the North Sea* (Sheffield, 2016).

Geoffrey N. Barrett, *Norwich Silver and its Marks 1565–1702: The Goldsmiths of Norwich 1141–1750* (Norwich, 1981).

David Bates and Robert Liddiard (eds), *East Anglia and its North Sea World in the Middle Ages* (Woodbridge, 2013).

Anthony Batty-Shaw, *Norfolk and Norwich Medicine: A Retrospect* (Norwich, 1992).

J. B. Black, *The Reign of Elizabeth 1558–1603* (1959 edn, Oxford).

Clifford and Yvonne Bird, *Norfolk and Norwich Clocks and Clockmakers* (Chichester, 1996).

Francis Blomefield, *Essay Towards a Topographical History of the County of Norfolk* (London, 1805 edn).

John Browne, *History of Congregationalism* (London, 1878).

J. S. Burn, *The History of the French, Walloon, Dutch and other Protestant Refugees settled in England* (London, 1846).

James Campbell, *Historic Towns: Norwich* (London, 1975).

Amy M. Charles, *The Shorter Poems of Ralph Knevet* (Ohio, 1966).

Penny Corfield, 'A provincial capital in the late seventeenth century: the case of Norwich', in Peter Clark (ed.), *The Early Modern Town* (London, 1976).

Basil Cozens-Hardy, *Maritime Trade of Blakeney, Norfolk 1587–90*, Norfolk Record Society vol. 8 (1936).

Basil Cozens-Hardy and Ernest A Kent, *The Mayors of Norwich 1403 to 1835* (Norwich, 1938).

Noel Currer-Briggs and Royston Gambier, *Huguenot Ancestry* (Chichester, 1985).

Alistair Duke, 'Eavesdropping on the correspondence between the Strangers, chiefly in Norwich, and their Families in the Low Countries 1567–70', *Dutch Crossing – Journal of Low Countries Studies*, vol. 38, no. 2 (2014a), pp.116–31.

Alistair Duke, *Private Correspondence between Flemish Strangers in England and their Families and Contacts in Flanders, 1566–1573* (2014b). There is a copy of this on the Norfolk Record Office bookshelves.

Raingard Esser, *Norwich Strangers' Book 1583–1600: A Systematic Namelist* (Norwich, 1990).

Raingard Esser, 'Social concern and calvinistic duty: the Norwich Strangers' community' (1992a): article from unidentified journal. There is a copy in the Norfolk Heritage Centre, Norwich.

Raingard Esser, 'The Norwich Strangers and the Sandwich connection: the second Pauline Leith lecture' (1992b). There is a copy of this on the Norfolk Record Office bookshelves.

Raingard Esser, 'News across the Channel: contact and communication between the Dutch and Walloon Strangers in Norwich and their families in Flanders 1565–1640', *Immigrants and Minorities*, vol. 14, no. 2 (1995), pp.139–52.

Raingard Esser, *Niederlanische Exulanten im England* (Berlin, 1996).

Raingard Esser, *Les étrangers dans la ville* (Paris, 1999).

D. H. Evans and Malcolm Atkin, 'Excavations in Norwich, 1971–1978, part III', *East Anglian Archaeology,* 100 (2002).

Glynis Fell, *The Spatial Impact of the Immigration of the Strangers*. Cambridge University BA dissertation, unpublished (1975). There is a copy in the Norfolk Heritage Centre.

Leonard Forster, *Janus Gruter's English Years* (Leiden and London, 1967).

Christopher Hanson-Smith, *The Flemish Bond: East Anglia and the Netherlands – Close and Ancient Neighbours* (Diss, 2004).

Helen Hoyte, *The Strangers of Norwich* (Aylsham, 2017).

W. Hudson and J. C. Tingey, *Records of the City of Norwich*, 2 vols (1906).

J. James, *History of the Worsted Manufacture in England* (1857).

Christopher Joby, 'The Dutch language in early modern Norfolk: a social study', *Journal of Low Countries Studies*, vol. 38, no. 2 (2014), pp. 152–88.

Christopher Joby, *The Dutch Language in Britain 1550–1702: A Social History of the Use of Dutch in Early Modern Britain* (Leiden, 2015).

Nelly J. M. Kerling, 'Aliens in the county of Norfolk, 1436–1485', *Norfolk Archaeology*, vol. 33 (1965).

R. W. Ketton-Cremer, 'The coming of the Strangers', in *Norfolk Assembly* (London, 1957).

R. W. Ketton-Cremer, *Norfolk in the Civil War* (Norwich, 1969).

John Kirkpatrick, *History of the Religious Orders and Communities and of the Hospitals and Castle of Norwich* (written about 1725, published Norwich, 1845).

Frederic Madden and others, *Collectanea Topographica et Genealogica* (London, 1834).

R. H. Mason, *History of Norfolk* (London, 1884).

Frank Meeres, *The Story of Norwich* (Andover, 2012).

Frank Meeres, *Norwich: A History and Celebration* (Salisbury, 2004).

Frank Meeres, *Strangers: A History of Norwich's Incomers* (Norwich, 2012).

Frank Meeres, 'Records relating to the Strangers at the Norfolk Record Office', *Journal of Low Countries Studies*, vol. 38, no. 2 (2014), pp.132–53.

G. Alan Metters, Victor Morgan, Elizabeth Rutledge and Barry Taylor (eds), *The Papers of Nathaniel Bacon of Stiffkey, vol. 6*, Norfolk Record Society, vol. 81 (2017).

W. J. C. Moens, *The Walloons and their Church in Norwich: Their History and Registers 1565–1832* (Lymington, 1887–8). He includes a transcript of Walloon baptisms 1595 to 1752, and Walloon marriages 1599–1611, with banns 1628–1691. He has rearranged the names into alphabetical order. He also includes lists of aliens in various lay subsidy rolls, but not that for 1576. Note that the names index at the back of the book does not include the baptisms on pages 1–113 of the second part of the book.

Victor Morgan, Elizabeth Rutledge and Barry Taylor (eds), *The Papers of Nathaniel Bacon of Stiffkey, vol. 5*, Norfolk Record Society vol. 74.

Frederick A. Norwood, *The Reformation Refugees as an Economic Force (*Chicago, 1942).

Geoffrey Parker, *The Dutch Revolt* (1979 edn, Harmondsworth).

Margaret Pelling and Charles Webster, 'Medical practitioners', in C. Webster (ed.), *Health, Medicine and Mortality in the Sixteenth Century* (Cambridge, 1979)

John Pound, *Tudor and Stuart Norwich* (Chichester, 1988).

John Pound, *The Norwich Census of the Poor, 1570*, Norfolk Record Society vol. 40 (1971).

John Pound, 'The social and trade structure of Norwich, 1525–1575', in Peter Clark (ed.), *The Early Modern Town* (London, 1976).

Carole Rawcliffe and Richard Wilson (eds), *Medieval Norwich* (London, 2004a).

Carole Rawcliffe and Richard Wilson (eds), *Norwich since 1550* (London, 2004b).

Douglas Rickwood, *The Origin and Decline of the Stranger Community in Norwich (with Special Reference to the Dutch Congregation) 1565–1700*, University of East Anglia, unpublished MA dissertation (1967a). There is a copy in the Norfolk Heritage Centre.

Douglas Rickwood, *The Norwich Stranger Settlement, University of East Anglia,* unpublished Masters' thesis (1967b). There is a copy in the Norfolk Heritage Centre.

Douglas Rickwood, *The Norwich Accounts for the Customs on Strangers' Goods and Merchandise,* Norfolk Record Society vol. 39 (1970).

Douglas Rickwood, 'The Norwich strangers 1565–1643: a problem of control', *Proceedings of the Huguenot Society of London*, 24 (1984).

Walter Rye, 'The Dutch refugees in Norwich', *The Norfolk Antiquarian Miscellany*, vol. 3 (1887), pp.185–248. This includes a full transcript (in the original Latin) of the 1568 census. Rye disclaims responsibility for it, saying it was done by another person (unnamed): I have compared it with the manuscript version in the Norfolk Record Office (NRO, DN/DIS 10) and found it extremely accurate.

Walter Rye, 'The Dutch Church: early register of baptisms 1598–1619', *East Anglian or Notes and Queries*, new series vols 12 (1907–8) and 13 (1909–10). This is a full transcript in the original mixture of Latin and Dutch. It is in date order, but scattered through the volumes in 24 parts. The pages have been xeroxed and put into a single volume available in the Norfolk Record Office.

L. F. Salzman, *English Industries of the Middle Ages* (1970 edn, London).

W. G. Sebald, *The Rings of Saturn* (Frankfurt, 1995, first trans. into English 1998).

Stephen S. Slaughter, *The Dutch Church in Norwich* (1933).

A. Hassell Smith, Gillian M. Baker and R. W. Kenny (eds), T*he Papers of Nathaniel Bacon of Stiffkey, vol. 1, 1576–1577*, Norfolk Record Society vol. 46 (1978 and 1979), pp.156–7.

Andrew Spicer, 'Southampton, Sea Beggars and the Dutch Revolt 1567–73', in T. Hermans and R. Salverda (eds), *From Revolt to Riches: Culture and History of the Low Countries 1500–1700* (London, 2017 edn).

John Strype, *A Survey of the Cities of London and Westminster* (1720), an updated version of *A Survey of London* by John Stowe (1598, 2nd edn 1603).

Helen Sutermeister, *The Norwich Blackfriars* (Norwich, 1977).

Johanna W. Tammel, *The Pilgrims and Other People from the British Isles in Leiden, 1576–1640* (Peel, Isle of Man, 1989). There is a copy of this on the Norfolk Record Office bookshelves.

Joan Thirsk, *Economic Policy and Projects* (1988 edn, Oxford).

Joan Thirsk, *Alternative Agriculture: A History* (Oxford, 1997).

Lucy Toulmin Smith, 'The Walloon Church in Norwich in 1589', *Norfolk Antiquarian Miscellany*, vol. 2 (1883), pp.91–148. This includes a full transcript (in the original French) of the French Book of Discipline, 1589.

Christine M. Vane, 'The Walloon community in Norwich: the first hundred years', *Proceedings of the Huguenot Society of London*, vol. 24 (1984).

Clive Wilkins-Jones, *Norwich City Library 1608–1737*, Norfolk Record Society vol. 72 (2008).

J. F. Williams, *Bishop Redman's Visitation 1597*, Norfolk Record Society vol. 17 (1946).

Fiona Williamson, *Social Relations and Urban Space, Norwich 1600–1700* (Woodbridge, 2014).

William Woods, 'Publications connected with the Dutch church in Norwich', in Norma Virgoe and Tom Williamson (eds), *Religious Dissent in East Anglia* (Norwich, 1993).

Keith Wrightson, *Earthly Necessities: Economic Lives in Early Modern Britain* (New Haven, Conn. and London, 2000).

Joyce Youings, *The Penguin Social History of Britain: Sixteenth-Century England* (Harmondsworth, 1984).

Index

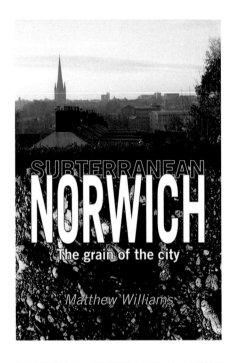
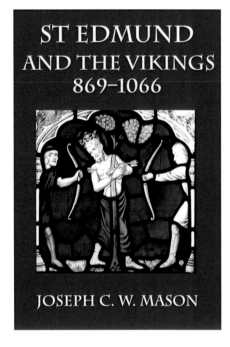
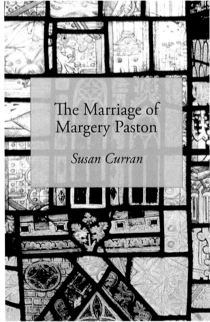
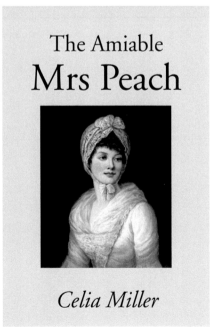